D1453872

THE AUTHORITY OF LAW

THE AUTHORITY OF LAW

Essays on Law and Morality

BY

JOSEPH RAZ

CLARENDON PRESS · OXFORD

1979

Oxford University Press, Walton Street, Oxford OX2 6DP

OXFORD LONDON GLASGOW
NEW YORK TORONTO MELBOURNE WELLINGTON
KUALA LUMPUR SINGAPORE JAKARTA HONG KONG TOKYO
DELHI BOMBAY CALCUTTA MADRAS KARACHI
NAIROBI DAR ES SALAAM CAPE TOWN

© *Joseph Raz 1979*

Published in the United States
by Oxford University Press,
New York

British Library Cataloguing in Publication Data

Raz, Joseph
  The authority of law.
  1. Law and ethics
  I. Title
  340.1'12   BJ55   79–40383

  ISBN 0–19–825345–1

*Printed in Great Britain by
Butler & Tanner Ltd.
Frome and London*

PREFACE

The law claims our allegiance and obedience. Every legal system claims authority. But what authority has the law over us? What authority should we acknowledge as due to the law? This is the main question this book attempts to answer. What kind of an answer can philosophy provide? Unrealistic expectations at the outset are bound to lead to unjustified disappointment. The question is of great practical importance in so many aspects of daily life. Its importance is growing as the law penetrates more and more into every corner of social and individual activity. But the deeper the law's penetration into various aspects of life the more complex the problem of the authority of law becomes and the more one despairs of the possibility of a general philosophical answer to it.

Consider any man in any of a large number of rather common situations. Consider, for example, a headmaster objecting to the routing of a bypass near his school. How should he behave? Should he confine himself to presenting his case in the local public inquiry? Or should he try to disrupt the inquiry since he knows that it is, by law, weighted against his cause? Should he organize a massive local sit-in? Or choose some other course of action? Since so many considerations have to be taken into account, their combination may well make the case unique. The nature of the harm the implementation of the proposed plan will cause, the benefits it will bring, the chances of having it changed by the various possible courses of action open to him, the danger that it will be replaced by a worse plan, the cost of his action to the school in terms of reputation, affecting, for example, possibilities of raising money from old members, its impact on his standing in the eyes of his students, its consequences to his personal and family life—do philosophers really examine or need to examine all these considerations?

The answer must be both yes and no. The difficulty of each individual case arises because of the particular way in which general considerations combine in it. Philosophical deliberation helps to determine which general considerations are relevant to practical decisions and it improves our understanding of their value and importance. This understanding is most valuable for making informed decisions in concrete cases, but it is insufficient. The actual decision must be based on complex judgments about the way these general considerations manifest themselves in the case at hand, and about the right way to resolve conflicts between them. Philosophy can provide guidance, but it is helpless to spare us any of the agony of the actual decision.

Legal philosophy provides only one part of the philosophical answer to practical questions. Clearly each concrete problem involves many other aspects as well. These may be discussed by other departments of the philosophy of practical reason. Legal philosophy itself is concerned only with the legal angle of all practical problems, namely with the way in which the fact that a certain action has some legal consequences should affect practical deliberation generally and moral considerations in particular. This is the question of the authority of law.

The book is divided into four parts. The second and third primarily criticize various attempts to establish a conceptual connection between law and morality which ensures an inescapable moral authority to the law. The last part provides a constructive argument establishing the character of the law's moral authority and contributing (though only too little) to the perennial question of the conditions the law must satisfy to be deserving of moral respect.

The first part provides an introduction to the argument of the book by supplying a philosophical analysis of the concept of legitimate authority. This analysis is presupposed in the last constructive part, especially in the essays entitled 'The Obligation to Obey the Law' and 'Respect for Law'. This is followed by several essays refuting, directly and by implication, a variety of traditional natural law arguments. Some of these arguments attempt to show that our criteria for identifying what is law and what is not assure the law of moral content. Essay 3 ('Legal Positivism and the Sources of Law') explains the reasons for rejecting any approach to the law which assumes that the determination of the legal validity of any standard of conduct involves a moral argument. Essay 4 ('Legal Reasons, Sources, and Gaps') explores some of the consequences of the alternative approach, generally known as 'legal positivism', which regards law as created by social sources so that the existence and content of legal systems can be determined on the basis of social fact without resort to moral argument. This essay defends the source-based conception of law from accusations of incoherence and explains why and in what sense all legal systems contain gaps calling for the exercise of discretion and for reliance on extra-legal considerations by courts in certain cases. The source-based conception of law is then described in greater detail in the fifth and sixth essays on 'The Identity of Legal Systems' and 'The Institutional Nature of Law'. Since the primary aim of the book is to examine arguments for the moral authority of laws, the discussion of the picture of law which emerges from the pursuit of legal positivism has not been carried very far. For a more completely articulated and defended explanation the reader is referred to the last two chapters of my *Practical Reason and Norms* (London, 1975).

One of the main stumbling blocks for legal positivists has been the use of normative language, i.e. the very same terminology which is used in moral discourse, in legal discourse. The fact that the law is described and analysed in terms of duties, obligations, rights and wrongs, etc., has long been regarded by many as supporting the claim of the natural lawyer that law is inescapably moral. The best positivist explanation of the use of normative language in law was suggested by Kelsen and is discussed in the seventh essay. The eighth ('Legal Validity') offers an outline of an account of legal discourse largely derived from Kelsen but free, I hope, from many of his obscurities, and dissociated from other essentially unrelated Kelsenian doctrines.

The second part of the book does not advance us far towards showing that law has moral authority. It rejects one kind of argument to that effect and in the process it defends a view of the nature of law and of legal discourse. The third part is similar in nature though less unified round a central theme. It is concerned with the refutation of three popular arguments. First, that an understanding of law inevitably involves an understanding of its functions and those cannot be described except in a morally loaded way. From this various consequences about the morality of law are often alleged to follow. Essay 9 offers an indirect refutation by showing how legal functions can be analysed in value-neutral terms. Second is the argument that since legal adjudication does and should invoke moral argument, law cannot be separated from morality. This argument has already been refuted in the essay on 'Legal Reasons, Sources, and Gaps', which establishes the possibility of conceptually separating in a general way law and value in adjudication. Essay 10 ('Law and Value in Adjudication') examines the adjudicative process more closely and explores the theme of the separability and connectedness of law and value in the courtroom. Finally, the argument (most closely connected with Lon Fuller) that there are certain procedural values inseparable from the law which form its internal morality is examined in the eleventh essay on 'The Rule of Law and its Virtue' and is seen to guarantee no inherent moral value to the law.

The second and third parts of the book are devoted to a refutation of some natural law arguments for the authority of law. It remains to the last part to develop a view of the authority of law consistent with legal positivism. Though some natural law arguments are consistent with legal positivism (see *Practical Reason and Norms*, ch. 5), I have tried to explain in Essay 12 that even they fail to establish the moral authority of law. The result is that one cannot explain why law has moral authority. It may have none. If a certain legal system has moral authority this cannot be just a result of its status as law or of features entailed by its legal aspect. It must base its moral claim on substantive features which it has, but which it is possible for a legal system to lack. Hence the real question is what should a legal system be like to have a justified claim to authority? This sounds very much like the question, what is a good legal system?—which obviously cannot be discussed here. Instead the implications and presuppositions of various moral attitudes to the law are examined (the essays on 'The Obligation to Obey the Law' and on 'Respect for Law') and I point rather dogmatically to a few moral features a law must possess to have authority, namely to be such that its authority will be consistent with individual autonomy (the essays on 'Conscientious Objection' and 'Civil Disobedience').

A word of explanation about the structure. The book is composed of independent essays for two reasons. The central problem of the book, the question of the authority of law and more broadly that of law and its relation to morality, touches on almost every aspect of our understanding of the law. I wanted to be free to explore some incidental questions (such as the nature of authority or of legal gaps) at greater length than would have been appropriate in a more closely woven book on law and morality. Furthermore, the many aspects of my central theme compel me to range widely over disparate issues (Essays 1, 11–15 belong essentially to political philosophy, Essays 2–10 to analytical legal philosophy) and to employ various styles of argument (Essays 1 and 4 in particular are very technical and many readers may prefer to skip them). I therefore thought it advisable to opt for a looser organization in which each essay is completely independent of the rest, so that readers can read any number and in any order.

The essay form also enabled me to incorporate in the book four articles not specifically written for it (Essays 5, 6, 7, 9) but which seemed to provide additional ingredients to its general argument. All the other essays were written with this book in mind, though several of them have been published before (Essays 4, 5, 7, 9, 11 appear here in a revised form and I have introduced minor changes in all essays). I wish to thank the following for permission to reprint the articles indicated:

The organizers of the World Congress of Legal and Social Philosophy 1977 (Essay 4); the editors of the *California Law Review* (Essay 5); the editor of the *Modern Law Review* (Essay 6); the editor of *The American Journal of Jurisprudence* (Essay 7); the editor of *Archiv für Rechts- und Sozialphilosophie* (Essay 8); Prof. A. W. B. Simpson and the Oxford University Press (Essay 9); The Liberty Fund and the editor of the *Law Quarterly Review* (Essay 11).

CONTENTS

I. LAW AND AUTHORITY

1. Legitimate Authority   3
2. The Claims of Law   28

II. THE NATURE OF LAW AND NATURAL LAW

3. Legal Positivism and the Sources of Law   37
4. Legal Reasons, Sources, and Gaps   53
5. The Identity of Legal Systems   78
6. The Institutional Nature of Law   103
7. Kelsen's Theory of the Basic Norm   122
8. Legal Validity   146

III. INTERNAL LEGAL VALUES

9. The Functions of Law   163
10. Law and Value in Adjudication   180
11. The Rule of Law and its Virtue   210

IV. MORAL ATTITUDES TO THE LAW

12. The Obligation to Obey the Law   233
13. Respect for Law   250
14. A Right to Dissent? I. Civil Disobedience   262
15. A Right to Dissent? II. Conscientious Objection   276

Index   290

Part I

Law and Authority

1

LEGITIMATE AUTHORITY*

THE PARADOXES

There is little surprise that the notion of authority is one of the most controversial concepts found in the armoury of legal and political philosophy. Its central role in any discussion of legitimate forms of social organization and of legitimate forms of political action makes the indefinite continuation of this controversy inevitable. The immediate relevance of the problem of authority to current controversial issues makes a dispassionate study of the subject all the more difficult. But beyond these extrinsic difficulties, the study of the concept of authority has to confront two major problems of intellectual origin: the methodological problem of how to avoid confusing the various quite distinct problems involving the notion of authority and the problem of the paradoxes of authority.

The paradoxes of authority can assume different forms, but all of them concern the alleged incompatibility of authority with reason or autonomy. To be subjected to authority, it is argued, is incompatible with reason, for reason requires that one should always act on the balance of reasons of which one is aware.[1] It is of the nature of authority that it requires submission even when one thinks that what is required is against reason. Therefore, submission to authority is irrational. Similarly the principle of autonomy entails action on one's own judgment on all moral questions. Since authority sometimes requires action against one's own judgment, it requires abandoning one's moral autonomy. Since all practical questions may involve moral considerations, all practical authority denies moral autonomy and is consequently immoral.[2]

---

* First published in Richard Bronaugh (ed.), *Philosophical Law* (Westport, Connecticut, 1978). I am indebted to J. E. J. Altham, K. Antley, L. J. Cohen, Philippa Foot, P. M. S. Hacker, and P. H. Nowell-Smith for their critical comments on an earlier version of the essay.

[1] For a version of this principle of reason see Davidson's principle of continence in his 'How Is Weakness of the Will Possible', in *Moral Concepts*, ed. J. Feinberg (Oxford, 1969).

[2] This argument does not apply to theoretical authority. There is nothing immoral

Arguments along these lines do not challenge the coherence of the notion of authority nor do they deny that some people are believed to have authority or actually have *de facto* authority. They challenge the possibility of legitimate, justified, *de jure* authority. Their paradoxical nature derives not from their denial of legitimate authority but from the fact that the denial is alleged to derive from the very nature of morality or from fundamental principles of rationality. Moreover the arguments challenge the legitimacy not only of political authority but of all authority over rational persons.[3] If the very nature of authority is incompatible with the idea of morality and rationality, then those who believe in legitimate authority are not merely wrong or mistaken in one of their moral beliefs. They are committed to an irrational belief or are guilty of a fundamental misapprehension of the concept of morality or of that of authority. This gives these arguments a much greater force. They are, for example, immune from most sceptical arguments. For even if there is no way of distinguishing between right and wrong substantive moral beliefs, at least we can clarify moral concepts and establish relations of entailment and incompatibility between them. If the very concepts of morality and rationality are incompatible with that of authority, then even the sceptic will be able to know that all authority is immoral and submission to it is irrational.

Paradoxically the very force of these arguments is their weakness. Many who may be willing to accept lesser challenges to legitimate authority will be reluctant to accept this most sweeping challenge. Many who may be ready to accept that many authorities are not legitimate, even that no political authority is ever legitimate, will be deterred by the thought that no authority can ever be legitimate. Many who may be ready to concede that those who believe in the possibility of legitimate authority are wrong will shy away from the thought that they are irrational or have no idea what morality is about.

---

in having authorities on how to cook, program a computer, reduce money supply, and so on, so long as one regards them as theoretical authorities only. Submission to theoretical authority may, however, be irrational, for arguments about the conflict between authority and reason are not confined to practical authority.

[3] They may be compatible with authority over small children and some mentally ill people.

It is not my aim to examine the ways in which authority can be defended or attacked. But since the arguments on which the paradoxes are based are said to derive all their force from the analysis of the concepts of authority, morality, and rationality, their examination is relevant to any attempt to clarify the notion of authority. I am concerned here with the nature of authority. I shall try to show why the concept of authority gives rise to the apparent paradoxes and why they are merely apparent. I am not the first to try to dissolve the paradoxes, and it is not part of my brief that all previous attempts to do so have failed. I think, however, that the analysis that follows, even if proving a known truth, does so in a novel way, which shows both the temptation and the fallacies of the paradoxes to best advantage.

A METHODOLOGICAL DETOUR

Some of the classical authors sought to explain the nature of authority by explaining the way in which people come to accept the authority of individuals or groups. Discussions of the concept were mixed with descriptions of the evolution of society, of conquests, or of social contracts. Modern authors have avoided this confusion, but discussion of the subject is still bedevilled with many methodological confusions. I shall describe briefly four of the common types of explanation and try to point to the lessons to be learned from their shortcomings.

1. The first standard explanation consists in specifying the conditions that are in fact either necessary or sufficient for holding effective (*de facto*) authority. But such explanations fail to elucidate the nature of authority in any way at all. To be sure, it is an important part of social theory to explain under what conditions people can obtain or hold authority, under what circumstances a community is likely to accept the authority of some persons. But they fail altogether to explain what these conditions are for, what it is to have authority or to be in authority.

2. The second type of explanation attempts to elucidate the nature of authority by describing the necessary or sufficient conditions for the holding of legitimate (*de jure*) authority.

This second pattern of explanation seems more promising. According to it the concept of authority is to be explained by explaining how claims to authority can be justified. The force of such explanations is clear. They do not presuppose that claims to authority can in fact ever be justified, but merely point out how they are to be justified. On the reasonable assumption that claims to authority are a way of justifying action, it seems almost inevitable that they differ from other justifications of action by the type of justificative arguments involved. In fact this conclusion is far from inevitable. Justifying claims may differ not only in the nature of the justifying argument invoked but also in the nature of the act justified.

There is a considerable plausibility in the idea that authority is to be explained by reference to the kind of act, for example, a claiming, which it justifies. We certainly need authority to perform some actions but not others, and it appears, at least prima facie, that to say that one has a certain authority is to indicate that one could be either justified or capable of doing certain actions, without committing oneself in any way as to the nature of that justification.

Here lies the major problem of justificative analyses of authority. None has so far succeeded in delineating the type of argument invocation of which is tantamount to a claim of authority. The fact that there are many different types of authority concerned with virtually every sphere of human activity makes one inclined to give up hope that such a delineation is possible. We can exemplify this difficulty by considering an interesting attempt made recently to provide a justificative analysis of authority. Richard Tuck has suggested that citations of political authority are statements designed to kill criticism of a political action but are not authentic justifications. They are based on the claim that (1) the action proposed or performed is right if somebody performs it; (2) it is neither right nor wrong that the person for whom authority is claimed should be that somebody; (3) that person in fact performed the action or proposes to do so.

Many will share Tuck's belief that nobody has a right to a position of (political) authority and that the only way to justify political authority is by the use of arguments of the type he outlines. But we all know that various writers have thought that some people are by nature slaves and that those who are by nature free have authority over them. Others have believed in the Divine Right of kings, and there are and were other theories asserting that some people have a right and a duty by nature or by reason to rule. Such people, let us assume, are wrong. But are they also guilty of misusing language, as Tuck's approach suggests?[4] Is the mistake one of moral and political theory, or is it also a mistake about the meaning of words, about the concept of authority?

All other justificative explanations have to overcome the same difficulty. It is not enough to establish that only arguments of a certain type can justify authority. One has to show that claiming authority on any other grounds is a misuse of language.

The criticism of the first two patterns of explanation points to a clear lesson: the analysis of authority cannot consist exclusively of an elucidation of the conditions under which one has either legitimate or effective authority. It must explain what one has when one has authority. This strongly suggests that authority is an ability to perform certain kinds of action.[5] The analysis I have proposed here is meant to vindicate this suggestion.

3. One popular theory that regards authority as ability to perform certain kinds of action identifies effective (*de facto*) authority with power over people. I shall suggest later that to have authority over people is to have normative power. But it is a different notion of power that is involved here. According to it to have power is to have influence, to be able to influence people's actions and their fortunes. A person has effective authority if he is powerful, if he can influence people's fate and their choices or options.[6] Legitimate authority can then be defined as justified effective authority.[7] It is effective authority that

---

[4] Richard Tuck, 'Why Is Authority Such a Problem?' in *Philosophy, Politics and Society*, 4th series, ed. P. Laslett, W. G. Runciman, and Quentin Skinner (Oxford, 1972).

[5] My distinction between explanation in terms of types of justification and those in terms of types of actions justified is in itself problematic. Characterizing having authority as ability to perform actions justified by arguments of certain kinds is justificative explanation and not explanation as an ability to perform acts of a certain kind.

[6] For a stimulating discussion of the notion of power as influence see S. Lukes, *Power: A Radical View* (London, 1974).

[7] It is sometimes defined as effective authority accepted by those subject to it or

should be preserved or obeyed (subject to various conditions and qualifications).

For several reasons, however, it seems that such theories put the cart before the horse. The notion of legitimate authority is in fact the primary one. For one thing not all legitimate authority is effective. Besides (as I will claim shortly), the notion of effective authority cannot be explained except by reference to legitimate authority. Several considerations should be borne in mind.

Though our concern is with practical rather than theoretical authority, an analysis maximizing the similarities between authority for action and authority for belief is, other things being equal, preferable. It seems clear that scientific genius can go unrecognized and that a man who is in fact the greatest authority in a certain field may have very little influence over people's research or their beliefs on issues within his competence.

Parents have authority over their children regardless of whether their children actually acknowledge their authority. Admittedly parental authority is usually recognized by other adults, but that is the wrong sort of recognition from the point of view of a recognition theory, which holds that it is recognition by the subjects that matters. Parental authority does not depend on recognition.

If theoretical authority does not entail recognition or enforcement, then there must be at least some cases of practical authority that also do not entail recognition or enforcement. There are practical authorities whose authority is based entirely on their being theoretical authorities: an expert doctor is an authority not only on the causes of illness but also on their cures. There are experts on the stock exchange and experts on navigation and many others who are authorities for action in their field even though their authority may be unrecognized and unenforced.

I share the belief that a legitimate political authority is of necessity effective at least to a degree. But this is a result of substantive political principles (e.g. that one of the main justifications for having a political authority is its usefulness in securing

---

based on their consent. These facts, however, are relevant, if at all, only to the extent that they show the authority to be a justified one.

social co-ordination, and that knowledge and expertise do not give one a right to govern and play only a subordinate role in the justification of political authority). It is not entailed by a conceptual analysis of the notion of authority, not even by that of the concept of political authority.

The analysis of legitimate authority is not by itself sufficient to explain our notion of authority. A complete account must include an analysis of effective authority as well. Having argued that the notion of legitimate authority does not presuppose that of effective authority,[8] it may be worth pointing out that the reverse is not true. The notion of legitimate authority is presupposed by that of effective authority. A person needs more than power (as influence) to have *de facto* authority. He must either claim that he has legitimate authority or be held by others to have legitimate authority. There is an important difference, for example, between the brute use of force to get one's way and the same done with a claim of right. Only the latter can qualify as an effective or *de facto* authority. But this is a problem that cannot be explored here.

4. Some people hold that authority must be defined by reference to rules: that a person has authority means that there is a system of rules, which confers authority on him. This mode of explanation is in fact a variant of the first and second patterns of explanation and is open to the same basic objection. It substitutes a claim as to when people have authority for a proper explanation of what it is to have authority. It states that people have authority only when it is conferred on them by some rules. But it does not provide any means of deciding which rules confer authority and which do not. Some rules will, it is true, confer authority quite explicitly. They have authoritative, binding formulations (enacted rules), and their authoritative formulations specify that they confer authority on a certain person. But the proposed definition does nothing to illuminate their meaning and effect.

The claim that all authority is conferred by rules is itself debatable. It is difficult to maintain that when a member of the

---

[8] This should not lead one to confuse authority with the right to have authority. A person may be entitled to have authority and yet not have it: he may be entitled to it and entitled to have it conferred on him by Parliament and yet not have it until it is so conferred on him.

public assumes authority in an emergency (for example, a fire in a theatre) his authority derives from any rules. It is not, however, my purpose here to discuss the ways authority can be acquired or defended. There are other objections to definitions of this type. Unless properly qualified they entail contradictions. If there are two systems of rules according to one of which a certain person has authority whereas according to the other he does not, then he both has and does not have authority. To avoid such a contradiction the proposed definition must be relativized. It cannot be taken to be a definition of having authority but of the relativized notion of having authority according to s where s is some system of rules. The relativized notion of authority, however, severs the connection between authority and practical reason.

Authority is a practical concept. This means that questions of who has authority over whom are practical questions; they bear on what one ought to do. In other words statements that some persons have authority may serve as premisses in practical inferences. The explanation of authority must explain the practical import of the concept. It must explain how it is capable of figuring in practical inferences.

What one ought to do depends on who has authority in a non-relativized sense. That a person has authority according to some system of rules is, in itself, of no practical relevance. Just as one can draw no conclusions as to what ought to be done from the fact that according to a certain person authority is vested in Parliament, so one cannot draw any such conclusions from the mere fact that according to some rules authority is vested in Parliament. Certain further assumptions may entail that if according to someone Parliament has authority, then Parliament does have authority. Similarly, further assumptions may allow a move from a statement of authority according to some rules to a non-relativized statement of authority. It would be a mistake, however, to build those further conditions into one's definition of 'authority according to some rules' so as to make the move to a non-relativized statement of authority always possible. The whole purpose of talk of relativized authority is to block the possibility of such a move, unless further assumptions are available. We need such a device to be able to talk of the views of other people about authority, of the situation according to rules accepted in some societies or proposed by some people. To do this we have in talk of relativized authority a way to refer to what those people or societies accept or propose as legitimate authority without endorsing those views. We simply state what authority is had by whom from a certain point of view.[9] In some circumstances the fact that some people hold certain views or endorse certain rules is enough to invest a person with authority. In others it is not. The move from a relativized statement of authority to a non-relativized one is never automatic and is not always possible.

These considerations suggest that the non-relativized notion is the primary one. The relativized notion is useful because it reveals the views of people or societies concerning non-relativized authority. Its explanation presupposes the non-relativized notion, which does not presuppose it. Our task then is to explain the notion of legitimate non-relativized authority in a way that shows its relevance to practical reasoning.

THE SIMPLE EXPLANATION

Several authors have analysed authority along the lines I have just suggested. On the whole there is a large measure of agreement between them but they differ greatly in important details. Robert Paul Wolff, to take one well-known example, says that 'authority is the right to command, and correlatively, the right to be obeyed'.[10] His definition is essentially sound, but it is both inaccurate and not perspicuous. It is inaccurate, for authority is a right to do other things as well. It can be a right to legislate, to grant permissions, to give authoritative advice, to adjudicate, and so forth. It is wrong to regard all these as commanding. Wolff's definition is not perspicuous since the notion of a right is even more complex and problematic than that of authority.

To be useful, the analysis must be made in terms of relatively simple concepts. From this point of view I think that the best existing explanation of authority is that offered by John Lucas: 'A man, or body of men, *has authority* if it follows from his saying "Let X happen", that X ought to happen.'[11] This definition

[9] The use of expressions such as 'according to law' is just one way of indicating that the statement is made from a point of view only. Often the context of utterance suffices to indicate this.

[10] Robert Paul Wolff, *In Defense of Anarchism* (New York, 1970), p. 4.

[11] John Lucas, *The Principles of Politics* (Oxford, 1966), p. 16.

is both perspicuous and general. It applies to all types of practical authority over persons and not merely to political authority. It makes clear that one can exercise authority not only by commanding but in other ways as well.[12]

Lucas explains authority as an ability to perform an action, and he regards the relevant action as that of changing the normative situation. I shall assume that if X ought to ϕ then he has a reason to ϕ and that if he has a reason to ϕ then he ought to ϕ. On this assumption Lucas's definition entails that a person has authority if his saying, 'Let X happen', is a reason for X to happen. This sounds somewhat incongruous. The reason is that Lucas's definition does not make clear that the authority he is defining is authority over persons. To make this assumption clear we can further amend his definition and say that X has authority over Y if his saying, 'Let $Y \phi$', is a reason for Y to ϕ. Let us call this the simple analysis.

Two comments are in place here. First, I do not claim that authority can be explained only in terms of reasons. The preference for a reason-based explanation is motivated by the belief that reasons provide the ultimate basis for the explanation of all practical concepts, namely, that all must be explained by showing their relevance to practical inferences. The preference for reason-based explanations of authority is one for trying to show the role of authority statements in practical reasoning directly rather than through the mediation of other concepts (such as rights). Second, a great variety of things are called reasons. That it rains, for example, is a reason for carrying an umbrella. So is the fact that one wants to be outside and not get wet. But in a perfectly straightforward sense both are just parts of one reason. We can distinguish between partial reasons and the complete reasons of which they are parts. It is in terms of complete reasons that the attempt to analyse authority will be made.[13] I shall argue below that the simple explanation fails

---

[12] His definition confines the exercise of authority to the use of optatives. It seems that authority can also be exercised through non-verbal behaviour and communication. But I am not concerned here with the examination of the different ways in which authority can be exercised.

[13] A complete reason on this account is not necessarily one whose justification is self-evident. That I promised to perform a certain action is, I believe, a complete reason to perform it. But, of course, one may well be challenged to justify such beliefs and must be ready to justify them. One must defend, in other words, the belief that promises

to distinguish adequately between intentional and non-intentional exercise of authority and that it does not pay attention to the distinction between being an authority and having authority. It also overlooks the fact that one needs authority to grant permissions and to confer powers. But first I shall examine some more far-reaching objections to it.

FIRST OBJECTION TO THE SIMPLE EXPLANATION

Is the utterance of an authority an absolute or a prima facie reason for doing as it demands? If we assume that it is an absolute reason, then it seems very unlikely that there are any legitimate authorities, and there seem to be very few *de facto* authorities. I, for example, believe that I am justified in taking the advice, commands, or rules issued by some people as reasons for action, but I cannot see that it is ever right to take anybody's word as an absolute reason to be followed under all circumstances. It seems to me that this is a widely shared view and that most people hold that under certain circumstances the instructions of authority need not be followed. Hence if authority is explained in terms of ability to issue absolutely binding instructions, then there seem to be very few recognized authorities in the world and none which is legitimate.

But are authoritative utterances prima facie reasons? Compare an order with a request and both with advice. All three are identified by the attitudes, beliefs, and intentions of their source, not by the way they are received by their addressee. The fact that one was ordered or requested or advised to take a certain action may be a reason to take it, and it may be held by the addressee to be so. Under different circumstances the fact that such utterances were made is no reason for action or is not held to be one. From the addressee's point of view there is no necessary difference between being ordered, being requested, and being advised except that they entail or imply different intentions, beliefs, or attitudes in the person issuing them.

One such difference is that the primary intention in advising is to convey information about what is morally right or wrong, what is lawful or unlawful, in one's interests or not, and so forth

---

are reasons for actions. For further discussion of the presupposition underlying my use of 'reasons' see *Practical Reason and Norms* (London, 1975), ch. 1.

or just about brute facts. If there is an intention to influence the addressee (and there need not be one) then it is to influence him by making him aware of the situation (for example, that he ought to ϕ or that ϕ-ing will secure the greatest income possible in the circumstances).

In short the adviser must intend his giving the advice to be taken as a reason to believe that what he says is true, correct, or justified. But he does not necessarily intend it to be taken as a reason for action, even though it may be the case that his giving the advice is a valid reason for action for the recipient.[14]

Requesting and ordering, on the other hand, entail intending that the act of requesting or ordering be taken as a reason to perform the act ordered or requested. What then is the difference between them? One such difference is relevant to our purpose. Suppose that a man makes a request and is told in reply that his request was considered, but on balance it was found that the reasons against the action requested overrode those for it including the request itself. He will no doubt be disappointed, but he will not feel that his request was disregarded. He has nothing to complain about. He must concede that whatever his hopes, he intended no more than that the action be taken on the balance of reasons, his request being one of them.[15] This is not so if he gave an order. A man who orders someone else does not regard his order as merely another reason to be added to the balance by which the addressee will determine what to do. He intends the addressee to take his order as a reason on which to act regardless of whatever other conflict-

---

[14] These remarks apply most naturally to 'advise that p'. Are they true of 'advise to ϕ'? This is a moot point, but it seems to me that 'I advise you to apply to Balliol', when used to advise, is used to make the same statement as is often made by 'Balliol is your best choice', or by 'On balance I think applying to Balliol is preferable to the alternatives'. 'Advise to ϕ', is reducible to 'advise that p'. But I shall not argue for this here.

[15] Some requests, such as pleas and beggings, intend also to induce new spontaneous desires to accede to them. A 'pure' request appeals to existing sympathies and to reason as sufficient to make it a reason for action for the addressee. It is wrong, however, to think of requests as merely intended to 'activate' a reason the addressee has (his sympathy or recognition of duty) by informing him of a need or a desire of the object of the request. Information of somebody's need, even if conveyed with the intention to move the addressee to action by activating existing reasons, does not amount to a request. One requests only when the act of communication itself is meant to constitute a reason. In special cases one has a right that one's requests be granted. There the divide between requests and commands is thin indeed and does on occasion boil down to the choice of language.

ing reasons exist (short usually of an emergency or other extreme circumstances).[16]

It may seem that the explanation of this difference is that a man issuing an order always intends it to be a very weighty reason and that is not always the case when people make requests. Apart from the fact that some requests are made with such an intention, this explanation seems unsatisfactory because it relies on an alleged difference in degree. If the difference indicated is the one crucial to the distinction between orders and requests, then it is unlikely to be one of degree only.

The crucial point of this objection is that one requires authority to be entitled to command but one does not need authority to be entitled to request. My point is not that everyone is entitled to request. Whether this is the case is a moral, not a conceptual, question. There is nothing in the concept of a request that entails that everyone is entitled to request. My point is that the fact that one is entitled to request does not entail that one has authority over the addressee of the request. Contrariwise, that one is entitled to command entails that one has authority over the addressee of the command. A request made by a person entitled to make it is a valid (prima facie) reason for its addressee. Similarly a command issued by a person entitled to issue it is valid. If we are to say no more than that a valid command is a reason for its addressee, then we fail to explain the difference between a command and a request and the reason for which only entitlement to the first entails having authority. To say that a valid command is a weightier reason than a valid request is both false and inadequate as an explanation of a distinction that is not merely one of degree.

SECOND OBJECTION TO THE SIMPLE EXPLANATION

The first objection was based on an argument to the effect that if authority is ability to change reasons by certain utterances,

---

[16] This statement has to be modified if it is to apply to orders (and requests) made in an institutional setting (such as the army). There conventional ways of commanding (or requesting) normally used to facilitate the identification of the agent's intentions are hardened and the agent's action invoking the convention counts as a command regardless of his true intentions. Such conventions presuppose that typically they will be used with the appropriate intention. When this presupposition fails they can no longer be regarded as conventions of commanding (or requesting).

then the utterances of authority are more than prima facie yet less than absolute reasons, which is an impossibility. The second objection is based on an argument to the effect that the utterances of (legitimate) authority though often reasons for action need not always be so. It consists of an appeal to our intuition based on a counter-example. Consider the following situation. I am driving my car in flat country with perfect visibility and there is no other human being, animal, or car for miles around me. I come to a traffic light showing red. Do I have any reason to stop? There is no danger to anyone and whatever I do will not be known to anyone and will not affect my own attitude, feelings, or beliefs about authority in the future. Many will say that there is not even the slightest reason to stop at the red light in such circumstances.[17] They insist that this in no way contradicts their acknowledgement of the legitimate authority of those who made the traffic regulations. This example seems sufficient to convince one that in this case or a similar case the utterances of authority can be held to be legitimate without holding them to constitute reasons for action.

I think that these objections are sufficient to undermine the simple explanation and yet the simple explanation is right in its basic insight—that authority is ability to change reasons for action. Both the simple explanation and the objections to it are based on an over-restricted view of reasons for action. I shall argue that if we regard authority as ability to change a certain type of reason, then the objections can be easily answered.

NORMATIVE POWER

Consider any situation in which an authority instructs a subordinate to follow the instruction of another whose authority does not derive from that of the first. A father telling his son to obey his mother is such a case. It differs from the father telling the son to obey his nanny, since the nanny's authority derives from that of the parents. An instruction to obey the nanny is, we may assume, her only source of authority. The mother's instructions are in any case authoritative. They are reasons for

---

[17] Further assumptions are required to show that I know that I have no reason to stop. For my purpose it is enough to establish that in fact I have no reason to stop. But in many situations these further assumptions obtain, and it is also true that for all I know there is no reason to stop.

action for the son. So are the father's instructions. His instruction to obey the mother is, therefore, a reason to act for a reason. It is a reason to act on the mother's instruction, which is itself a reason anyway. I shall call a reason to act for a reason a positive second-order reason. There are also negative second-order reasons, that is, reasons to refrain from acting for a reason. I shall call negative second-order reasons exclusionary reasons. To get an example of an exclusionary reason we need only reverse the father's instruction and assume that he orders his son not to act on his mother's orders.[18] Now the son has a reason for not acting on a reason.

There is one important point to bear in mind concerning second-order reasons: they are reasons for action, the actions concerned being acting for a reason and not acting for a reason. If P is a reason to ϕ then acting for the reason that P is ϕ-ing for the reason that P. Not acting for P is not ϕ-ing for the reason that P. This is compatible with ϕ-ing for some other reason as well as with not ϕ-ing at all. I am not assuming that whenever one fails to act on a reason one does so intentionally. One may fail to act on a reason because one does not know of its existence. These clarifications make it plain that in the examples I am assuming that in telling his son to obey his mother, the father tells him not merely to do what she tells him to do but also to do it for the reason that she tells him so. Similarly I am assuming that when the father tells his son not to obey his mother, he is not telling him never to do what his mother tells him to do but merely never to take her instructions as reasons for action.

Sometimes a person may have a reason for performing an action and also a reason for not acting for certain reasons against that very action. The son, in our example, may know that his only coat is ugly. This is a reason against wearing it. It conflicts with his mother's instruction to wear a coat when he goes out at night. But the reason against wearing the coat is reinforced indirectly by the father's order to disregard the mother's instruction. In this and many other cases the fact that is a reason (the father's order) for disregarding certain reasons (the mother's instruction) for ϕ-ing (wearing the coat) is dif-

---

[18] I am assuming that he is entitled to make such an order—a matter that can be subject to dispute but that need not detain us here.

ferent from any fact that is a reason (the coat's ugliness) for not ϕ-ing. But sometimes the same fact is both a reason for an action and an (exclusionary) reason for disregarding reasons against it. I shall call such facts protected reasons for an action.

I will define normative power as ability to change protected reasons. More precisely, a man has normative power if he can by an action of his exercise normative power. An act is the exercise of a normative power if there is sufficient reason for regarding it either as a protected reason or as cancelling protected reasons and if the reason for so regarding it is that it is desirable to enable people to change protected reasons by such acts, if they wish to do so.[19]

I shall assume that power is used by making what I shall call 'power-utterances'. There are three ways in which the power-holders can change protected reasons that are important to our purpose. The first is by issuing an exclusionary instruction, that is, by using power to tell a person to ϕ, the power-utterance is a reason for that person to ϕ and also a second-order reason for not acting on (all or some) reasons for not ϕ-ing. Exclusionary instructions are, therefore, protected reasons. The second way of exercising power is by making a power-utterance granting permission to perform an action hitherto prohibited by an exclusionary instruction. I shall call such permissions 'cancelling permissions' for they cancel exclusionary reasons. The third form of using power is by conferring power on a person. This does not in itself change protected reasons, but it enables a person to change them. The power a person has can be restricted in many ways—in the way it can be exercised, the persons over whom it is held, the actions with respect to which the power-holder can make power-utterances, and so forth.

Given these clarifications it is evident that there is a close relation between normative power and authority. On the simple explanation of authority power is a special case of

---

[19] Cf. my 'Voluntary Obligations and Normative Powers', in *Proceedings of the Aristotelian Society*, Supp. Vol. 46 (1972), 79–102, and my *Practical Reason and Norms*, sec. 8, where the notion is more fully explained as well as given a more general definition. In this book, however, I erred in suggesting that a normative power is ability to change exclusionary reasons. Comments made by Philippa Foot forced me to realize that it is ability to change protected reasons (or exclusionary permissions). All mandatory rules are protected reasons.

authority. Authority is ability to change reasons. Power is ability to change a special type of reasons, namely protected ones. However, in the light of the objections to the simple explanation, we should regard authority basically as a species of power. To provide a comprehensive defence of this view requires showing that rules and commands are protected reasons and that all authoritative utterances are power-utterances. This is not a task that can be accomplished in this essay. Instead I shall try to provide a persuasive case showing, first, that the two objections fail against this view and, second, that the paradoxes can be explained away by it.

POWER AND AUTHORITY

We should distinguish between authority over persons and authority to perform certain actions. The two overlap but are distinct notions. Everyone who is an authority has authority over people, but not everyone who has authority is an authority. The difference is not of great philosophical moment, but its neglect can be a source of endless confusion. A person is an authority if he has relatively permanent and pervasive authority over persons, that is, either authority over a large group of people or with respect to various spheres of activity, or both.

Since power is the ability to change protected reasons for action and as reasons for action are reasons for some persons or others, we can divide powers into powers over oneself and powers over others. The most important species of power over oneself is the power to undertake voluntary obligations. Power over others is authority over them. There is one exception to this characterization. Sometimes we say that a person has authority over himself. This is a degenerate case of authority: an extension by analogy from the central cases of authority over others. It is interesting to note that when speaking of a person's authority over himself, we always refer to his power to grant himself permissions or powers. We never refer thus to one's power to undertake voluntary obligations.

One of the main obstacles to an analysis of authority is the frequent failure to distinguish between authority to perform an action and authority over persons.[20] A person has authority to

[20] This confusion undermines much of Richard Tuck's analysis in 'Why Is Authority Such a Problem?'

perform an action if he has been given permission to perform it or has been given power to perform it by somebody who has power to do so. Thus, I have authority to open your mail if the censor has given me permission to do so, assuming that he has power to do so.

My authority to open your mail is not authority over you. I cannot change your normative situation in any way though the censor changed it by giving me the authority to open your mail, thereby diminishing your right to privacy. I can also have authority to sign cheques in your name, which is a power I have because you gave it to me. This last example shows that the source of a person's authority to perform an act must have power to confer it, but he need not have authority over the person on whom he confers authority. To give me authority to sign cheques in your name you need power, but that you have such a power does not entail that you have any authority over me. It may well be that you have none.

The authority to act is, however, closely related to authority over persons, albeit in a somewhat more indirect way. When we consider the cases in which we are granted permissions or powers, it is evident that not all of them can be described as having authority to act. Only when the interests of another person will be affected by the act do we speak of it as authorized. But this is not a sufficient condition. I am permitted to open a supermarket that will lead to someone's bankruptcy, and yet it is not the case that I have authority to open the supermarket. I am permitted to do so simply because there is not and never was a prohibition against doing so. One has authority to do only those things that one is given permission to do by somebody who has authority over the person whose interests are affected.

We can now define X *has authority to* φ as: there is some Y and there is some Z such that,

(1) Y permitted X to φ or gave him power to do so
(2) Y has power to do so
(3) X's φ-ing will affect the interests of Z and Y has authority over Z.[21]

---

[21] Normally X, Y and Z will be different persons. A person may, however, give authority to another to affect his own interests or give himself authority to affect the interests of another.

REFUTING THE OBJECTIONS

The distinctions between being an authority and having authority and between authority to act and authority over persons are not directly connected with my claim that authority over persons, the basic concept of the three, is a species of normative power. These distinctions must be preserved by any account of authority. The advantage of the power analysis of authority is that it successfully meets the objection to the simple explanation and dissolves the paradoxes of authority.

Take the first objection first. What is the difference between orders and requests? Authority over persons is ability to change protected reasons for their actions. In most discussions of the concept of authority attention is focused on issuing orders and laying down rules as the standard manifestations of authority. These are, indeed, the standard cases of the intentional invocation of authority. It is, however, important to see that authority can be exercised without the person having authority intending to invoke it. This is true of political as well as of other kinds of authority and is a very important channel for the influence of authority to be felt. I shall take advice given by authority as a typical case in point.

Advice, whatever the hopes of the adviser may be, is given with the intention that its utterance will be taken as a reason for belief, not for action.[22] But the recipient of the advice may regard it as both a reason for action and an exclusionary reason for disregarding conflicting reasons. Consider the standard grounds for seeking advice. These are usually to gain information relevant to the solution of some practical problem facing one or for comparing one's own evaluation of the weight and importance of various factors with that of other people as a means of checking one's own views and calculations. But sometimes advice is sought for entirely different reasons. A person may be faced with a problem involving considerations concerning which he has little knowledge or understanding. He may turn to an expert, to an authority, for advice despite the fact that he has no way of assessing the reasons pointed out by the

---

[22] Advice differs from other cases of conveying information primarily in being given with the belief that it is or may be relevant to an actual or hypothetical question facing the recipient in his own estimate or in the opinion of the adviser and in being either intended by the adviser or expected by the recipient to be taken into account in the resolution of that practical problem.

authority against other conflicting reasons of which he may be aware. He may decide to follow the advice given without trying to work out whether it indicates reasons that tip the balance. If he does so he is in fact excluding all the conflicting reasons of which he is aware from his considerations. He is regarding the advice both as a reason to perform the action he was advised to perform and for not acting on conflicting reasons. A person may be justified in holding the advice he received to be a protected reason, even though advice is not given with an intention to be taken as a protected reason.

Orders, on the other hand, are given with the intention that their addressees shall take them as protected reasons. Many people can give an order without being entitled to do so. They are entitled to do so only if they have authority (power) over the addressee with respect to the subject-matter of the order. The order may be a valid first-order reason for performing the act even if it is not a valid exclusionary reason not to act on conflicting reasons, and it may be both even though the person who issued it has no authority to do so. But it always is a valid first-order reason and an exclusionary reason if he has the authority to give it.

Exclusionary reasons may exclude action for all or only for some kinds of the conflicting reasons. Exclusionary reasons differ in scope, that is, in the extent to which they exclude different kinds of conflicting reasons. Therefore, to maintain that orders are both first-order and exclusionary reasons is not tantamount to maintaining that they are absolute reasons. They may not exclude certain conflicting reasons, and when this is the case one must decide what to do on the balance of the non-excluded first-order reasons, including the order itself as one prima facie reason for the performance of the ordered action.

What then is the difference between an exclusionary reason and a first-order reason of a weight sufficient to override all the conflicting reasons that are excluded by the exclusionary reason and no others? There are two answers to this crucial question. First, exclusionary reasons exclude by kind and not by weight. They may exclude all the reasons of a certain kind (such as, considerations of economic welfare), including very weighty reasons, while not excluding even trivial considerations belonging to another kind (such as, considerations of

honour). Second, regardless of the different impact of exclusionary and weighty reasons on what ought to be done, all
things considered, they also differ in the way we view them.
Some facts are weighty reasons overriding conflicting reasons;
others are not to be compared with conflicting reasons. Their
impact is not to change the balance of reasons but to exclude
action on the balance of reasons.

This difference in function, regardless of any possible difference in what ought to be done, all things considered, explains
the difference between orders and requests. Valid orders are
not necessarily more weighty or important reasons than valid
requests. There could be orders that exclude few conflicting
considerations and that do not exclude and may be overriden
by certain requests. A request may be a reason of sufficient
weight to justify sacrificing one's life. The difference is not in
importance but in mode of operation. A request is made with
the intention that it shall be taken as a reason for action and
be acceded to only if it tips the balance. Orders are made with
the intention that they should prevail in certain circumstances
even if they do not tip the balance. They are intended to be
taken as reasons for excluding certain others that may tip the
balance against performing that action.

Put it another way. For every order, if we know what the person who issued it thinks is the correct outcome of all possible
practical conflicts in which it may be involved, we can ascribe
to him the view that his order has just the weight that would
justify all those consequences. But in doing this we have not
advanced at all toward explaining the difference between
orders and requests in general. This can be done if there is a
certain constant weight, or range of weights, that is characteristic of all orders and distinguishes them from requests. But in
fact both orders and requests span the whole range of possible
weights both in the eyes of those who issue them and of others.
Having assumed that the difference between them lies in their
practical implications, I submit that it consists in the fact that
orders but not requests are protected reasons.

There is a minimum that an order must exclude to be an
order. It must at least exclude considerations of the recipient's
present desires. Often orders exclude much more besides, but
never do they exclude less. In appropriate circumstances one

may be able to justify one's not having followed an order on the ground that the order was not intended to apply to the case. It was never intended, one could claim, that one should obey even if it turns out that there was a strong moral reason for not doing so or if obeying would severely damage the recipient's interests or be unlawful.[23] When such considerations amount to a justification and lead the agent not to follow the order, he cannot be said to have obeyed it but neither did he disobey it. It was not intended that he should follow it in such circumstances. But it is never a justification that the agent had a desire, however strong, for something inconsistent with his following the order. Many parents' orders come near to the minimum exclusion, being intended to exclude only consideration of the child's present desires in order to avoid argument on what is best, given his strong desire to perform or to avoid some action. But parents' orders often exclude a consideration of the child's own interests and may exclude much more besides.

That is the explanation of the fact that it is more presumptuous to order than to request. If you request you submit yourself to the addressee's judgment on the balance of reasons, while at the same time trying to add a reason on one side of that balance. But one who commands is not merely trying to change the balance by adding a reason for the action. He is also trying to create a situation in which the addressee will do wrong to act on the balance of reasons. He is replacing his authority for the addressee's judgment on the balance.

Similar considerations refute the second objection which denies that authoritative instructions are always reasons for action. There is a sense in which if one accepts the legitimacy of an authority one is committed to following it blindly. One can be very watchful that it shall not overstep its authority and be sensitive to the presence of non-excluded considerations. But barring these possibilities, one is to follow the authority regardless of one's view of the merits of the case (that is, blindly). One may form a view on the merits but so long as one follows the

---

[23] This is not always an acceptable justification. Many legal orders, for example, are given with the intention that they shall be followed in the face of conclusive moral reasons against performing the ordered act. It may be that one should never regard such orders as binding and that no one has legitimate authority to issue such orders. But this in no way affects my point that such orders are often given. In the intention of the man giving the order it is to be taken as excluding even moral considerations.

authority this is an academic exercise of no practical importance. We can go further than that and say that sometimes the very reasons that justify the setting up of an authority also justify following it blindly in a stronger sense—that is, following it without even attempting to form a judgment on the merits. This is the case, for example, with some traffic regulations. We all know the benefit from allowing traffic lights to regulate one's action rather than acting on one's own judgment. But we tend to forget that a significant part of the benefit is that we give up attempting to form a judgment of our own. When I arrive at a red traffic light I stop without trying to calculate whether there is, in the circumstances, any reason to stop. From our vantage point we have invented an example in which the question does not arise since the answer (there is no reason) is plain. But for the man in our example the question does arise; he has to discover whether there is no reason to stop. And if he is to inquire in this case, he has to inquire in many other cases. For us it looks ridiculous to hear him say, 'I am bound to follow authority regardless of the merits of the individual case,' for we know in advance what the merits are and forget that he has to find that out, and not only now but in many other cases as well. Only when it is justified to prevent this, is it also justified to accept authority in this respect, even if once in a while this makes one look ridiculous to the gods.

The last remarks in response to the objection to the simple view of authority help to explain both the force of the paradoxes and the way to overcome them. The paradoxes, I should hasten to say, pose no problem to the simple view of authority. On this view, the commands of legitimate authority are facts of the world that are reasons for action. They are essentially like the weather and the stock exchange in being facts that are reasons for certain actions and against others. One no more abandons reason or forfeits one's autonomy if one follows the commands of authority than if one follows trends on the stock exchange.

This solution not only gets rid of the paradoxes but also presents them as simple mistakes. If, however, authority over persons is normative power over them, then we can explain the temptation that the paradoxes present without succumbing to it. I shall examine the paradoxes as presented by Robert Paul Wolff: 'Men', he says 'can forfeit their autonomy at will. That is to say, a man can decide to obey the commands of another without making any attempt to determine for himself whether what is commanded is good or wise.'[24] Whatever the relevance of the second sentence to the problem of autonomy, it is true that accepting authority inevitably involves giving up one's right to act on one's judgment on the balance of reasons. It involves accepting an exclusionary reason.[25]

Wolff is anxious to emphasize that his view does not require people to disregard orders and commands altogether. The following shows both the strength and the weakness of his position.

For the autonomous man, there is no such thing, strictly speaking, as a command. If someone in my environment is issuing what are intended as commands, and if he or others expect those commands to be obeyed, that fact will be taken account of in my deliberations. I may decide that I ought to do what the person is commanding me to do, and it may even be that his issuing the command is the factor in the situation which makes it desirable for me to do so. For example, if I am on a sinking ship and the captain is giving orders for manning the lifeboats, and if everyone else is obeying the captain because he is the captain, I may decide that under the circumstances I had better do what he says, since the confusion caused by disobeying him would be generally harmful. But insofar as I make such a decision, I am not obeying his command; that is, I am not acknowledging him as having authority over me. I would make the same decision, for exactly the same reasons, if one of the passengers had started to issue 'orders' and had, in the confusion, come to be obeyed.[26]

Wolff is making two valid and important points here. (1) Because an order is always given with the intention that it be taken as both an exclusionary reason and a first-order reason, its addressee has more options than either to disregard the order altogether or to obey it as he was intended. He may hold it to be a valid first-order reason, given the circumstances of its utterance, while denying that it is an exclusionary reason. (2) This means that an anarchist can reject the legitimacy of all authority while giving some weight to the instructions of *de*

[24] Wolff, *In Defense of Anarchism*, p. 14.

[25] Wolff is wrong in saying that accepting authority involves giving up the right or the attempt to form a judgment on the balance of reasons. Only action on that judgment is excluded (if it involves relying on excluded reasons which are not overridden).

[26] Wolff, *In Defense of Anarchism*, pp. 15–16.

facto authorities. He can take such instructions to be first-order reasons without conceding the legitimacy of the authority. For it is only by acknowledging that such instructions are also valid exclusionary reasons that one accepts the legitimacy of the issuing authority. Only such an acknowledgement amounts to submission to authority for only it contains the necessary element of the denial of one's right to act on one's own judgment on the merits.

Reformulating Wolff's contentions in this way does show that there is more in them than simple confusions. He sees correctly that legitimate authority involves a denial of one's right to act on the merits of the case. But the reformulation also shows where he went wrong. He tacitly and correctly assumes that reason never justifies abandoning one's autonomy, that is, one's right and duty to act on one's judgment of what ought to be done, *all things considered*. I shall call this the principle of autonomy.[27]. He also tacitly and wrongly assumes that this is identical with the false principle that there are no valid exclusionary reasons, that is, that one is never justified in not doing what ought to be done on the balance of first-order reasons. I shall call this the denial of authority.

This confusion is natural if one conceives of all reasons as essentially first-order reasons and overlooks the possibility of the existence of second-order reasons. If all valid reasons are first-order reasons then it is a necessary truth that the principle of autonomy entails the denial of authority, for then what ought to be done all things considered is identical with what ought to be done on the balance of first-order reasons. But since there could in principle be valid second-order reasons, there is nothing in the principle of autonomy that requires the rejection of all authority.

The question of the legitimacy of authority takes the form that it was always assumed to take: an examination of the grounds that justify in certain circumstances regarding some utterances of certain persons as exclusionary reasons. There is no short cut that will make such an inquiry redundant by showing that the very concept of legitimate authority is incompatible with our notion of rationality or morality.

[27] It is clear that this principle of autonomy is not really a moral principle but a principle of rationality.

2

THE CLAIMS OF LAW

Can the very abstract analysis of authority in the previous essay be applied to the law? Do we have any reason to expect the notion of authority to play an important role in our understanding of the law or in shaping our attitude to it? Two preliminary objections must be tackled first.

(1) It is a popular view that the law enjoys *de facto* or effective authority. Its analysis involves these concepts but not necessarily that of a legitimate authority. This is a mistake. To hold that a government is *de facto* government is to concede that its claim to be government *de jure* is acknowledged by a sufficient number of sufficiently powerful people to assure it of control over a certain area. A person has effective or *de facto* authority only if the people over whom he has that authority regard him as a legitimate authority. This would usually, though not necessarily always, imply that he claims legitimate authority for himself. It is enough that others regard him as legitimate authority. This condition may have to be weakened. It may be unnecessary for the relevant population genuinely to believe that the person having effective authority is a legitimate authority; it is enough if, for whatever reasons, they avow such a belief. Furthermore, we could well find situations in which only some of the population acknowledge the authority of the relevant person, provided they are sufficiently prominent or powerful to enable him to impose his rule on the others. The reasons for which the relevant population accepts the authority of a person vary and do not belong to the anlaysis of the concept of a *de facto* authority. The population may acknowledge the legitimate authority of a person on the ground that he is the person in control (and that any attempt to change things will lead to chaos, etc.). This should not lead to the conclusions that control is enough and that acceptance of a claim to legitimate authority is not a logically necessary condition for the existence of a *de facto* authority. We need not concern ourselves with the precise conditions for being an effective authority. They probably differ with respect

to different types of effective authorities: legal, political leadership, ecclesiastical, etc. A common factor in all kinds of effective authority is that they involve a belief by some that the person concerned has legitimate authority. Therefore, the explanation of effective authority presupposes that of legitimate authority.[1]

(2) Authority was analysed in the context of a person in authority and his authoritative utterances. Such an analysis could in principle apply to a legislator and his acts of enactment. But not all law is enacted. Customary rules can be legally binding. Can they be authoritative despite the fact that they are not issued by authority? It is possible to talk directly of the authority of the law itself. A person's authority was explained by reference to his utterances: he has authority if his utterances are protected reasons for action, i.e. reasons for taking the action they indicate and for disregarding (certain) conflicting considerations. The law has authority if the existence of a law requiring a certain action is a protected reason for performing that action; i.e. a law is authoritative if its existence is a reason for conforming action and for excluding conflicting considerations. 'Reason' here means a valid or justifiable reason, for it is the legitimate authority of the law which is thus defined. The law enjoys effective authority, as we saw it, if its subjects or some of them regard its existence as a protected reason for conformity.

These clarifications show that it makes sense to refer to the authority of the law and that if its analysis involves the notion of effective authority it also involves that of legitimate authority. This may seem sufficient to show that the notion of authority is inextricably tied up with that of law. It is indeed plain that to determine our proper attitude to the law we must examine whether the law has authority over us which we should acknowledge. But need we use the concept of authority in explaining the nature of law? Does the concept play a part not only in determining our obligation to the law but also our understanding

---

[1] This view is in fact incorporated in most current analyses of authority. If it appears at first sight controversial, this is only because it is implicit rather than explicit in many popular accounts of *de facto* authority. It is generally agreed that authority cannot be based on force or threat of force alone; that it is dependent on influence, acceptance, etc. Further analysis will show that these notions presuppose a claim to authority and its recognition.

of it? The answer is affirmative, for it is an essential feature of law that it claims legitimate authority.

This may sound unduly mysterious, but it can in fact be given fairly precise meaning. We should concentrate on the circumstances in which non-conforming behaviour is or is not a breach of law. We need to establish first that the law claims that the existence of legal rules is a reason for conforming behaviour. This should not be confused with the false claim that the law requires conformity motivated by recognition of the binding force, the validity of the law. It is a truism that the law accepts conformity for other reasons (convenience, prudence, etc.). If pronouncements from the Bench may be taken as its mouthpiece,[2] it sometimes welcomes reliance on other (for example, independent moral) reasons for doing that which the law requires. Suppose, however, that—apart from the law itself— there are insufficient reasons for doing as the law requires. Suppose that on balance (excluding the existence of the law from the balance) one ought not to perform the required act, and that that is the view of both the law's subjects and of the judge. Failure to perform the act in such circumstances is a breach of the law. Does this mean that the law requires action against reason? No, it merely means that the law holds itself, i.e. the existence of the relevant legal rule, to be a reason which tips the balance and provides a sufficient reason for the required act. The way to interpret the fact that conformity is required even in the absence of other reasons for it is that the law itself is presented as such a reason. It does not matter if compliance is motivated by acknowledgment of such a claim. What matters is the nature of the claim itself.

The law's claim to legitimate authority is not merely a claim that legal rules are reasons. It includes the claim that they are exclusionary reasons for disregarding reasons for non-conformity. By and large I shall disregard this aspect of the law's claimed authority in the following essays. A few remarks may, however, be in place here. Many legal systems include doctrines specifically designed to allow individuals to deviate from an otherwise binding legal requirement if they consider themselves bound by strong reasons to do so. The rights of freedom of conscience and of conscientious objection are but prominent

---

[2] The legitimacy of so doing is explained in Essay 3 and other essays of Part II.

examples of such doctrines. In many countries prosecutorial discretion is meant by law to take account of such considerations. But in all legal systems the recognition given by law to such non-legal reasons is limited and is itself strictly regulated by law: non-legal reasons do not justify deviation from a legal requirement except if such justification is allowed by a specific legal doctrine.

It may be thought that the law ought to give recognition to all relevant considerations, that failure to do so is a moral defect in the law. In a sense it is a moral defect that the law sometimes does not enable courts to recognize the relevance of certain considerations. But if so, it is an inevitable defect. Perhaps many of the considerations not currently recognized by, for example, English courts should be recognized by them. But it is practically impossible for the law to recognize all the considerations relevant to cases to which it applies. If the law has moral authority then this authority must be established by showing, among other things, that it is better not to enable courts to apply certain considerations than not to have law at all.

The practical inability of the law to give full weight to all the reasons which may affect an agent is particularly obvious when the costs of enforcing proper recognition of such reasons or of the likely abuse of such a law if not adequately enforced seem to outweigh the benefits. This is likely to happen on numerous occasions. When concentrating attention on individual cases it is often felt that the arguments for making the case an exception to the rule are overwhelming and individuals or at the very least the courts must be given powers to recognize such exceptions, i.e. to have a general power to exempt from the law on grounds of hardship or justice. This may be justified with respect to certain legal problems. But in many areas this cure will be worse than the disease. It may be better to cause hardship in a few cases than to lead to great uncertainty in many. Uncertainty frustrates expectations, prevents planning, encourages abuses of the law by encouraging attempts to exploit its vague margins, and very often policing such laws involves prying into the private affairs of individuals. In matters where these considerations are important and where serious hardship or injustice is rare, certainty is at a premium and the courts are justifiably denied exemptive powers. The result is that very weighty reasons for deviating from the legally required act on a specific occasion may have been excluded. Another cause for non-recognition is oversight. In drafting the law it may not have been realized that very pressing reasons for deviating from it exist or will exist in the future in a certain class of cases to which it applies. The slowness of the reforming and legislative processes often prevents law from being amended even after many are aware of its shortcomings.

I have mentioned practical inability and oversight as reasons for the law's failure to give full weight to all the reasons which may affect a case. These observations are made to explain not to justify. It is not here claimed that such reasoning always or indeed ever justifies the authority of the law. I shall return to this question in Part IV below.[3] The purpose of these remarks was merely to outline the kinds of argument normally invoked to explain and defend the fact that the law sometimes disregards valid and weighty reasons, for the problem is not how to justify these facts but how to interpret them.

The considerations mentioned are typical exclusionary reasons. Suppose there is a law requiring one to ϕ. Let us assume that there is a very pressing reason, R, for not-ϕ-ing on a particular occasion. The law requires one not to act on that reason. Is it because it claims absolute weight for itself which defeats R or is it because the law claims to itself the status of a protected reason which excludes R? One should look for the standard reasons for which R is rejected by the law. Those are the reasons expressed by the courts as justification for not excusing someone who acts on R and breaks the law and on similar occasions. My claim is that these reasons are those I mentioned above and other related reasons. Some will, therefore, be arguments that allowing everyone to act for R will have, on the whole, worse consequences because of the rate of failure to do so properly (people will be often wrong in thinking that R exists in their situation, etc.).

But the fact that trying to act for a certain reason (R) for ϕ-ing is more likely, because of the rate of failure to do so properly, to do more harm than good is not a reason for not-ϕ-ing.

---

[3] There is more than one question of justification involved. One must distinguish between 'Is the law (or legislator) right to claim such authority in those circumstances?' and 'Is the individual morally bound to acknowledge that authority?' Sometimes an affirmative answer to the first question will be combined with a negative answer to the second.

It is a reason for not acting for R. Indirectly it weakens the case for ϕ-ing, but directly it is an exclusionary reason: a reason for excluding R. Similarly, the fact that though the rule that one should ϕ should be changed (because all things considered one should not ϕ) it should not be changed here and now or by me is not a reason for ϕ-ing which overrides the reasons for not-ϕ-ing but rather a reason why I should disregard those reasons for not-ϕ-ing. It is the essential exclusionary character of a rule that it resists permanent revision. It is immune from the claim that it should be re-examined with a view to possible revision on every occasion to which it applies.[4] This regulation of the appropriate method of revising rules is based not on the belief that until revised the reasons for the act required outweigh all conflicting reasons, but on the more rational and less mysterious belief that until it is revised it is justifiable to exclude such conflicting reasons.

One last caveat: what is excluded by a rule of law is not all other reasons, but merely all those other reasons which are themselves not legally recognized. We should not conceive of the law as a set of isolated norms each having its own separate and independent function, but as a set of (potentially conflicting or reinforcing) reasons which together determine what is required by law.

If this analysis is correct then the law claims authority. The law presents itself as a body of authoritative standards and requires all those to whom they apply to acknowledge their authority. This is of course not a very novel thesis. In one way or another it is common to think that the law claims authority. The purpose of this essay and of the previous one was to interpret that common notion, give it precise meaning, and vindicate it by integrating it to a wider thesis about the nature of authority and other known facts about the law. By doing this the central problem of this book was defined and presented. Since the law claims authority should its claim be acknowledged? Is it justified? Is there an obligation to submit to the authority of the law; if not, is it at all permissible to do so? Is the legitimacy of the authority of the law conditional on a legal recognition of a right of dissent?

[4] Cf. *Practical Reason and Norms*, ch. 2.

Part II

The Nature of Law and Natural Law

Part II

The Nature of Law and Some Special Cases

3

LEGAL POSITIVISM AND THE SOURCES OF LAW*

1. THE NATURE OF LEGAL POSITIVISM

The perennial and inexhaustible nature of the controversy concerning the positivist analysis of the law is due in no small measure to the elusive meaning of 'positivism' in legal philosophy. True, it is well established that legal positivism is essentially independent (even though not historically unrelated) both of the positivism of nineteenth-century philosophy and of the logical positivism of the present century. But the great variation between different positivist theories of law and the large variety of philosophical motivations permeating the work of the non-positivists indicate the difficulty, perhaps the impossibility, of identifying legal positivism at its source—in a fundamental positivist philosophical outlook. The easiest approach to the continuing controversy concerning legal positivism is through the particular theses or groups of theses round which it revolves.

Three areas of dispute have been at the centre of the controversy: the identification of the law, its moral value, and the meaning of its key terms. We could identify these as the social thesis, the moral thesis, and the semantic thesis respectively. It should be understood, however, that in each area positivists (and their opponents) are identified by supporting (or rejecting) one or more of a whole group of related theses rather than any particular thesis.

In the most general terms the positivist social thesis is that what is law and what is not is a matter of social fact (that is, the variety of social theses supported by positivists are various refinements and elaborations of this crude formulation). Their moral thesis is that the moral value of law (both of a particular law and of a whole legal system) or the moral merit it has is a contingent matter dependent on the content of the law and the circumstances of the society to which it applies. The only

---

* My thinking on the problems discussed in this essay was greatly influenced by conversations with R. M. Dworkin and J. M. Finnis, who disagree with many of my conclusions.

semantic thesis which can be identified as common to most positivist theories is a negative one, namely, that terms like 'rights' and 'duties' cannot be used in the same meaning in legal and moral contexts. This vague formulation is meant to cover such diverse views as: (1) 'moral rights' and 'moral duties' are meaningless or self-contradictory expressions, or (2) 'rights' and 'duties' have an evaluative and a non-evaluative meaning and they are used in moral contexts in their evaluative meaning whereas in legal contexts they are used in their non-evaluative meaning, or (3) the meaning of 'legal rights and duties' is not a function of the meaning of its component terms—as well as a whole variety of related semantic theses.

Of these the social thesis is the more fundamental. It is also responsible for the name 'positivism' which indicates the view that the law is posited, is made law by the activities of human beings. The moral and semantic theses are often thought to be necessitated by the social thesis. In crude outline the arguments run as follows: Since by the social thesis what is law is a matter of social fact, and the identification of law involves no moral argument, it follows that conformity to moral values or ideals is in no way a condition for anything being a law or legally binding. Hence, the law's conformity to moral values and ideals is not necessary. It is contingent on the particular circumstances of its creation or application. Therefore, as the moral thesis has it, the moral merit of the law depends on contingent factors. There can be no argument that of necessity the law has moral merit. From this and from the fact that terms like 'rights' and 'duties' are used to describe the law—any law regardless of its moral merit—the semantic thesis seems to follow. If such terms are used to claim the existence of legal rights and duties which may and sometimes do contradict moral rights and duties, these terms cannot be used in the same meaning in both contexts.

I have argued elsewhere[1] that both arguments are fallacious and that neither the moral nor the semantic theses follow from the social one. The claim that what is law and what is not is purely a matter of social fact still leaves it an open question whether or not those social facts by which we identify the law or determine its existence do or do not endow it with moral

[1] *Practical Reason and Norms*, pp. 162 ff., and see also Essay 8 below.

merit. If they do, it has of necessity a moral character. But even if they do not, it is still an open question whether, given human nature and the general conditions of human existence, every legal system which is in fact the effective law of some society does of necessity conform to some moral values and ideals. As for the semantic thesis, all the positivist has reason to maintain is that the use of normative language to describe the law does not always carry the implication that the speaker endorses the law described as morally binding. Put somewhat more precisely this means that normative language when used to state the law does not always carry its full normative force. To this even the non-positivist can agree. This does not justify the view that terms like rights and duties are used with a different meaning in legal and moral contexts.

It is not the purpose of the present essay to explore these arguments. I mention them only to indicate the extent to which the version of positivism that will be argued for here is a moderate one which need not conflict with the natural lawyer's view concerning the semantic analysis of normative terms and the relation between law and morality. The following are but some examples of views usually associated with natural law theories which are comparable with the version of positivism defended below:

(a) 'A legal duty' means a duty which one has because the law requires the performance of that action.

(b) There is a necessary connection between law and popular morality (i.e. the morality endorsed and practised by the population).

(c) Every legal system's claim to authority is justified.

Whether or not these views are true, they are certainly compatible with the social thesis which is the backbone of the version of positivism I would like to defend. The social thesis is best viewed not as a 'first-order' thesis but as a constraint on what kind of theory of law is an acceptable theory—more specifically it is a thesis about some general properties of any acceptable test for the existence and identity of legal systems.

The (Strong) Social Thesis. A jurisprudential theory is acceptable only if its tests for identifying the content of the law and determining its existence depend exclusively on facts of human behaviour capable of being described in value-neutral terms, and applied without resort to moral argument.

This formulation is less clear than it might be. A more clear and lucid statement requires a fuller theoretical elaboration and is likely, therefore, to be more controversial. The above formulation strives to get at the core motivation and the basic idea underlying the various formulations of the social thesis and accepts the inevitable cost in lack of precision. Some clarification may nevertheless be called for.

First, the thesis assumes that any complete theory of law includes tests for the identification of the content and determination of the existence of the law. This seemed self-evident to many philosophers of law who saw it as one of their main tasks to provide such tests. Other equally influential legal philosophers were never stirred to do so and felt that such tests are no part of legal philosophy or are fruitless or impossible. Lon Fuller is the most eminent of those contemporary philosophers who have taken such a view. The reasons for dissenting from such positions will be indicated briefly in the next section. It is best to regard such theories as incomplete theories of law. For one reason or another most, if not all, theories of law are incomplete in that they do not propose answers to some questions which fall within the province of jurisprudence.

Secondly, the thesis assumes that there is a sufficiently rich vocabulary of value-neutral terms. It does not assume that there is a clear and sharp break between value-laden and value-free terms. Nor is it committed to any side in the naturalist/anti-naturalist dispute. That the test is *capable* of being described in value-neutral terms does not mean that no value or deontic conclusions are entailed by it. To assert that is to take an anti-naturalist position.

Thirdly, the thesis does not require disregarding the intentions, motivations, and moral views of people. Value-neutrality does not commit one to behaviousism.

Finally, it is worth noting that the social thesis can be divided into two: *A*—A social condition is necessary for identifying the existence and content of the law: A rule is a legal rule only if it meets a social condition. *B*—A social condition is sufficient for identifying the existence and content of the law: A rule is a legal rule if it meets the social condition.

2. THE SOCIAL THESIS

I have claimed that the social thesis has always been at the foundation of positivist thinking about the law and that its semantic and moral consequences have all too often been misunderstood. It is not to my purpose here to expound and defend any particular view about the tests by which the existence and content of law is to be identified.[2] But since acceptance of the social thesis does give shape to theories of law which endorse it, it is important to reflect once again upon the reasons supporting the social thesis. In so doing I will inevitably commit myself to certain more definite views about the social conditions for the existence and identity of legal systems.

A. The most general and non-theoretical justification of the social thesis is that it correctly reflects the meaning of 'law' and cognate terms in ordinary language. This claim can be and has been illustrated often enough. It seems fundamentally sound as an essential part of every defence of the social thesis and yet in itself it is inconclusive. The word 'law' has non-legal uses: laws of nature, moral laws, laws of various institutions, the laws of thought, etc. Several of these have problematical status; moreover there are no clear demarcation lines in linguistic usage between the different kinds of law. Hence the dispute about the character of international law, for example, cannot be determined by appeal to ordinary language.

For similar reasons usage is too amorphous to give adequate support for the social thesis. It certainly suggests that law has a social base, that Nazi Germany had a legal system, etc. But it is not sufficiently determinate to establish beyond dispute that social facts are both sufficient and necessary conditions for the existence and identity of the law.

Finally, we do not want to be slaves of words. Our aim is to understand society and its institutions. We must face the question: is the ordinary sense of 'law' such that it helps identify facts of importance to our understanding of society?

B. The social thesis is often recommended on the ground that it clearly separates the description of the law from its evaluation. This, it is alleged, prevents confusion and serves clarity

---

[2] See Essays 5 and 6 below and my *Practical Reason and Norms*, Sections 4.3–5.2, where I suggested various modifications and elaborations on Hart's ideas as expounded in *The Concept of Law* (Oxford, 1961).

of thought. This is true, but it presupposes the thesis rather than supports it. If the law is to be identified by social tests then trying to identify it without clearly separating social facts from evaluative considerations is misleading and often downright wrong. But if the identification of the law involves, as many natural lawyers believe it does, evaluative as well as social conditions then to distinguish between the two in identifying the law is misleading and wrong.

C. Adhering to the social thesis eliminates investigator's bias. It requires that the investigator should put aside his evaluative and deontic views and rely exclusively on considerations which can be investigated and described in a value-neutral way. This again, though true, presupposes the social thesis and is one of its results rather than its foundation. For in this respect too it must be admitted that if those natural lawyers who reject the social thesis are right then involving the investigator's sense of values (it will not then be called bias) is the only proper way for identifying the law. This does not mean that on this view the law is what it is because the investigator believes in certain values. It does, however, mean that the proper way for identifying the law is to inquire into the validity and implications of certain values.

D. There are, no doubt, many other reasons and variations on reasons which have been proposed in support of the social thesis and many of them have at least some truth in them. But the main justification of the social thesis lies in the character of law as a social institution. Some social institutions may have to be understood in ways which are incompatible with an analogous social thesis applied to them. But the law, like several others, is an institution conforming to the social thesis. To see this, it is necessary to specify in a general way the main ingredients of the tests for existence and identity for a legal system and to identify those with which the social thesis is concerned. The tests for identity and existence of a legal system contain three basic elements: efficacy, institutional character, and sources.

Efficacy is the least controversial of these conditions. Oddly enough it is also the least studied and least understood. Perhaps there is not much which legal philosophy can contribute in this respect. Though I believe there are at least some, however elementary, difficulties which need to be explored.[3] Since this essay is not concerned with the precise details of the efficacy condition these difficulties can be overlooked. Suffice it that all agree that a legal system is not the law in force in a certain community unless it is generally adhered to and is accepted or internalized by at least certain sections of the population. This condition is simply designed to assure that the law referred to is the actual law of a given society and not a defunct system or an aspiring one. It is the least important of the conditions. It is not disputed by natural lawyers. And it does not help to characterize the essence of law as a kind of human institution. It distinguishes between effective and non-effective law and not between legal and non-legal systems. Consider, by way of analogy, social morality. The same condition applies. No morality is the social morality of a population unless it is generally conformed to and accepted by that population. Here the condition of efficacy does not illuminate the nature of morality. It merely tells an effective morality from one which is not.

More important and also more controversial is the second component of the tests for existence and identity—the institutionalized character of the law. Again, the many controversies about the precise nature of the institutional aspect of law can be side-stepped here. It is widely agreed (and by many natural lawyers as well) that a system of norms is not a legal system unless it sets up adjudicative institutions charged with regulating disputes arising out of the application of the norms of the system. It is also generally agreed that such a normative system is a legal system only if it claims to be authoritative and to occupy a position of supremacy within society, i.e. it claims the right to legitimize or outlaw all other social institutions.

These institutionalized aspects of law identify its character as a social type, as a kind of social institution. Put in a nutshell, it is a system of guidance and adjudication claiming supreme authority within a certain society and therefore, where efficacious, also enjoying such effective authority. One may think that there is much more that can be said about the sort of social institution that law is. Why be so sparing and abstract in its description? No doubt the features of law mentioned can and

[3] See my *The Concept of a Legal System* (Oxford, 1970), ch. 9, for some of the puzzling aspects of many common views about efficacy.

should be elaborated in much greater detail. But when articulating a general test for existence and identity for the law one probably should not go beyond this bare characterization. The rest belongs properly to the sociology of law, for it characterizes some specific legal systems or some types of legal systems (modern capitalist, feudal, etc.), and not necessarily all legal systems.[4]

'Law', as was mentioned already, is used in many different contexts and is applied to norms of great variety and diversity. Lawyers quite naturally focus their professional attention on a certain range of uses: those which are tied to institutions of the type described. Many legal philosophers have suggested that the philosophical analysis of law should follow the legal profession and should pin its analysis to this kind of institution. This is quite natural and completely justified. Given even the very sketchy and rudimentary characterization proposed above, it is amply clear that law thus understood is an institution of great importance to all those who live in societies governed by law, which nowadays means almost everybody. There is more than enough justification to make it a subject of special study (which need not and should not neglect its complex interrelations with other institutions and social forces). There is also sufficient reason to encourage the general public's consciousness of law as a special type of institution.

Many natural law theories are compatible with all that was said above concerning the institutional nature of law. Yet it must be pointed out that such an institutionalized conception of law is incompatible with certain natural law positions; and this for two reasons. In the first place, it is a consequence of the institutionalized character of the law that it has limits. Legal systems contain only those standards which are connected in certain ways with the operation of the relevant adjudicative institutions.[5] This is what its institutionalized character means.

---

[4] The main possible addition to the facts I mentioned are sanctions, the use of coercion or of force, and the existence of institutions for law-enforcement. See on this H. Oberdiek, 'The Role of Sanctions and Coercion in Understanding Law and Legal Systems', *American Journal of Jurisprudence* (1975), p. 71; Raz, *Practical Reason and Norms*, pp. 154–62.

[5] Kelsen thought the relation is simple: Laws are norms addressed to courts (see, for example, *The General Theory of Law and State* (New York, 1945), p. 29. Others suggest more indirect connections. Most notable is Hart's idea that laws are standards courts are bound to apply and use in adjudication: *The Concept of Law*, pp. 89 ff.

Hence the law has limits: it does not contain all the justifiable standards (moral or other) nor does it necessarily comprise all social rules and conventions. It comprises only a subset of these, only those standards having the proper institutional connection.[6] This is incompatible with the view that law does not form a separate system of standards and especially with the claim that there is no difference between law and morality or between it and social morality.

A second and perhaps more radical consequence of the conception of law as an institutional system is that one cannot impose moral qualifications as conditions for a system or a rule counting as legal which are not reflected also in its institutional features. If law is a social institution of a certain type, then all the rules which belong to the social type are legal rules, however morally objectionable they may be. Law may have necessary moral properties, but if so, then only on the ground that all or some of the rules having the required institutional connections necessarily have moral properties. To impose independent moral conditions on the identity of law will inevitably mean either that not all the rules forming a part of the social institution of the relevant type are law or that some rules which are not part of such institutions are law. Either way 'law' will no longer designate a social institution.

3. THE SOURCES OF LAW

Most positivists are ambiguous concerning one interesting point. While their general terms suggest an endorsement of the strong social thesis, their actual doctrines rest on efficacy and institutionality as the only conditions concerning the social foundation of the law. Let the combination of these two conditions be called the weak social thesis. It is easy to show that the weak and the strong theses are not equivalent. Suppose that the law requires that unregulated disputes (i.e. those with

---

[6] Cannot a society have judicial institutions instructed to apply all social rules and cannot we envisage such a society lacking a clear differentiation between social morality and ideal or critical morality? Such societies are possible and probably have existed. This, however, merely shows that from their point of view there was no distinction between law and morality (unless they were made conscious of the distinction by observing other communities). We who have the distinction can still apply it to them when judging that, as things stand in their community, law encompasses the whole of their social morality. But things could have been different even for them.

respect to which the law is unsettled) be determined on the basis of moral considerations[7] (or a certain subclass of them, such as considerations of justice or moral considerations not fundamentally at odds with social morality). Suppose further that it is argued that in virtue of this law moral considerations have become part of the law of the land (and hence the law is never unsettled unless morality is). This contention runs directly counter to the strong thesis. If it is accepted, the determination of what is the law in certain cases turns on moral considerations, since one has to resort to moral arguments to identify the law. To conform to the strong thesis we will have to say that while the rule referring to morality is indeed law (it is determined by its sources) the morality to which it refers is not thereby incorporated into law. The rule is analogous to a 'conflict of law' rule imposing a duty to apply a foreign system which remains independent of and outside the municipal law.

While all this is clear enough, it is equally clear that the contrary view (according to which morality becomes part of the law as a consequence of the referring law) does not offend against the requirement of efficacy. For here too the bulk of the legal system may be conformed to. Nor is this view inconsistent with the institutional aspect of law: morality becomes law, on this view, by being tied to the relevant institutions. Finally, the allegation that morality can be thus incorporated into law is consistent with the thesis of the limits of law, for it merely asserts that source-based laws may from time to time incorporate parts of morality into law while imposing perhaps various conditions on their applicability. Having said that I should add that the result of admitting the view under consideration is that some non-source-based moral principles are part of almost every legal system, since most legal systems require judges to apply moral considerations on various occasions.

The difference between the weak and the strong social theses is that the strong one insists, whereas the weak one does not, that the existence and content of every law is fully determined by social sources. On the other hand, the weak thesis, but not the strong one, builds into the law the conditions of efficacy and

[7] Note that the reference is to morality, not to social morality. Social morality is based on sources: the customs, habits, and common views of a community.

institutionality. The two theses are logically independent. The weak thesis though true is insufficient to characterize legal positivism. It is compatible with—

   (a) Sometimes the identification of some laws turns on moral arguments,

but also with—

   (b) In all legal systems the identification of some laws turns on moral argument.

The first view is on the borderline of positivism and may or may not be thought consistent with it. But whereas the first view depends on the contingent existence of source-based law making moral considerations into the criteria of validity in certain cases (as in the example above), the second view asserts a conceptual necessity of testing law by moral argument and is clearly on the natural law side of the historical positivist/natural law divide.

   I will argue for the truth of the strong social thesis (thus excluding both (a) and (b)).[8] I shall rename the strong social thesis 'the sources thesis'. A 'source' is here used in a somewhat technical sense (which is, however, clearly related to traditional writings on legal sources). A law has a source if its contents and existence can be determined without using moral arguments (but allowing for arguments about people's moral views and intentions, which are necessary for interpretation, for example). The sources of a law are those facts by virtue of which it is valid

---

[8] The weak social thesis provides all the ingredients by which one determines whether a normative system is a legal system and whether it is in force in a certain country. In other words, the weak social thesis provides a complete test of existence of legal systems, a test by which one determines whether there is a legal system in force in a country. It also contributes (that is, the institutional character of law contributes) some of the ingredients which make up the test of identity of a legal system (i.e. the test by which one determines whether two norms belong to the same legal system), but here it is insufficient and has to be supplemented by the strong social thesis, i.e. by the claim that all laws have social sources.

   E. P. Soper, 'Legal Theory and the Obligation of the Judge: The Hart/Dworkin Dispute', *Michigan L. Rev.* 75 (1977) p. 511 f., and D. Lyons, 'Principles, Positivism and Legal Theory', *Yale L.J.* 87 (1977) p. 424 f., argue that legal positivism is consistent with (a). Supporters of such a conception of the law have to provide an adequate criterion for separating legal references to morality, which make its application a case of applying pre-existing legal rules from cases of judicial discretion in which the judge, by resorting to moral consideration, is changing the law. I am not aware of any serious attempt to provide such a test.

and which identify its content. This sense of 'source' is wider than that of 'formal sources' which are those establishing the validity of a law (one or more Acts of Parliament together with one or more precedents may be the formal source of one rule of law). 'Source' as used here includes also 'interpretative sources', namely all the relevant interpretative materials. The sources of a law thus understood are never a single act (of legislation, etc.) alone, but a whole range of facts of a variety of kinds.

What are the reasons for accepting the sources thesis? Two arguments combine to support it. The one shows that the thesis reflects and explicates our conception of the law; the second shows that there are sound reasons for adhering to that conception.

When discussing appointments to the Bench, we distinguish different kinds of desirable characteristics judges should possess. We value their knowledge of the law and their skills in interpreting laws and in arguing in ways showing their legal experience and expertise. We also value their wisdom and understanding of human nature, their moral sensibility, their enlightened approach, etc. There are many other characteristics which are valuable in judges. For present purposes these two kinds are the important ones. The point is that while it is generally admitted that both are very important for judges as judges, only the first group of characteristics mentioned is thought of as establishing the legal skills of the judge. The second group, though relevant to his role as a judge, is thought of as reflecting his moral character, not his legal ability. Similarly, when evaluating judgments as good or bad, lawyers and informed laymen are used to distinguishing between assessing judicial arguments as legally acceptable or unacceptable and assessing them as morally good or bad. Of many legal decisions we hear that they are legally defective, being based on a misinterpretation of a statute or a case, etc. Of others it is said that though legally the decisions are acceptable, they betray gross insensitivity to current social conditions, show how conservative judges are, that they are against trade unions, or that in their zeal to protect individuals they go too far in sacrificing administrative efficiency, etc.

These distinctions presuppose that judges are, at least on

occasion, called upon to rely on arguments revealing their moral character rather than their legal ability. (It is unreasonable to suppose that the judge's moral character reveals itself only when he is wrong in law. It affects decisions too often for that to be a reasonable hypothesis.) As indicated above, the use of moral judgment is regarded not as a special case of applying law or legal arguments, but is contrasted with them. This is manifested in the way the two kinds of tests evaluating judges and judgements are related to two further distinctions. The first is that between applying the law and creating, innovating, or developing the law. It is a common view that judges both apply the law and develop it. And though their two functions are extremely hard to disentangle in many cases, yet sometimes, at least, it is clear of a case that it breaks new ground, while of many others it may be equally clear that they merely apply established law. The important point is that it is our normal view that judges use moral arguments (though perhaps not only such arguments) when developing the law and that they use legal skills when applying the law (though not only legal skills are used when they have to decide whether to apply a precedent or distinguish or overrule it. I shall disregard this problem in the sequel and will return to it in Essay 10 below).

Finally there is the distinction between settled and unsettled law. All lawyers know that on some questions the law is unsettled. Sometimes they say on such cases that no one knows what the law is—as if there is law on the question which is very difficult to discover. But most of the time they express themselves more accurately, saying that this is an open question, that the law is unsettled, etc. (On the interpretation of these expressions, see Essay 4.) It is primarily in deciding cases regarding which the law is unsettled (as well as in distinguishing and reversing settled law) that judges are thought to develop the law using moral, social, and other non-legal arguments. It is when deciding cases where the law is settled that the judges are thought of as using their legal skills in applying the law.

The sources thesis explains and systemizes these distinctions. According to it, the law on a question is settled when legally binding sources provide its solution. In such cases judges are typically said to apply the law, and since it is source-based, its application involves technical, legal skills in reasoning from those sources and does not call for moral acumen. If a legal question is not answered by standards deriving from legal sources then it lacks a legal answer—the law on the question is unsettled. In deciding such cases courts inevitably break new (legal) ground and their decision develops the law (at least in precedent-based legal systems). Naturally, their decisions in such cases rely at least partly on moral and other extra-legal considerations.

One need not assume complete convergence between the distinctions mentioned above and the sources thesis. If, in fact, the sources thesis coincides with the way these distinctions are generally applied, it has explanatory power and is supported to that extent. It can then be regarded as being a systemizing or a tidying-up thesis where it goes beyond the ordinary use of these distinctions. This argument for the sources thesis is not an argument from the ordinary sense of 'law' or any other term. It relies on fundamental features of our understanding of a certain social institution, the primary examples of which are contemporary municipal legal systems but which extend far beyond them. It is not part of the argument that a similar conception of legal systems is to be found in all cultures and in all periods. It is part of our ways of conceiving and understanding the working of social institutions. There is nothing wrong in interpreting the institutions of other societies in terms of our typologies. This is an inevitable part of any intelligent attempt to understand other cultures. It does not imply that in interpreting alien institutions you disregard the intentions, beliefs, or value-schemes of their participants. It only means that at some stage you classify their activities, thus interpreted, in terms of a scheme for analysing social institutions of which the participants themselves may have been ignorant.

Still, it may be reassuring to know that the sources thesis is not merely a reflection of a superficial feature of our culture. I shall argue briefly that the sources thesis captures and highlights a fundamental insight into the function of law. It is a commonplace that social life requires and is facilitated by various patterns of forbearances, co-operation, and co-ordination between members of the society or some of them. The same is true of the pursuits of goals which the society or sections in it may set themselves. Different members and different sections of a society may have different views as to which schemes of co-operation, co-ordination, or forbearance are appropriate. It is an essential part of the function of law in society to mark the point at which a private view of members of the society, or of influential sections or powerful groups in it, ceases to be their private view and becomes (i.e. lays a claim to be) a view binding on all members notwithstanding their disagreement with it. It does so and can only do so by providing publicly ascertainable ways of guiding behaviour and regulating aspects of social life.[9] Law is a public measure by which one can measure one's own as well as other people's behaviour. It helps to secure social co-operation not only through its sanctions providing motivation for conformity but also through designating in an accessible way the patterns of behaviour required for such co-operation. This fact has been emphasized by many a natural lawyer for it forms part of the justification of the need for positive law. Locke is a prominent and well-known example. Hart more than anybody else emphasized the point among legal positivists.

To prevent misunderstanding let me elaborate some of the crucial steps in the argument. Many societies (large or small) have a relatively formal way of distinguishing between expressions of views, demands, etc., and authoritative rulings. Such a distinction is an essential element in our conception of government, be it in a family, in a loosely organized community, or in the state. Not all authoritative rulings are laws, not all systems of such rules are legal systems. But marking a rule as legally binding is marking it as an authoritative ruling. This marking-off of authoritative rulings indicates the existence in that society of an institution or organization claiming authority over members of the society that is holding them bound to conform to certain standards just because they were singled out by that purported authority regardless of whether or not they are justifiable standards on other grounds. Since it is of the very essence of the alleged authority that it issues rulings which are binding regardless of any other justification, it follows that it

---

[9] I do not mean to suggest that all laws are open. Secret laws are possible provided they are not altogether secret. Someone must know their content some of the time. They are publicly ascertainable and they guide the behaviour of the officials to whom they are addressed or who are charged with their enforcement by being so.

must be possible to identify those rulings without engaging in a justificatory argument, i.e. as issuing from certain activities and interpeted in the light of publicly ascertainable standards not involving moral argument.

If the first argument for the sources thesis was that it reflects and systemizes several interconnected distinctions embedded in our conception of the law, the second argument probes deeper and shows that the distinctions and the sources thesis which explicates them help to identify a basic underlying function of the law: to provide publicly ascertainable standards by which members of the society are held to be bound so that they cannot excuse non-conformity by challenging the justification of the standard. (Though, of course, in many countries they are free to act to change it.) This is the reason for which we differentiate between the courts' applying the law, i.e. those standards which are publicly ascertainable and binding beyond a moral argument open to the litigants, and the activity of the courts in developing the law relying on moral and other rational considerations. In making this a test for the identification of law, the sources thesis identifies it as an example of a kind of human institution which is of decisive importance to the regulation of social life.

4

LEGAL REASONS, SOURCES, AND GAPS*

It is common ground to all legal positivists that the law has social sources, i.e. that the content and existence of the law can be determined by reference to social facts and without relying on moral considerations. This view led early positivists such as Bentham, Austin, and to a degree also the American Realists to a reductivist interpretation of legal statements. They claimed that legal statements are synonymous with statements about what certain people commanded or willed, or about the chances that a man may come to harm of a certain kind, or about the likelihood that courts will reach certain decisions. Professor Hart, while accepting the sources thesis, mounted a most formidable criticism of reductivism. He argued that legal statements are deontic or practical. They are used to demand and justify action and thus function in discourse and argument in ways which no theoretical statements could.[1]

Professor Hart's arguments are convincing and there is no need to elaborate them here. His own several attempts to reconcile the sources thesis, according to which all laws have a source, with his rejection of reductivist explanations of legal statements are less successful.[2] More illuminating in this respect is Kelsen's work: Kelsen never succumbed to the reductivist temptation but developed a most ingenious way of combining the sources thesis with anti-reductivism.[3] Unfortunately, his discussion is so obscure that he is very often mistaken for a reductivist.

* Published in *Archiv für Rechts- und Sozialphilosophie, Beiheft* 11 (1979).

[1] For Hart's repeated attempts to come to grips with the problem of reductivism see especially 'The Ascription of Responsibility and Rights', *Proceedings of the Aristotelian Society* 49 (1948–9), 171; *Definition and Theory in Jurisprudence* (Oxford, 1953), and *The Concept of Law* (Oxford, 1961).

[2] For a recent penetrating analysis of the development of Hart's views on the issue and a powerful criticism of his views see G. P. Baker, 'Defeasibility and Meaning' in P. M. S. Hacker and J. Raz (eds.), *Law, Morality and Society* (Oxford, 1977).

[3] His views remain the same in *General Theory of Law and State* (New York, 1944) and *Pure Theory of Law*, 2nd ed. (Berkeley, 1967).

Kelsen's theory, though containing invaluable insights, is defective on various counts.[4] The purpose of the following remarks is to contribute[5] to an anti-reductivist explanation of legal statements, based on the sources thesis. Such an explanation, it will be argued, presupposes the possibility of gaps in the law and a proper understanding of the relation between law and legal adjudication.

1. PROFESSOR DWORKIN'S REFUTATION OF POSITIVISM

If the law is based on sources, what is the law on matters not referred to in any source? If a person has a legal right only if its existence can be traced back to a legal source, what is his situation if no source confers it on him? Is it then the law that he does not have it? Is that the case even if there is no law (traceable to a source) denying him the right? Are there gaps in the law? What does it mean to say that there is a legal gap in a situation in which the judge is instructed how to find a solution by the law (e.g. 'Act as if you are a legislator')?

These and similar questions are the subject of many jurisprudential writings.[6] Professor Dworkin has attempted to show that endorsement of the sources thesis makes these questions insoluble and that therefore legal positivism is an incoherent doctrine.[7] His argument can serve as an introduction to an appreciation of the problem facing the supporter of the sources thesis.

1.1 The Refutation. Professor Dworkin's argument is lengthy and designed to allow for various ways of interpreting the sources thesis. The following version of it seems to capture the main thrust of his attack: Assume that p is a variable ranging over legal propositions and that $S(p)$ asserts the existence of a

---

[4] I have argued against reductivist interpretations of Kelsen in Essay 7 below and in 'Kelsen's General Theory of Norms', *Philosophia* (1976), where his views are also criticized.

[5] For other pieces of the jigsaw cf. 'Legal Validity' below.

[6] Cf. Alchouron and Bulygin, *Normative Systems* (Vienna, 1971), for an excellent discussion from which I have greatly benefited. My conclusions differ from theirs mainly because they do not allow for normative conflicts (which do not amount to inconsistencies) or for truth-value gaps. Nor do they draw the conclusions that I do from the sources thesis.

[7] See his 'No Right Answer?' in Hacker and Raz (eds.), *Law, Morality and Society*, some of the arguments of which he repeats in 'Can Rights be Controversial?', *Taking Rights Seriously* (London, 1977).

source for p. Assume a reductivist version of positivism by which p means the same as $S(p)$. It follows that

(1) $\vdash \quad p \leftrightarrow S(p)$.

This entails both

(2) $\vdash \quad -p \leftrightarrow -S(p)$ (counterposition of (1)).
(3) $\vdash \quad -p \leftrightarrow S(-p)$ (Substitution in (1)).

Therefore (1) entails

(4) $\vdash \quad -S(p) \leftrightarrow S(-p)$.

That is, it is a theorem that whenever p has no source (e.g. p has not been enacted nor made the *ratio decidendi* of a binding decision, etc.) *not-p* has a source (e.g. it has been enacted that *not-p*). This conclusion is patently false. In England, for example, there is no source for the legal proposition that it is legally prohibited to kill any butterfly, but neither is there a source for its contradiction, i.e. that it is not legally prohibited to kill any butterfly. (1) must be rejected for it entails a false conclusion.

1.2 Positive/Negative Solution.   A legal positivist cannot accept an interpretation of the sources thesis which entails (1). What routes are available to him to escape Professor Dworkin's criticism? Three different solutions will be outlined briefly in this section. In the next section I shall argue in greater detail for a fourth. First, one may insist that different categories of legal propositions should be distinguished. (1) must be restricted to one category and not every legal proposition should be allowed to be substituted for p in it. In particular, positive legal propositions should be distinguished from negative ones. The sources thesis concerns positive propositions only and negative ones cannot, on this view, be substituted for p in (1). This would block the inference of (3) and therefore of (4) from (1). Let us assume that we follow such a line of reasoning and distinguish between positive legal propositions (Pp being a variable ranging over them only) and negative ones (Np). A negative proposition is true if and only if the corresponding positive one is false and false if and only if the corresponding positive proposition is true.

Hence:

(5) ⊢ $Np \leftrightarrow -Pp$.

The sources thesis is understood as entailing

(6) ⊢ $Pp \leftrightarrow S(Pp)$.

There is an additional theorem for negative propositions:

(7) ⊢ $S(Np) \rightarrow Np$.

  (5) and (6) entail

(8) ⊢ $-S(Pp) \rightarrow Np$ (counterposition of (6) and substitution of equivalents in it).

Thus there will be two consistent theorems for relating negative propositions and sources ((7) and (8)) and one for positive proposition (6).

  This move would not be more than a trick unless positive and negative legal propositions can be distinguished in such a way that there is an independent reason for treating the resulting kinds of propositions differently. Such reasons, fortunately, have often been pointed to before. It is a feature of legal language that whereas one needs a law or some legal source to support a claim that a person is under a duty, is lawfully married, or that a contract or a will is valid, absence of a source for the contrary suffices to show that no duty, marriage, or contract, etc., exist. A valid contract must be made, the validity of marriage depends on certain formal steps being taken, a law is needed to impose a duty, etc. But there need be no making of uncontracts for there not to be a contract, no ceremony for two persons to remain unmarried to each other, and no law to confer a non-duty on a person.

  Pointing to the obvious asymmetries between positive and negative legal propositions is not explaining them. Nor can it be denied that many cases create problems. Does one need a source to have a right, or does one have a right unless there is a source denying it? Such problems call for further clarifications which in themselves shed more light on the nature of the sources thesis.[8]

---

  [8] Cf. my brief discussion in *The Concept of a Legal System* (Oxford, 1970), pp. 170–2. The discussion of this issue below is merely an elaboration of the points made there.

1.3 The True/False Solution. The sources thesis can, but need not, be defended through reliance on the distinction between positive and negative statements. If one does not wish to rely on (6) and (7) with their presupposition of a distinction between negative and positive legal propositions, one can accept (9) and (10) instead:

(9) $S(p)$ is a logically necessary and sufficient condition for the truth of p.

(10) $S(-p)$ is a logically necessary and sufficient condition for the falsity of p.

This solution is offered by Professor Dworkin himself. Since $-(p \& -p)$ and since (9) entails that $S(-p)$ is necessary and sufficient for the truth of $-p$ this solution entails:

(11) $\vdash S(-p) \rightarrow -S(p)$ and therefore

(12) $\vdash -(S(-p) \& S(p))$.

(12) may seem counter-intuitive. It means that if $-p$ has a source (say it was enacted) then p has no source (was not enacted nor made a binding precedent, etc.). Cannot there be a situation in which both p and *not-p* have been validly enacted? In such a case $S(-p) \& S(p)$ is true, though its negation is entailed by (9) and (10). But all this objection amounts to is that sources have to be defined so that $-S(-p)$ is part of the source of p. The possibility of a negative condition like this being part of a source is no more than the possibility of repeal by enacting the opposite of the previous law, for example, repealing a permission by enacting a prohibition or a prohibition by enacting a permission. Since a source sufficient to establish the truth of a legal proposition must guarantee that the law on which it is based has not been repealed, it must include such negative conditions $(-S(-p))$ wherever this form of repeal is legally recognized. If one is to preserve the logical consistency of legal language then one must postulate that where positive law fails to provide a rule of precedence, i.e. a rule determining which of two conflicting enactments, etc., are ineffective (or which of them is repealed) then both are ineffective so that neither $S(p)$ nor $S(-p)$ are true.[9]

[9] The same stipulation must be made in the version of the positive/negative solution presented above. My own position as set out below does not require this kind of stipulation.

The true/false solution differs from the negative/positive solution in presupposing the possibility of legal gaps. In a sense even Dworkin's positivist does not rule out the possibility of legal gaps. But with him as well as with the positive/negative solution in the version given above, legal gaps depend on non-legal gaps. According to them, if it could be the case that neither $S(p)$ nor $-S(p)$, then it could also be that neither p nor $-p$. This possibility is open under the true/false solution as well, but to it is added the possibility of gaps not deriving from non-legal gaps but arising whenever it is neither the case that $S(p)$ nor that $S(-p)$. When this is the case, there is neither a source for p nor for $-p$. Since unlike the negative/positive solution, the true/false solution does not distinguish between positive and negative propositions and requires a source for either, it must and does concede the possibility that for some p neither p nor *not-p* have a source. In such a case neither p nor *not-p* will be either true or false.

Notice that such a gap does not prevent one from defining a permission as the negation of a prohibition. 'x is legally permitted to ϕ' means the same as 'it is the law that x is not prohibited to ϕ' (*LPer x*, $\phi = df.$ *L — Pr x*, ϕ). But this should be distinguished from: it is not the law that x is prohibited to ϕ ($-LPr\ x$, ϕ). According to the true/false solution it cannot be the case that one is legally permitted to do that which one is legally prohibited from doing:

(13) ⊢ $- (LPr\ x, \phi\ \&\ LPer\ x, \phi)$.

For by definition

(14) ⊢ $LPr\ x, \phi \leftrightarrow L - Per\ x, \phi$.

But it is possible that an act is neither prohibited nor permitted:

(15) ⊢ ◇ $((-LPr\ x, \phi)\ \&\ (-LPer\ x, \phi))$.

When an action is neither legally prohibited nor legally permitted there is a legal gap. (15) is just a special case of the general case of legal gaps allowed by the true/false solution where neither p nor $-p$ is true.

The true/false approach may be thought the most faithful to the sources thesis since it regards no legal statement as true unless it has a source. Dworkin's positivist and the positive/

negative solutions allow that negative legal propositions can be true even if they have no source other than the absence of a source for their contradictory proposition.

In 'No Right Answer?' Professor Dworkin denies that the true/false solution is part of an acceptable theory of law: 'Everything turns on the question of which ground-rules of assertion the participants in the legal practice in fact follow, and we can easily imagine ground-rules very different from those that positivism presupposes' p. 74). By this he must mean that the courts of a certain country may follow a practice of respecting certain considerations rather than others on grounds other than their sources, i.e. grounds determined not by social facts but by moral values.[10] This is, of course, possible. The point of the sources thesis is not that courts never rely on sourceless considerations, but rather that when doing so they are not relying on legally binding considerations but exercising their own discretion. Professor Dworkin does not refute legal positivism. He prefers to ignore it. But his oversight is nevertheless helpful. It draws attention to the problem of the relation between law and judicial jurisdiction. If the sources thesis entails that there is jurisdiction despite gaps, it is bound to explain how such jurisdiction is exercised.

1.4 The Prima Facie Solution. The prima facie solution has not been explored by legal philosophers. It is based on the idea that binding, valid laws may conflict and that such conflicts are not inconsistencies. They show that a law has prima facie force only. What is conclusively required by law in any given situation cannot, therefore, be judged by consulting one law only but is often the result of the operation of various laws, some of which may well conflict. Consequently two kinds of legal propositions should be distinguished: propositions about what is prima facie the case and propositions about what is conclusively the case.[11]

---

[10] Professor Dworkin must mean that if his argument is even to appear to have any force against the sources thesis which he stated to be his target in this section of his article.

[11] Professor Dworkin's 'The Model of Rules I', *Taking Rights Seriously*, which was first published in *Chicago Law Review* (1967) did a great deal to draw the attention of legal philosophers to the prima facie character of many laws. Cf. also my 'Legal Principles and the Limits of Law', *Yale L.J.* 81 (1972), 823, for an argument that the prima facie character of law is more extensive and radical than Professor Dworkin allows.

The prima facie solution interprets the sources thesis as applying to prima facie legal propositions ($Pf\,p$, for short). (1) is therefore rejected in favour of:

(16) ⊢ $Pf\,p \leftrightarrow S(p)$.

It entails the equivalent of (2), namely

(17) ⊢ $-S(p) \leftrightarrow -Pf\,p$.

But the equivalent of (3) becomes

(18) ⊢ $S(-p) \leftrightarrow Pf - p$.

There is nothing which could count as a source of $-Pf\,p$. One
can legislate that there is a prima facie duty to ϕ, but one cannot
legislate that there is no prima facie duty to ϕ (as distinct from
'there is a prima facie duty not to ϕ'). If there is no prima facie
duty to ϕ, this cannot be the result of a special source. It can
only result from the absence of a source for the contrary (as
in (17)). Hence Dworkin's refutation does not apply.

In several respects the prima facie solution is a close relative
of the positive/negative solution. According to both, where
$-S(p)\ \&\ -S(-p)$ (or $-S(Pp)\ \&\ -S(Np)$) there is no legal gap,
as the true/false solution dictates. Both therefore allow that certain legal propositions are true even without a source and both
confine this to negative propositions ($-Pf\,p$ or Np). Yet the
prima facie solution is not committed to a general categoriza-
tion of all propositions into negative and positive. It relies instead on a distinction between internal and external negations
of prima facie propositions and on the view that the absence
of a prima facie legal state of affairs does not require a source.[12]

By introducing the notion of a prima facie proposition, however, this solution can dispense with theorem (12) which states
that $-(S(-p)\ \&\ S(p))$. This theorem (and theorem (11)) can-

---

[12] This absence of distinction between Pp and Np leads to some apparently counter-
intuitive results such as (i) ⊢ $-S(Per\,x, \phi) \leftrightarrow -Pf(Per\,x, \phi)$. That is, if there is no source
permitting x to ϕ then it is not the case that prima facie x is permitted to ϕ. But this
is not really paradoxical. Assume that (ii) either $S(Pr\,x, \phi)$ or $-S(Pr\,x, \phi)$. If (iii) $S(Pr\,x,
\phi)$ then (iv) $Pf(-Per\,x, \phi)$ and in such a case (i) is not paradoxical. If (vi) $-S(Pr\,x,
\phi)$ then (vii) $-Pf(Pr\,x, \phi)$ (by (18)). According to (15) (when adapted to Pf proposi-
tions) (vii) entails $Pf(Per\,x, \phi)$. The prima facie permission results from the absence
of a prohibition. That it does not result from the absence of an explicit permission
is not on reflection surprising.

not be derived from (16) and (18). All that follows from them is

(19) ⊢ $(S(-p)$ & $S(p)) \rightarrow (Pf\, p$ & $Pf-p)$.

If the antecedent is true then there are conflicting legal rules, but no contradiction. The rejection of (11) and (12) seems to be an advantage. Whether or not the admission that the law may contain gaps is an advantage, it should be mentioned that the prima facie solution, while rejecting the claim that there are gaps where the law is silent, opens the possibility of a new kind of gap, i.e. through the existence of insoluble conflicts. If $Pf\, p$ & $Pf-p$, and if there is not sufficient ground to determine how the conflict is to be resolved, then neither p nor $-p$ is the true conclusive legal position. In such a case we say that the law is unsettled and this means that it contains a gap.

2. SOURCES AND LAWS

2.1 Open Questions. The various solutions outlined in the above discussion give rise to many new questions. If the negative/positive solution is viable it must provide a test by which all legal statements can be identified as either positive or negative. If the true/false solution is to survive it must explain why it is thought that closure rules like: 'Whatever is not prohibited is permitted', 'If a contract is not legally valid then it is legally invalid', 'If a person is not guilty he is innocent', etc. are often thought to be universally valid. It is their supposed validity which provides the intuitive grounds for accepting the positive/negative solution. But the true/false solution is based on a rejection of these closure rules as universally valid (they may still be 'locally' valid, for some legal system) for it asserts that a man can be neither guilty nor innocent, a contract neither valid nor invalid, an act neither prohibited nor permitted. If the negative/positive and the true/false solutions are incompatible, much more needs to be said about their precise detail before judgment can be passed about the success of either of them.[13] The prima facie approach brings with it its own problems and in particular the problem of the relation between prima facie and conclusive judgments.

Beyond these, and similar questions which are specific to

[13] As will emerge below, the two solutions are compatible if properly interpreted.

different solutions, there are the more important questions which are common to all these solutions and to other possible ones: What is the exact nature of the relation between a law and its source? Does the sources thesis entail the possibility of gaps, and if so, on what grounds? How is the existence of gaps related to the existence or absence of jurisdiction to adjudicate in such cases?

Three solutions were outlined above to demonstrate the main routes a legal positivist may take and some of the main problems and consequences involved in each route. For the rest of the present essay a solution will be developed, different from those presented above, but essentially a variation of the prima facie solution. In developing it is hoped that some of the problems mentioned above will be at least partially answered.

2.2 Legal Statements.   Sources are normally thought of as sources of law. The occurrence of an event of a certain kind creates a law. Certain legal statements are true in virtue of that or other laws alone. These are pure legal statements. Other legal statements are true because of the existence of the laws and of other facts, such as the making of contracts, wills, the commission of offences and other wrongful acts, the exercise of public or private powers, the performance of duties. These are applied legal statements.

The usefulness of 'interposing' laws between sources and statements is self-evident. First, it distinguishes law-creating facts and other facts relevant for the truth of some legal statements, such as the commission of wrongs or of private transactions. It does, in other words, play a major role in forging the network of distinctions between private and public law. Laws are also one of the devices enabling us to refer to the content of the law without referring to the circumstances of its creation, the details of which are irrelevant for most practical purposes. When one wants to talk about what is commanded, rather than about who and when and how commanded, one refers to commands and all one needs to know is that they were properly issued in one way or another. For similar reasons we talk more often of laws than of legislative acts, etc., as imposing duties.

For present purposes, however, omitting laws and discussing

directly the relations between sources and legal statements sim-
plifies matters without distorting any essential facts. But it is
important to remember that 'sources' here means not just law-
creating acts but all sorts of facts which make legal statements
true or false. What, then, are legal statements? They are
expressed in many forms, but most commonly through the use
of the operators 'It is the law that ...' or 'Legally ...' or by
the adjective 'legal' ('He has a legal right to ...', etc.). Often
no linguistic indication is given to show that a sentence is used
to make a legal statement: 'You ought not to do that' may be
used to make a legal statement. Ultimately it is impossible to
identify legal statements by their form or through any linguistic
indicators. They are identified by the nature of their truth-conditions. This point will be taken up again below. Though there
is no linguistic form the use of which is necessary to express legal
statements, all of them can be expressed by deontic sentences
(i.e. sentences about what is or is not to be done, what rights,
duties, permissions, liberties, powers people have or lack, what
transactions were effected, etc.) preceded by 'Legally ...' or
'It is the law that ...' and sentences obtained from such sentences by the operations of sentential, quantificational, and
modal logic. Such sentences can be viewed as the canonical
form of legal statements. ($L\,p$ will indicate *Legally p* in formal-
ized formulations.)[14]

A statement is not a statement of law in the abstract but a
statement of English Law or of German Law, etc. So the operators should be 'It is English law that ...', etc., but reference
to the particular system can be omitted in the present discussions so long as it is remembered that all legal statements are
statements of different particular legal systems.

Legal statements, like deontic statements generally, are logically stratified. Statements of legal reasons for action form the
most elementary stratum. Permissions, duties, and powers are
explained in terms of reasons; rights are explained in terms of
duties, permissions, and powers, legal transactions in terms of
rights and powers, etc. To analyse the nature of legal gaps in

---

[14] Note that 'there is a law that p' entails 'legally p' and normally implies that p
is part of the content of a single law. As explained above, for the purposes of the present
discussions such statements are assimilated to other legal statements and are not treated
as a special category.

full, one has to examine each kind of statement separately. But in fact, once the problem of gaps is analysed for reason-statements, all the rest follows, given an adequate analysis of the other deontic concepts. The present discussion will therefore be confined to the case of reasons.

Three kinds of reason-statements will be discussed:

(1) p is a reason for x to ϕ or ($p\,R\,x$, ϕ) for short.
(2) There is a reason for x to ϕ or ($R\,x$, ϕ) for short.
(3) There is a conclusive reason for x to ϕ or ($R_c\,x$, ϕ) for short.

Statements of kind (1) will not be analysed here. Statements of kind (2) are true if and only if a corresponding statement of type (1) is true. There could be a reason to ϕ and at the same time a conflicting reason not to ϕ. There is a conclusive reason for x to ϕ if there is a reason for x to ϕ which overrides all conflicting reasons, is not excluded by exclusionary reasons, nor cancelled by any cancelling conditions. There cannot be conflicting conclusive reasons; i.e.

(20) $\vdash \quad -(R_c\,x,\ \phi\ \&\ R_c\,x,\ \overline{\phi})$.

At the same time it is not to be assumed that in every case to which reason applies there is a conclusive reason either for the action or against it. That is

(21) '($R_c\,x$, ϕ) $\vee$ ($R_c\,x$, $\overline{\phi}$)' is false.

There are many kinds of permissions. For present purposes two kinds should be considered:

(22) x has explicit permission to ϕ ($Per_e\,x$, ϕ) $=df$. There is a fact with some force to cancel reasons for no-ϕ-ing ($\overline{\phi}$-ing).
(23) x has a conclusive permission to ϕ ($Per_c\,x$, ϕ) $=\underline{df}$. It is false that there is a conclusive reason for x to $\overline{\phi}$ (i.e. $-R_c\,x$, $\overline{\phi}$).

A conclusive permission to act is the contradictory of a conclusive reason for refraining from that act. Hence the following is a logical truth:

(24) $\vdash \quad (R_c\,x$, $\phi) \leftrightarrow -(Per_c\,x$, $\overline{\phi})$.

In the main the definition of a conclusive permission follows the customary approach to permissions. The notion of an explicit permission is less familiar. Philosophers and logicians often think of 'permissions' as a nominalization of the deontic 'may'. But in ordinary discourse 'permission' means some act of granting permission and a person is permitted to act only if he is granted permission to do so. 'Explicit permission' is meant to explicate this notion of granted or obtained permissions. 'He allowed me to enter the room' imports that there was a reason why I should not which his permission cancelled. But a permission can be granted not only to cancel an existing reason but also to forestall possible reasons by cancelling them in advance: The manager and his secretary may object to a person's having access to the files. If either does object then the person has a reason not to approach the files. A journalist seeks to consult the files. He has no reason not to, since so long as no objection is made the files are available to the public. Anticipating that the secretary may object he obtains the permission of the manager. The permission cancels the force of the secretary's objection (if and when it materializes).

These are the only kinds of deontic statements to be discussed here. All other and more complex kinds of deontic statements are explained by pointing out their logical relations with these elementary forms of statement. Therefore though the following is a discussion of one particular kind of statement, the considerations invoked apply to all legal statements of all kinds.

2.3 Sources as Reasons.   Statements of the form *LR x, φ*, i.e. there is a legal reason for *x* to *φ* (which mean the same as 'Legally *x* ought to *φ*', 'It is the law that *x* ought to *φ*'), are true, according to the sources thesis, because of the existence of a source, i.e. an appropriate social fact specifiable without resort to moral argument. But the relation between the statement of a source and the corresponding legal statement is not identity of meaning but that between ground and consequence. Two common answers to 'Why ought one to *φ*?' are 'Because there is a new law to that effect' or 'Because last year Parliament decreed so'. Both come to much the same thing (but see section 2.4). Since reference to laws is not examined in this essay, only the second kind of answer is of present concern. It calls attention to the very familiar fact that the making of contracts, marriages, laws, etc., are reasons for action. One ought to do as one contracted to do because one contracted to do so. One ought to maintain a certain person because one married him. One ought to pay income tax because Parliament enacted so, etc. Legal sources are reasons for action. If s is a variable ranging over statements of social sources, then $s\,LR\,x$, ϕ ('s is a legal reason for x to ϕ') is the general form of statements of legal reasons. Such statements are true if and only if s is true and is a statement of the appropriate social condition according to the doctrine of identity.

Because the existence of the appropriate source is a reason for x to ϕ, its existence is the ground for the truth of statements of the form 'Legally x ought to ϕ' ($LR\,x$, ϕ). These are essentially existential statements asserting that there is some fact which is a legal reason for x to ϕ ($LR\,x$, ϕ is essentially the same as $(\exists s)\,s\,LR\,x$, ϕ). The existence of the source is the ground for the truth of a statement of what one ought, legally, to do, in the same way in which the existence of an appropriate instance is the ground for the truth of an existential statement. On this interpretation the sources thesis entails:

(25) Statements of the form $p\,LR\,x$, ϕ are true only if statements of social facts specifiable without recourse to moral argument are substituted for p.

The sources thesis entails a similar condition concerning explicit permissions:

(26) Statements of the form $LPer_e\,x$, ϕ are true only if there is a social fact specifiable without recourse to moral argument which has the force to cancel legal reasons.

The facts alluded to are facts like an Act of Parliament repealing a legal prohibition or duty, a constitutional guarantee of certain freedoms, a licence to use a certain property given by one person to another. The sources thesis, it should be remembered, is a thesis about the law not about practical reason in general. Theses (25) and (26) are not meant as an assertion that only social facts can be reasons or permissions but that only such facts can be legal reasons and legal permissions.

It follows that while there is always a source for statements of the form $LR\,x$, ϕ, there is no source for the negative statements: $-LR\,x$, ϕ, $L-R\,x$, ϕ. Whether there is a difference between 'it is not the case that one legally ought to ϕ' and 'it is the law that it is not the case that one ought to ϕ' will be considered below. Intuitively, the negation of a legal reason is nothing more than the absence of a legal reason. It does not make sense to look for a source for the absence of a reason, legal or otherwise. This is but a reflection of the fact that $-(p\,LR\,x$, $\phi)$ has no source either.

Here Professor Dworkin's refutation is avoided in a new way: by denying that there could be a source for a certain kind of legal statement. This claim may seem surprising and, therefore, a further explanation may be in place. It is often said, for example, that though a permission can be inferred from the absence of a prohibition, it can also result from a direct law granting it. Hence permissions can have sources. This, of course, has not been denied. What has been denied is that permissions of the same kind can be either based on a source or be sourceless. Explicit permissions are always source-based, conclusive permissions never are. The enactment of a law repealing a legal prohibition is an explicit permission:[15] it cancels a reason. The granting of a prospective permission confers an immunity: it is a fact with force to cancel the force of certain facts as reasons. A constitutionally guaranteed liberty gives one immunity against parliamentary legislation through having the force to cancel reasons arising out of parliamentary legislation. Normally when one has an explicit permission, one has a conclusive permission too. Hence often ordinary statements about freedoms, liberties, rights, and permissions do not, and have no need to, distinguish between these two kinds of permissions. Once the distinction is drawn it follows from the definitions that explicit permissions always depend on sources whereas conclusive ones never do.

Conclusive legal reasons are ordinary legal reasons, and thus are themselves social facts. They are undefeated reasons and thus depend also on the absence of defeating facts. The sources

---

[15] It may be worth noting that the cancelling permissions discussed in the first essay are a subclass of explicit permissions. Since, as was pointed out in the second essay, all legal reasons are protected reasons, all explicit legal permissions are cancelling permissions and the ability to grant them is a normative power.

thesis requires that the way conflicts of reasons are to be resolved is also determined, to the extent that it is legally determined at all, by social facts. Such facts are also legal sources.

2.4 Ultimate Legal Rules.   The claim that legal sources are reasons for action raises as many questions as it solves. Are legal sources moral reasons or prudential reasons, or is there a special and distinct kind of reasons which legal reasons exemplify? Do ordinary legal statements import moral approval of the law? These questions cannot be explored here (they are indirectly answered in Essay 8 below). But suppose one asks why is a certain legislative act a reason for action? Is it not because of moral grounds that a policeman's order, for example, is a reason for action? Be that as it may, some of these grounds are legal while others may not be. The policeman's order is a valid reason because, generally, policemen act to preserve the peace and are reliable. This is not a legal ground. Another ground for accepting that the policeman's order is a reason for action is that Parliament conferred on him power to give such orders. There may or may not be non-legal grounds for accepting legal sources as reasons, but there are always such legal grounds. Or almost always, for in the end one gets to ultimate legal rules.

Suppose it is asked of English law why is it true that parliamentary legislation is binding on the courts. The answer is that this is so because of the practice of the courts which follows a rule to that effect and because the rules practised by the courts of a legal system are rules of that system according to the doctrine of identity. Here (as in the case of all ultimate rules) the courts' practice is what makes the rule a legal rule and is thus its source. But the relation of source to rule and to the action the rule requires is different in the case of ultimate rules from that relation in the rest of the law.

With the rest of the law both the rule and its source could with equal justice be regarded as the reason for doing as the rule prescribes. Ultimate rules are likewise reasons for the action they require, but not so their source. That the English courts hold themselves bound to apply statutes is not the reason why they ought to do so. The rule that they should apply statutes is such a reason. The practice is no more than proof (constitutive proof) that the rule is a legal rule. It is neither a ground for the validity of the rule nor for the action it prescribes. It is this fact which establishes the character of the rule as an ultimate *legal* rule. The fact that a rule is an ultimate legal rule means no more than that there is no legal ground, no legal justification for its validity. It does not imply that there is no ground or justification for the rule, only that if such ground exists it is not a legal one. With ordinary legal rules their source is the legal ground of their validity and a reason for behaving as they prescribe. That Parliament so enacted is a ground for the validity of the law and a reason for the required behaviour. These are legal reasons for their character as grounds of validity is itself determined by another law. By definition ultimate legal rules are not similarly grounded on legal reasons. The absence of a further law determining the grounds of validity of the ultimate rules is precisely what makes them *ultimate* legal rules.

Because further legal rules (themselves grounded in social facts) determine which facts create rules and are thus, with those facts, the grounds of validity of the rules, they can be used to identify the rules for the validity of which they are a ground. Since all the grounds are social facts or legal rules grounded in social facts, this identification is in accord with the sources thesis. There are no legal grounds for the validity of ultimate rules; no justification of them is provided by law. If they are identifiable by social facts, i.e. if they have sources, these facts cannot be the legal grounds for their validity. Therefore they cannot be legal reasons for doing as they require. They are identifying criteria only. The courts themselves use them as such. English courts look for their own practices when asking whether they are bound by a fraudulently obtained Private Act or by an Act of Parliament binding future Parliaments. But they refer to the source of the law in the practice of the courts in order to identify the precise content of the ultimate legal rule which binds them, not in order to justify it. Therefore, though the ultimate rule itself is the reason for the action it requires, its sources are not.[16]

---

[16] Hart was right in asserting that the rule of recognition, like all other rules, rests on social sources. Kelsen, however, was right in insisting that the relation between ultimate rules and their sources is different from that between ordinary rules and their sources. Positivists often claim that controversy is proof that the law is unsettled. By the analysis presented here, this is true of ultimate rules but not of others.

3. LEGAL GAPS

3.1   The Nature of Gaps.   There is a gap in the law when a legal question has no complete answer. Understanding a question is knowing what counts as a correct answer. This does not mean knowing which is the correct answer. It means knowing which statements are possible answers, i.e. which statements would be, if true, the correct answer. A legal question is a question all the possible answers to which are legal statements. A legal gap exists if none of the possible complete answers to a legal question is true.

Where a question lacks an answer it has various correct secondary answers such as 'This question has no answer', 'There is no law on this matter', 'The law is unsettled', etc. It also may have partial answers. This is so in particular where some of the possible complete answers are false while the others are neither true nor false. The existence of partial answers and of secondary answers is compatible with the existence of a legal gap, i.e. with the absence of a complete answer.

A court may or may not have jurisdiction over a given legal question. It has jurisdiction over a question when it is entitled to look for its answer and rely on it in rendering decision. Essentially this means that it has jurisdiction when its decision as to the right answer to the question is *res judicata* (if the answer is an applied legal statement) or when it is the basis on which the courts proceed to create the *res judicata* (if the answer is a pure legal statement). On the basis of this definition we can distinguish two kinds of gaps in the law:

Jurisdictional Gaps.   A legal system is jurisdictionally complete if its courts have jurisdiction over all legal questions. It has a jurisdictional gap if its courts lack jurisdiction over certain legal questions.

Legal Gaps.   A legal system is legally complete if there is a complete answer to all the legal questions over which the courts have jurisdiction. It contains a legal gap if some legal questions subject to jurisdiction have no complete answer.

It is possible, of course, to have a wider concept of legal gaps, according to which the mark of a gap is the existence of any unanswered legal question. But the narrower concept defined here is the more important one. Gaps present legal and philosophical problems only if they arise from questions over which there is jurisdiction. A legal system is a normative system providing for its own application through judicial bodies, and judicial bodies play a crucial role in any doctrine of identity for legal systems. Since the law is identified through the eyes of the courts, legal gaps should be so identified too. Yet 'a legal question' should not be identified as any question a court may answer in rendering decisions. It is not to be taken for granted that all the questions courts are concerned with are legal questions. A legal question is identified independently by the character of its answers: only legal propositions are possible complete answers to a legal question and legal propositions of a given legal system are identified by their truth-conditions as determined by the doctrine of identity.

In every case there is one legal question which encompasses all the others: What decision does the law require in this case? A complete answer is provided by pointing to a decision which the law requires. When no decision is required by law the question is unanswerable and there is a legal gap. In such a case the question will have secondary, and possibly partial, answers only, such as 'the law is unsettled', 'the law requires nothing'. It is here assumed that the question is not addressed to the court's own jurisdiction and therefore 'the law requires a decision that there is no jurisdiction' is not an answer to this question.

When the court's decision turns on whether or not a person ought (conclusively) to perform a certain action, there are two possible complete answers:

(1) $LR_c x, \phi$, the law conclusively requires that action; and
(2) $LPer_c x, \overline{\phi}$, i.e. the law conclusively permits the omission of that action.

If neither proposition is true there is a legal gap for there is no decision required by law. It follows that there are two possible kinds of legal gaps:

(1) '$LR_c x, \phi$' is neither true nor false and '$LPer_c x, \overline{\phi}$' (i.e. '$L - R_c x, \phi$') is neither true nor false.
(2) '$(-LR_c x, \phi) \& (-LPer_c x, \overline{\phi})$' is true.

Both are situations of gaps if the questions to which the relevant propositions are answers are (at least if they have complete answers) within the jurisdiction of the courts.

3.2 Indeterminacy and Gaps.   Whether or not there is a legal reason to perform a certain action is a matter of identifying which legal reasons there are and whether they are reasons for that action. Ultimately it is a question of interpreting the precise import of certain facts such as acts of legislation, judicial decisions, etc. Whether a certain executive act is a legal reason (i.e. whether it creates a binding legal norm) is a matter of interpreting a parliamentary legislative act which conferred legislative powers on the executive as well as of interpreting the executive act itself. The same is true of deciding whether that executive act is a reason for a certain action. To a considerable extent these questions revolve round the interpretation of the language used and the intentions with which certain acts were performed. What do the words of the contract, will, company memorandum, or statute mean and what did those who formulated them intend, are the most familiar (though not the only) questions involved in identifying and interpreting legal reasons.

Questions of intention and meaning may have no answer. It may be neither true nor false that in making the remark a person intended to insult his colleague, and then it is also neither true nor false that he did not so intend. Similarly it may be neither true nor false that this is a dwelling or a motor vehicle. It may be neither true nor false that this man is bald. Where the facts which are legal reasons are indeterminate, through vagueness, open texture, or some other factors, certain legal statements are neither true nor false.[17] Such indeterminacy may make it neither true nor false that this structure

---

[17] Normally indeterminacy of intention creates a legal gap only if reflected in the use of indeterminate language. Closure rules—on which see below—come into operation in most other cases. Sometimes, however, gaps arise because of indeterminate intentions independently of the language employed. Suppose that a statute requires 'ship-owners' to ϕ. Years after its enactment a new kind of vessel is developed which is beyond doubt a ship, but it is neither true nor false that the legislator intended the obligation to apply to the owners of such vessels. Many legal systems hold that the plain language of the statute is at least a prima facie reason for such owners to ϕ. But a system's rules of interpretation may make such questions depend exclusively on the legislator's intention (and they may regard the language employed merely as presumptive evidence of its intentions). In such a system the law on the question is indeterminate.

is liable to tax as a dwelling, etc. A cause of legal gaps of the first type is the indeterminacy of language, of intention, and of other facts. It is worth noting that this kind of legal gap is not the law's peculiarity. They are totally dependent on and derive from gaps in statements of an ordinary and not a particularly legal kind such as statements about intentions and language. It is the indeterminacy of ordinary everyday facts which generates legal gaps.

Are such gaps inevitable? It seems that the sources thesis makes them unavoidable since it makes law dependent on human action with its attendant indeterminacies. In 'No Right Answer?' Professor Dworkin denies that vagueness inevitably leads to gaps. In part, his view presupposes a rejection of the sources thesis and does not therefore affect the present argument. But, in part, he relies on the possibility of rules of interpretation for handling vague terms such as 'if a statute uses vague language it must be taken to have changed the legal *status quo ante* only to the extent justified by the indisputable core of the language employed' (p. 68). This suggestion rests, however, on a fallacious view of vagueness. It assumes that whereas a term which is not vague divides all cases into those to which it applies and those to which it does not, a vague term divides all cases into three sets: those to which it applies 'by its indisputable core meaning' those to which it clearly does not apply, and those in between. It is as if a term is vague because it draws two sharp dividing lines instead of one. The truth is that all, and not only some, nouns, verbs, adverbs, and adjectives of a natural language are vague. And though a vague term clearly applies to some cases, clearly fails to apply to some, and doubtfully applies to others, yet it is often impossible to draw general boundary lines between the three categories. It is a test of adequacy of any account of vagueness that it recognizes as a central type of it the cases where vagueness is 'continuous'.

Terms are vague in this sense if besides cases on the borderline between the area covered by the concept and that which it does not cover there are borderline cases between those covered by the term and those which belong to the borderline and there are borderline cases between those to which the term does not apply and those on the borderline, and so on indefinitely. With respect to a vague term of this kind one is on occasion uncertain

whether a case is a borderline case or not. The prevalence of
vague terms of this kind makes it impossible to prevent gaps
due to vagueness in the way suggested by Professor Dworkin.[18]
It does not seem plausible to suppose that other rules of interpretation conforming to the sources thesis will fare any better.
This should not be taken to mean that rules of interpretation
are of no use in solving problems of interpretation arising from
vagueness and indeterminacy. It only means that they cannot
solve all such problems and that they themselves sometimes give
rise to new problems.

3.3 Conflict and Gaps   The gaps discussed above are gaps of
truth-value in statements of reason making it impossible to
know whether there is a reason for a certain action. But even
where that problem does not arise, indeterminacy due to the
very same kinds of factor makes it impossible to resolve some
conflicts of legal reasons. According to the sources thesis the
weight or strength of legal reasons is, just like its content, totally
determined by social facts. Those do for the most part provide
enough indications as to how to resolve conflicts of legal reasons.
Sometimes, however, no sufficient indication is provided. In
such cases, though there is no special problem as to which legal
reasons apply, there is none which is conclusive.

    There are two kinds of situation in which neither of two con-

[18] There is no denying of course that the law can reduce drastically the number of
indeterminate cases in the ways suggested by Professor Dworkin (though this is not
necessarily a very desirable goal).
    Note that on some semantic theories this view of vagueness entails the existence of
an infinite number of truth-values, generated as in the following diagram:

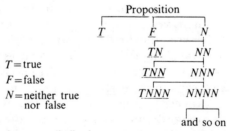

Possible truth-values are underlined.
    P is TNN if it is true that it is indeterminate whether P is indeterminate. P is NNN
if it is indeterminate whether P is NN, etc. Only combinations beginning with T are
truth-values. (If V is any iteration of F, T, and N then $VTV=VV$ and FV is equivalent
to a disjunction of all the other iterations of the same level as V.)

flicting reasons is conclusive. One is where the two are equally balanced. They cancel each other and it is false that there is a conclusive reason for the act and false that there is a conclusive reason for its omission. '$(L - R_c x, \phi)$ & $(L - R_c x, \overline{\phi})$' is true and it follows that '$(LPer_c x, \overline{\phi})$ & $(LPer_c x, \phi)$' is true. This kind of situation involves no unresolved conflict nor any legal gap.

Completely different is a situation of unresolved conflict. It arises when conflicting reasons fail to override each other, not because they are equally matched, but because they are not matched at all: for whatever reason, the conflicting reasons are incommensurate as to strength. Neither is stronger nor are they equal in strength. In such a case it would be wrong to say that the agent is permitted to perform the act. But it would be equally wrong to say that he is not permitted to perform it. The only intuitively correct description of his state is that he is neither permitted nor not permitted to perform the act. This is possible only if the statement that he is permitted as well as its negation are neither true nor false. It follows that '$LR_c x, \phi$' and '$LR_c x, \overline{\phi}$' are equally neither true nor false. Hence unresolved conflicts give rise to legal gaps and these, like all other gaps due to indeterminacy in the sources, are gaps of the first kind.

There is yet a third way in which the sources thesis is responsible for legal gaps and it too arises out of conflict situations. The law may make certain legal rules have prima facie force only by subjecting them to moral or other non-source-based considerations. Let us assume, for example, that by law contracts are valid only if not immoral. Any particular contract can be judged to be prima facie valid if it conforms to the 'value-neutral' conditions for the validity of contract laid down by law. The proposition 'It is legally conclusive that this contract is valid' is neither true nor false until a court authoritatively determines its validity. This is a consequence of the fact that by the sources thesis courts have discretion when required to apply moral considerations.

3.4 Closure Rules. Because of the sources thesis indeterminacy in sources always leads and absence of sources for sufficient conflict reserving rules may lead to legal gaps of the first kind. Can there be legal gaps of the second kind? Gaps of the second kind can exist only if it is possible that $(-LR_c\,x,\ \phi)$ & $(-LPer_c\,x,\ \overline{\phi})$. That is, if it is possible that

(27) $(-LR_c\,x,\ \phi)$ & $(-L-R_c\,x,\ \phi)$.

But it is a logical truth that

(28) $\vdash\ \ -(LR_c\,x,\ \phi)\leftrightarrow(L-R_c\,x,\ \phi)$.

From (27) and (28) follows

(29) $(L-R_c\,x,\ \phi)$ & $(-L-R_c\,x,\ \phi)$.

(29) is a contradiction. Hence (28) entails the rejection of (27) and with it of the possibility of gaps of the second kind. The derivation of (28) is simple. First, $L-R_c\,x,\ \phi\rightarrow-LR_c\,x,\ \phi$. It cannot be true that legally there is a conclusive reason to perform an act and at the same time that legally there is no such conclusive reason. Therefore

(30) $\vdash\ \ LR_c\,x,\ \phi\rightarrow-L-R_c\,x,\ \phi$.

$L-R_c\,x,\ \phi\rightarrow-LR\,x,\ \phi$ follows from (30) by counterposition. Next the derivation of $-LR_c\,x,\ \phi\rightarrow L-R_c\,x,\ \phi$. Assume that the antecedent is true, i.e. that $LR_c\,x,\ \phi$ is false. Can it also be that $L-R_c\,x,\ \phi$ is false? If $-LR_c\,x,\ \phi$, then it is not the case that there is a fact which is a conclusive legal reason to ϕ. But if there is no conclusive legal reason to ϕ, can it fail to be the law that there is no conclusive reason to ϕ? This would have been a real possibility had there been a need for a special kind of fact to make true negative statements of reasons of the form $-R\,x,\ \phi$ (as was confusedly imagined to be possible by the negative/positive solution. Cf. (7) above). But it has already been established (in section 2.2) that such propositions are verified by the absence of reasons only and it is precisely that absence which is entailed by $-LR_c\,x,\ \phi$. Hence $-LR_c\,x,\ \phi\rightarrow L-R_c\,x,\ \phi$, Q.E.D.

(28) is logically equivalent to (31):

(31) $\vdash\ \ (-LR_c\,x,\ \phi)\leftrightarrow(LPer_c\,x,\ \overline{\phi})$.

This is a rendering of the familiar closure rule that whatever is not legally prohibited is legally permitted and vice versa. So far as (31) is concerned both implications are equally valid. The primacy of the implication from left to right (i.e. whatever is not prohibited is permitted) is due to the positive/negative distinction underlying the whole position, i.e. one needs some facts to have reasons, but none is needed for there not to be a reason. Thus the present approach validates this and several other closure rules and by accepting them rejects the possibility of the second type of legal gaps.

The outcome of this discussion is that legal gaps are not only possible but, according to the sources thesis, inescapable. They arise, however, where the law speaks with an uncertain voice (simple indeterminacy) or where it speaks with many voices (unresolved conflicts). Contrary to much popular imagining, there are no gaps when the law is silent. In such cases closure rules, which are analytic truths rather than positive legal rules,[19] come into operation and prevent the occurrence of gaps.[20]

[19] They are analytic truths concerning *legal* propositions derivable from the sources thesis. They cannot be derived in normative systems where such a thesis does not hold.

[20] I am grateful to Simon Blackburn, Ronald Dworkin, and Mary Tiles for instructive comments on earlier drafts of this essay.

5

THE IDENTITY OF LEGAL
SYSTEMS*

Laws are part of legal systems; a particular law is a law only if it is part of American Law or French Law or some other legal system. Legal philosophers have persistently attempted to explain why we think of laws as forming legal systems, to evaluate the merits of this way of thinking about the law and to make it more precise by explicating the features that account for the unity of legal systems. Various theories have been suggested but none has been accepted as completely satisfactory, and the continuing debate owes much to the intricacy of the problems involved. This intricacy is partly due to a considerable cloudiness in the understanding of the problems themselves. I will attempt, through this essay, to clarify the nature of the problem of the unity of municipal legal systems. My primary aim is not to answer all the relevant questions, but rather to formulate them more precisely, for I believe that in philosophy a clear conception of a problem is half the way to its solution.

The term 'a legal system' is not a technical legal term. It may occasionally figure in courts' decisions, but any term can appear there. Although it is occasionally used in legal argument, it has not the character of a technical legal term such as 'floating charge' or 'fee simple' or 'consideration'. Nor is the concept important to the day-to-day administration of law, as are the concepts of contract, ownership, right, duty, and the like. The term is primarily used in thinking about the law, not in the actual use and application of the law. It is commonly used in books of jurisprudence or comparative law, not in books about property law, torts, or copyright.

Therefore, when trying to clarify the notion of a legal system, the legal theorist does not aim at defining clearly the sense in which the term is employed by legislators, judges, or lawyers.

* First published in *California Law Review* (1971). I am indebted to Professor H. L. A. Hart for many discussions on the problems dealt with in this essay and for his illuminating comments on a first version of it.

He is, rather, attempting to forge a useful conceptual tool, one which will help him to a better understanding of the nature of law. This does not mean that he should not try to model the concept in a way that would be useful to the solution of certain legal problems. Rather, it means only that even if he does this, he will not be trying to elucidate the meaning of a technical legal term, but instead to provide the legal practitioner with a concept that may help him in tackling some nagging legal problems. But should it really be the goal of the legal theorist to help solve legal problems by moulding a precise concept of the identity of a legal system? To what kind of legal problems may such a concept be relevant? And if this is not his goal, what is? Providing an answer to these questions is the main purpose of this essay.

To try to answer these questions we should first distinguish between two possible concepts of the unity of a legal system, which I call the material unity and the formal unity. The material unity of a legal system consists in its distinctive characteristics; it depends on the content of its laws and on the manner in which they are applied. When trying to explain the characteristic features of a legal system we are not, of course, looking for the detailed regulation of every legal institution. Rather, we are looking for the all-pervasive principles and the traditional institutional structure and practices that permeate the system and lend it its distinctive character. To distinguish the problem of formal unity from that of material unity, I shall call the former the problem of the identity of legal systems.

THE PROBLEM ISOLATED

The identity of the system is found in the criterion or set of criteria that determines which laws are part of the system and which are not. Some proposed answers to the problem of identity are well known; perhaps the best-known are: A law is part of a legal system if and only if it was enacted directly or indirectly by the sovereign of that system (Austin), or if and only if it is authorized by the basic norm of the system (Kelsen), or if and only if it ought to be recognized according to the rule of recognition of the system (Hart). These three philosophers were not concerned with the material unity of legal systems. They did not think that the unity of the system depends on the content or spirit of its laws, or on the traditions and practices of its most important legal institutions. Instead, they hoped to formulate a test that would enable them to determine whether any two laws belong to the same legal system or not.

A more or less clear concept of the identity of a legal system is presupposed by any investigation into its material unity. The investigator needs to know which laws and institutions form the system before he can inquire into its distinctive characteristics. He does not need, however, a complete and precise list of the laws of the system. It suffices for his purposes to be able to identify the bulk of the laws. Indeed, the investigation into the material unity of a legal system may even help to decide some borderline cases concerning its identity. When all other indicators fail to provide an answer, it may be reasonable to decide that a norm is part of a certain legal system on the ground that it closely resembles in spirit and manner of application the rest of the laws in that system, or that since it is diametrically opposed to the character of the system it should not be regarded as a part of it.

In describing the problem of identity as a quest for criteria that determine which laws belong to a legal system, it is normally assumed that the notion of a law is clear and uncontroversial. In fact this is far from being the case. The problem of the individuation of laws—the question of what is one complete law—is one of the most controversial in jurisprudence. It would, therefore, be desirable to separate the problem of identity of legal systems from that of the individuation of laws. This can easily be achieved by reformulating the problem in the following way: The problem of identity of legal systems is the quest for a criterion or set of criteria that provides a method for determining whether any set of normative statements is, if true, a complete description of a legal system.

With the help of certain technical terminology, it is possible to side-step the problem of individuation. A statement is a normative statement if and only if the existence of a norm is a necessary condition for its truth. A normative statement is pure if and only if the existence of certain norms is sufficient for its truth. The set of all the pure statements referring to one legal system is called the 'total set' of that system, and every set of pure statements that is logically equivalent to the total set of a system is a complete description of that system. The problem of identity is a search for criteria for a complete description of any legal system, and it is irrelevant whether any statement in the description describes just one complete law or not. Therefore, a theory concerning the nature and principles of individuation of laws need not be presupposed in an examination of the problem of identity.

By stipulating that the criteria identify sets of statements that are complete descriptions *if true*, the problem of the existence of legal systems may be separated from the problem of identity. It is the business of criteria of existence of legal systems to provide a method for determining when a complete description is a true description—to determine whether the legal system described actually exists. This task should be clearly separated from that of formulating the criteria of identity.[1]

The problem of identity has two quite distinct aspects: the aspect of the scope of a legal system and the aspect of its continuity. Questions of scope arise when we consider whether the conventions of the constitution, a valid contract, the regulations of a limited company or of a trade union, for example, are part of the legal system. Questions of continuity concern the various ways in which a legal system ceases to exist and is replaced by a new system. Does, for example, a revolution, or a *coup d'état*, or a declaration of independence, terminate the existence of one legal system and signal the emergence of a new system?

A momentary legal system is a legal system at a particular point of time. The problem of scope is the search for criteria of identity of momentary legal systems, whereas the problem of continuity is the search for criteria providing a method for determining whether two momentary legal systems are part of one, continuous, legal system. I will show that somewhat different considerations apply to each of these problems.

These preliminary clarifications make it clear that problems of identity are here considered as jurisprudential problems, the solution of which lies in providing sets of criteria of identity, which, if successful, provide methods of determining the identity of *all* municipal legal systems. Thus conceived, the problem is very different from that facing a legal practitioner looking for an answer in a *particular* legal system to a certain

[1] Cf. J. Raz, *The Concept of a Legal System*, pp. 49, 70.

legal problem. Consider, for example, a judge who must render a decision in a particular case before him. Some answers that might satisfy the legal philosopher will not help the judge. A legal philosopher may say, and some philosophers have said, that what judges do about disputes is the law; but this is unlikely to be of much help to a judge wondering what he should do about a dispute. Does this prove that this jurisprudential criterion is false or pointless? The answer to this question depends on one's position on the fundamental problem posed above: What purpose do legal philosophers have in constructing theories concerning the identity of legal systems? They do not mean merely to elucidate the current meaning of a legal term; what, then, is their purpose?

One possible answer is that the goal is to forge a concept that will help the courts and other people concerned with the law to find answers to certain legal problems. There is a sense in which this is trivially true of all jurisprudential problems. Jurisprudence strives to improve our understanding of the law, and in one way or another, however remotely or indirectly, an improved understanding of the law is bound to affect the operation of the law and to help legal practitioners. But the above-mentioned contention should not be taken in this sense, for its intent is to claim that there are certain specific legal problems the solution of which will directly benefit from a jurisprudential analysis of the identity of legal systems.

Several legal problems can be thought to be relevant to the concept of identity. Some relate to the scope of the legal system, that is, to the problem of the identity of momentary systems. Most legal systems distinguish between procedures of proving matters of fact and procedures of arguing about points of law before the courts. Many legal systems stipulate that ignorance of law is no excuse for committing an offence whereas (reasonable) mistake of fact is. Many legal systems include laws to the effect that a general law is valid only if published in a manner specified by law. All of these legal provisions can give rise to disputes turning on the question: Is some rule part of the legal system or not? Should the defence have proved the rule as a fact or is the rule part of the legal system? There are other doctrines that may also bring the question of the scope of the legal system before the courts. For example, are internationally binding treaties to which the state is a party, part of the municipal law of that state? Are the rules of public international law part of the law of the land?

Questions pertaining to the continuity of legal systems may arise before the courts in different contexts. A successful *coup d'état* or the establishment of a new state may give rise to various problems: Are previous laws still in force? Do persons who previously held high office still hold it or should they be renominated? Can the new regime or state claim taxes and debts owed to the old one? Can a person who committed an offence before the change be prosecuted after it has occurred? And so on.

Some, perhaps most, of the problems mentioned have obvious solutions and present no difficulty to the lawyer or judge. It is the nature of the question, the considerations relevant to a correct answer, that matter. Its degree of difficulty is immaterial. Nor is it part of the claim that such problems are always decided according to the courts' conception of the scope or continuity of a legal system. Other legal considerations may be involved, and the courts may explicitly or implicitly decide the issues on the other grounds.[2] It follows that even when faced with such problems, the courts' opinions on the question of identity are not always clear from the actual decision in the case. The arguments used to justify the decision are a much better indication and even they may be open to different interpretations.

It may be suggested that legal theorists, when dealing with the problem of identity, should aim to help formulate a systematic answer to legal problems of the kind mentioned. They should take account of existing legal solutions. They should, for example, regard the fact that foreign law, when applied by courts according to the rules of private international law, must be proved by expert witnesses as an indication that it is not part of the legal system under which these courts operate. Legal theorists should generalize such particular legal solutions, elucidate the reasons for their adoption, and on this basis formulate a theory of identity that will help solve difficult and novel

---

[2] For example, the courts may decide that a certain law is part of the system and is valid, and the provision making validity dependent on publication should be construed to include an exception for laws of this kind.

problems of this kind as well as provide guides for evaluating the merits of accepted solutions.

In pursuing such a task the theorist may find himself torn between two conflicting considerations. On the one hand, he is striving to reveal an underlying unity in the solutions, whether accepted or proposed, of many diverse legal problems. On the other hand, he must face the fact that each solution bears different legal consequences and arises in a different context, and therefore each solution might well be guided by different considerations. The purpose of making validity depend on publication may be different from the law's purpose of declaring that a mistake of law is no excuse. The theorist cannot take for granted that examination of the various legal problems relating to the identity of the legal system will lead to any unified criterion of identity. Still less can he assume that conclusions reached in the study of one legal system will be applicable to any other legal system. Different legal systems uphold different ideals of justice, maintain a different balance between conflicting interests, and pursue somewhat different goals. They exist in different societies living under different conditions. They are, therefore, likely to adopt different solutions to the problem of identity.

These remarks do not show that an investigation into the various legal criteria of identity accepted in a certain legal system and their underlying rationale is not worth pursuing. Rather, they merely warn against hasty generalizations and against uncritical application of accepted solutions to novel cases. They also draw attention to the fact that while pursuing such an investigation the theorist is engaged to a considerable extent in a critical task. He does not merely enumerate legal criteria, he rather inquires into their justifications and on this basis attempts to reach a sound generalization that will help solve new or difficult cases reasonably.

It is probably these features of this particular purpose of a doctrine of identity that account for the fact that none of the great positivist legal philosophers interested in problems of identity regarded their inquiries as designed to further this purpose. Positivist jurisprudence conceived the problem of identity as a descriptive problem of general jurisprudence. They wanted to find criteria for identifying the laws of any legal system; they were not interested in the correct or desirable solution to any set of specific legal problems. Bentham, Austin, Gray, The American Realists, Kelsen, Hart—none of them had any great interest in any of the legal problems enumerated above. They did not regard them as relevant to their theories because they were pursuing a different goal. The attempt to achieve a reasonable and systematic solution to a set of related legal problems of the type enumerated is a possible aim of a legal theorist. It is not, however, an aim that has been important in the history of jurisprudence.

THE PROBLEM CLARIFIED

What, then, were the aims of legal philosophers when dealing with problems of identity? There are three main issues that bear on the problem when considered as one of analytic jurisprudence:

> First, the relation between the existence of a law and its efficacy;
> second, the distinction between making a new law and applying an existing one; and
> third, the relation of law and the state.

Together these issues determine the answer to the problem of identity. Although each one of them has engaged the mind of some of the legal philosophers who have discussed the problem of identity, failure to consider all three partially accounts for the fact that no satisfactory solution to the problem has been found. This section is an examination of the three issues.

A. The Relation of Existence and Efficacy of Laws

The question of the relation of existence and efficacy of laws is one of the most fundamental questions concerning the nature of law. It concerns the conditions for the existence of laws, but since laws exist only in legal systems, to ask whether a law exists is to ask whether it is part of the legal system concerned: the question refers to the problem of identity. There are two extreme positions on this issue. At the one extreme is the claim that a law created in the appropriate manner exists and is valid; its efficacy or inefficacy does not affect its existence and validity unless another law of that system makes efficacy a condition of continued existence of laws. Diametrically opposed to this is the argument that laws exist because and to the extent that they are socially accepted and followed; social customs are laws even if not enacted, whereas enacted law is not valid if it has no roots in social practices. Some theorists offer various compromise solutions. Kelsen, for one, says:

A general legal norm is regarded as valid only if the human behaviour that is regulated by it actually conforms with it, at least to some degree. A norm that is not obeyed by anybody anywhere, in other words a norm that is not effective at least to some degree, is not regarded as a valid legal norm. A minimum of effectiveness is a condition of validity.[3]

Lasswell and Kaplan also prefer a compromise solution, although placing a much heavier stress on efficacy than does Kelsen's solution. Lasswell and Kaplan argue: 'Laws are not made by legislatures alone, but by the law-abiding as well: a statute ceases to embody a law (except in a formal sense...) in the degree that it is widely disregarded.'[4]

There is an element of truth in both views. Laws guide human behaviour, help people in planning and deciding on their future course of action, and provide standards for evaluating past or planned actions. A law, the existence of which is unknown, or that is never acted on by the police nor enforced by judges or juries, does not guide the behaviour of most people, not even that of law-abiding people. There seems, therefore, to be no reason to regard it as part of the legal system, since its complete inefficacy has deprived it of the main characteristic of law, that of guiding behaviour. Furthermore, not only do parliaments often modify the law in response to a change in social practice and to conform with prevailing opinions and customs, but some social practices that were not adopted by the legislature have characteristics of laws—they guide behaviour and very often they affect courts' decisions, sometimes without the judges even being aware of this.

As against these arguments, proponents of the opposite view argue that although both laws and social practices guide beha-

---

[3] H. Kelsen, *The Pure Theory of Law*, p. 11.
[4] H. Lasswell and A. Kaplan, *Power and Society* (New Haven, 1950), p. 75.

viour, this is no reason to amalgamate the two. The concept 'a law' was traditionally used to refer to norms, whether or not they conform with social practices, that have the characteristic of being part of a system of norms united by its relation to legal institutions. Social practices differ from laws because they are not institutionalized. The contention that laws are laws because they were enacted by legal institutions clarifies this basic fact about the law, focusing attention on its institutionalized nature. Even legal custom is not law until it is recognized and declared to be law by the courts. Efficacy, therefore, does not affect the validity and existence of laws. To claim otherwise is to confuse law with social customs and to disregard the basic fact about the law—that it is created by institutions. There is, no doubt, a relation between law and social practices, but it is at most a causal relation. Legislatures and courts may, consciously or unconsciously, be affected in making new laws by prevailing customs and practices; the existence of laws may also affect social customs and habits and even modify opinions. There is, however, no logical connection between law and social practice.

Both arguments are attractive, and it is very tempting to accept a compromise solution, as Kelsen, Lasswell, Kaplan, and others have done. There is, however, yet another possible solution to the problem, which is not a combination of the first two yet incorporates the sound elements of both. This solution shifts the emphasis on to the law-applying institutions, and makes recognition by law-applying organs a necessary condition of the existence of laws. This in turn makes the institutionalized nature of law an indispensable part of the criteria of identity: a law is part of the system only if it is recognized by legal institutions. The emphasis is, however, on the law-applying rather than the law-creating institutions.

Such an approach may be justified by three reasons, the third of which underlies the other two. First, although law-creating institutions are of the greatest importance in modern societies, where law is conceived as the outcome of deliberate human decision as to what society should be like, they played a minor role or did not even exist in primitive societies, where the laws were conceived as immutable and were in fact changed mainly by slowly evolving customs. Law-applying institutions are, on the other hand, a constant feature of law in every type of society and their existence should be regarded as a defining character- istic of law.

Secondly, since most legal systems recognize diverse sources of law, the only way to determine which are the law-making institutions and procedures of a given legal system is to establish which sources of law are recognized by the courts. Hence only the courts of a legal system can provide the clue to its criteria of identity.

Thirdly, it is an essential feature of legal systems that they are institutional, normative systems. It is, therefore, reasonable to take the law to consist of those norms, rules, and principles, that are presented to individuals and institutions as guides to their behaviour by the body of legal institutions as a whole. When the actions of law-creating and law-applying organs con- flict, the actions of the law-applying organs are those that affect the considerations of the law's subjects; they have final auth- ority to declare what is the law.[5]

The third rationale also preserves the importance of efficacy to the definition of law. Efficacy, however, is relevant only in so far as it affects the practices of the law-applying institutions. If, for example, the courts consistently refuse to act on a law, that law is not part of the legal system the courts operate, despite the fact that it was lawfully enacted and was never repealed. If the courts consistently interpret a statute in a way deviating from its original meaning, their reading of it, not its original sense, becomes the law. According to this approach, then, the existence of the law is logically related to the practice of the law-applying organs. The condition of a law's membership in a legal system is, however, a counterfactual: if presented with the appropriate case the courts would act on the law. This may be true even though they are never—or seldom—presented with the appropriate case. Prosecutions in criminal cases may seldom be made, and civil cases may always be settled out of court in a way contrary to the law. Therefore a law may be valid even though it is largely inefficacious.

These remarks do not spell out any solution to the problem of the relation between efficacy and existence of laws. Rather, they merely delineate an approach to the problem, defining a

[5] See generally J. Raz, op. cit., pp. 191–2, 201–2.

certain type of possible solution.[6] A large number of authors—
among them Holland, Gray, Salmond, Holmes, Llewellyn, and
Hart—opted for this approach and adopted some solution that
comes within its scope, although they differed greatly in the
details of their theories as well as in the reasons that led to their
adoption. The outline of an argument for some solution such
as is offered above does not represent the reasons of all of
them; it may not even represent the reasons of anybody
but myself. But what we all have in common is the emphasis
on law-applying organs in our criteria of identity of legal
systems.

Since the aim of this essay is to clarify problems rather than
examine or propose detailed solutions, there is no need here to
compare the various solutions to the problem of identity that
fall within the delineated approach. Attention should, however,
be drawn to two claims that, although made by some of the
above-mentioned writers, were rejected by others, and are not
a necessary concomitant of all theories of identity of this type.
First, to claim that a law is part of a system only if it is acted
on by the law-applying organs does not entail that these organs
create the law. They may be, and on most occasions are, merely
recognizing and enforcing laws previously created by legislation, precedent, or custom. Secondly, that a law is part of a
system only if recognized by the courts does not entail that laws
are descriptions or predictions of what the courts are doing or
will do. Courts are composed of human beings and the causes
of their actions are open to analysis and prediction by psycho-
logists, sociologists, and other scientists just as much as are the
causes of other people's actions. Their judgments are, however,
the fruits of deliberate decisions based on the evaluation of
reasons for the various alternatives. Moreover, the courts write
down the reasons that, in their opinion, justify their decisions,
and it is by examining the courts' opinions that one finds the
laws on which they act. The laws themselves are, therefore,
normative. They guide the actions of the courts as much as
those of ordinary people. Their existence is ultimately based on

[6] Various problems are not even mentioned here. What is a law-applying organ?
What is a court? Are the actions of all law-applying organs relevant to the criteria
of identity? I refer in the text sometimes to courts, sometimes to law-applying organs,
but I do not wish to express any opinion on these questions here. See further Essay
6 below.

social practices, but this is common to all positive norms and does not detract from their normativity.

B. The Distinction Between Making a New Law and Applying an Existing One

The statement that a law is part of a legal system only if it is recognized by the law-applying organs—the courts—of the system means only that it would have been acted on by the courts had they been presented with the appropriate problem. That a court would apply a law if faced with a case to which the law applies is an indication that either the law exists in the legal system or that the law will be made by the courts when they have an opportunity to do so. Recognition by the courts or other law-applying organs is not a complete criterion of identity because these organs often have power to make new laws, and often what law they are going to make can be determined in advance. As a first step towards completing the criterion,[7] one must incorporate in it reference to the fact that the law would not only be recognized by the courts but would be recognized as a previously existing law. It is not a new law that they would make when faced with an appropriate case. For this reason the distinction between applying an existing law and creating and applying a new one is the second jurisprudential issue involved in the problem of identity. Of the major legal theorists Hart is the only one to face this problem, and a brief discussion of the relevant aspects of his theory will clarify the nature of the issue.

Hart argues that the distinction between the application of a new law and the application of a previously existing one turns on the existence or absence of a duty to apply the law. If and only if the court applies a law that it is under a duty to apply is it acting on a previously existing law; on the other hand, when it applies a rule that it has no duty to apply it is not acting on a previously existing law.[8] This is a consequence of Hart's

[7] Hypothetical recognition by the courts is not, strictly speaking, even a necessary condition for a law's membership in a legal system, for a law may belong to a legal system even if the courts have power to change it and it is known that they will do so, given an appropriate opportunity. The precise relation between the courts' practices and the identity of the legal system is clarified by the discussion in this part of Hart's theory of the rule of recognition. See pp. 91–5 below.

[8] In such cases the court transforms the rule into a law of the system if and only

doctrine of the rule of recognition. In every legal system, he argues, there is of necessity a rule of recognition that identifies the laws of the system;[9] the criterion of identity of legal systems can be formulated as follows: A legal system consists of a rule of recognition and all the laws identified by that rule. Hart's discussion of the rule of recognition falls short of the high standard of lucidity characterizing the rest of his book and requires interpretation, which will be limited to the doctrine's effects on the problem of identity.[10]

A rule of recognition is 'a rule for conclusive identification of primary rules of behaviour'.[11] Here, as occasionally elsewhere, Hart states that the rule identifies only primary rules. It is quite clear, however, that his rule of recognition is a rule for the identification of all the other rules of the system, and only them. It specifies 'some feature or features possession of which by a suggested rule is taken as a conclusive affirmative indication that it is a *rule of the group*'.[12] This means that the rule of recognition of a system constitutes its criterion of validity: 'To say that a given rule is valid is to recognize it as passing all the tests provided by the rule of recognition and so as a *rule of the system*.'[13] The rule of recognition provides also the means for the resolution of conflicts between laws.[14] This is conceived by Hart as an essential part of the rule's function in identifying the laws of the system, for it is a condition of the validity of a rule that it does not conflict with a superior rule.

How does the rule of recognition fulfil its function? The rule is unique among the rules of the legal system.[15] It is a necessary rule in the sense that every legal system necessarily has one and only one rule of recognition and a set of rules which does not include a rule of recognition is not a legal system.[16] Furthermore,

---

if as a result of its recognition by the court in this case there arises a duty to apply it in other cases: that is, if the system has some rule of precedent.

[9] H. L. A. Hart, *The Concept of Law*, pp. 92–120.

[10] The rule of recognition is also central to Hart's theory of the existence of legal systems. Cf. ibid., pp. 109–13. This aspect of the doctrine will be disregarded in the present discussion.

[11] Ibid., p. 92.

[12] Ibid. (emphasis added).

[13] Ibid., p. 100 (emphasis added; cf. ibid., pp. 102, 106).

[14] Ibid., pp. 92–3, 98, 103.

[15] Ibid., p. 107.

[16] Cf. ibid., p. 93.

all the other laws exist and are part of the legal system only if they fulfil conditions laid down in the rule of recognition. The existence of the rule of recognition itself cannot, of course, be ascertained in this manner. 'Its existence is a matter of fact [and] ... must consist in an actual practice.'[17] Hart offers a detailed analysis earlier in his book of what it means for a rule to exist as a matter of fact—as a social practice;[18] this analysis is quite clearly meant to apply to the rule of recognition.

Whose practice constitutes the conditions for the existence of the rule of recognition? Hart's answer is far from clear. Often he refers to 'the practice of courts, legislatures, officials or private citizens'.[19] On occasion, while including reference to the behaviour of private citizens, he attributes special importance to the practice of the courts.[20] Finally, we are told—and this should be regarded as Hart's position—that the behaviour of the population is not part of the conditions for the existence of the rule of recognition. Its existence consists in the behaviour of the 'officials' of the system,[21] by which he presumably means law-applying officials.[22]

Hart holds that the conditions for the existence of social rules are practices of those people to whom the rules are addressed. It follows, then, that the rule of recognition is addressed to the officials of the legal system.[23] Furthermore, Hart's explanation of social rules is basically an explanation of duty-imposing rules. The only other type of rules Hart recognizes are power-conferring rules, but he does not consider what social practices constitute the existence of a customary power-conferring rule.

[17] H. L. A. Hart, *The Concept of Law*, pp. 107–8; cf. p. 245.

[18] Cf. ibid., pp. 54–6. For a discussion of Hart's explanation of a social rule see J. Raz, op. cit., pp. 147 ff.

[19] H. L. A. Hart, op. cit., p. 104 n. 9. See also ibid., pp. 98, 106.

[20] Ibid., p. 105.

[21] Ibid., pp. 110, 113.

[22] This interpretation is confirmed by H. L. A. Hart, 'Kelsen's Doctrine of the Unity of Law', in *Ethics and Social Justice*, ed. Kiefer and Munitz (New York, 1970).

[23] There is no clear statement in the book on this issue. The rule is often said to be used by officials and individuals (cf. H. L. A. Hart, *The Concept of Law*, pp. 97, 98, 104), but it is quite clear that it is addressed to officials and applies only to them. It follows that if every legal system has a rule of recognition it also has officials and rules of change and adjudication investing officials with legal powers. That is the reason for my claim above that Hart's theory should be counted with the theories which emphasize the institutional nature of law. Occasionally, however, Hart tends to deny that institutions are an essential part of every legal system. Cf. ibid., p. 93; Hart, 'Kelsen's Doctrine of the Unity of Law', p. 195.

Therefore, since the rule of recognition is a customary rule, it must be interpreted as duty-imposing. Besides, all the legal powers of officials are conferred on them by the rules of change and adjudication, authorizing them to make new laws and to settle disputes. To claim that the rule of recognition is a power-conferring rule is to confuse it with either rules of change or rules of adjudication.[24]

The rule of recognition imposes an obligation on the law-applying officials to recognize and apply all and only those laws satisfying certain criteria of validity spelled out in the rule, which criteria include indications of how conflicts of laws are to be resolved.[25] From Hart's examples it would seem that although he thinks that the criteria of validity most commonly refer to the mode of origin of the laws, this is not always the case.[26]

The jurisprudential criterion of identity implied by this theory is: A legal system consists of a rule of recognition and all the laws that ought to be applied according to it. When the courts apply a rule that they were not obliged to apply they may make it thereby into a law (if there is in the system a rule of precedent that will oblige all courts henceforth to apply it), but they do not apply an existing law and the rule was not part of the system before its application.

Hart's rule of recognition is subject to criticism on a few points and requires some clarification. One should remember that clear conceptual distinctions do not entail the existence of clear instances of the concepts involved. Therefore, the absence of clear instances should not deter one from striving

---

[24] It is commonly assumed that by secondary rules Hart means power-conferring rules. This interpretation is supported by some passages in his writings. Cf. Hart, Book Review, *Harvard Law Review* 78 (1965), pp. 1281, 1292. This interpretation, however, conflicts with other aspects of his theory and does not represent his present views. It is true that all the primary rules are duty-imposing, but not all the secondary rules are power-conferring. The rule of recognition is an exception. Rules of change, adjudication, and recognition are called secondary because they presuppose the existence of primary rules, whereas primary rules can exist without secondary ones, albeit not as a legal system. This is an explanation of the terminology, not a criterion for determining which rules are primary and which are secondary. This is determined by their social function—whether they are rules of change, adjudication, and recognition—not by their normative character.

[25] The logical form of a rule of recognition is: All law-applying officials have a duty to apply all and only laws that satisfy the following criteria: . . .

[26] Cf. H. L. A. Hart, *The Concept of Law*, pp. 92, 94, 97, 98.

to formulate clear conceptual distinctions. The courts, in most cases brought before them, probably neither merely apply an existing law nor do they merely initiate a new law. They may be doing a little of both. But this does not detract from the ability of a clear distinction between applying existing law and creating a new one to shed light on legal processes.

The application of the rule of recognition to concrete cases may be beset by similar problems. Hart makes it quite clear that the rule of recognition, like any other rule, is necessarily open-textured and vague to some extent. It may also be incomplete,[27] for it may not include an accepted answer to some legal questions, such as the validity of rules of public international law within the municipal legal system. The existence of a rule of recognition does not entail that all the legal problems, the solution of which may depend on the nature of the criteria of validity, such as the problems mentioned above, have found their solution in the system. So long as the rule is incomplete some such problems will remain unanswered, but when the courts are faced with such unsolved problems and accept a certain solution they modify the rule of recognition. This should surprise no one. The rule of recognition, being a customary rule, is constantly open to change.

Asserting that there is in every legal system a rule of recognition does not involve one in the task of giving a systematic and reasonable account of the limits of a legal system based on accepted or proposed solutions to a whole host of legal problems, as described above. However, any attempt to articulate the details of the criteria of validity incorporated in any rule of recognition of any legal system means embarking on precisely this endeavour. Attempting to formulate criteria of validity based on complex court practices that are in a constant state of change and that are necessarily vague and almost certainly incomplete, involves not only legal perceptiveness and theoretical skill, it demands sound judgment and reasonable value-decisions as well. Hart's theory leads one to the point where the boundaries between analytic and critical jurisprudence, between general and particular jurisprudence, begin to blur. But he himself does not cross the boundary. Rather, he provides

---

[27] H. L. A. Hart, *The Concept of Law*, pp. 144–50.

conceptual tools for dealing with particular and critical problems, but he does not deal with those problems himself.

There is no reason to suppose that the rule of recognition refers to all the criteria of validity of a legal system, and it is clearly wrong to think that it determines them all. A criterion of validity is a set of conditions set by law, satisfaction of which is sufficient for being a law of the system. All the laws of a legal system, except the rule of recognition the existence of which is a matter of social practice, are valid; they exist in the system because they satisfy some criterion of validity. Besides the rule of recognition, other laws can also set criteria of validity. All the laws conferring legislative powers, for example, determine criteria of validity; so also does a law stipulating conditions that a social custom must fulfil to be legally binding.[28]

That the rule of recognition sets up some criteria of validity is clear. There must be in every system some criteria of validity that, although legally binding, are not legally valid, hence they must be set in the rule of recognition. There is, however, no reason to think that all the criteria must be stipulated in that rule. The fact that all the criteria of validity are determined in laws that, directly or indirectly, are valid according to criteria determined in the rule of recognition, guarantees that by imposing a duty to apply the laws satisfying its criteria of validity, the rule of recognition imposes a duty to apply all the laws of the system.

Furthermore, there is no reason to suppose that every legal system has just one rule of recognition. It may have more. Imagine a legal system in which no valid law makes custom or precedent a source of law, but in which, nevertheless, both custom and precedent are sources of law. It follows that the criteria for the validity of laws created by custom or precedent are determined by rules of recognition imposing obligations on the courts to apply such laws. But we should not assume that there is just one rule of recognition rather than two—one relating to each source of law—simply because the

---

[28] Because it is a condition for being a law of a legal system that the courts ought to apply it, it follows that criteria of validity are conditions for the duty of the courts to apply laws. Therefore, since the courts have a duty to apply lawfully enacted laws, laws conferring powers of legislation give rise to criteria of validity. They are not, however, the only type of law that does so. The rule of recognition is just one example of a law setting criteria of validity that is not a power-conferring law.

system must contain means of resolving conflicts between laws of the various sources.[29] First, as was pointed out above, the rule of recognition, even if it is one rule, may be incomplete, which means that the system may not include any means of resolving conflicts. Perhaps the problem has never arisen and there is no generally accepted solution to it. Secondly, there may be two or more rules of recognition that provide methods of resolving conflicts; for example, the rule imposing an obligation to apply certain customs may indicate that it is supreme, whereas the rule relating to precedent may indicate that it is subordinate.[30]

In most legal systems courts have authority to settle at least some of the disputes to which there is no clear solution in the laws of the system. Courts have a duty to apply the laws of the system when they are applicable and to exercise discretion in order to decide (partially) unregulated disputes—disputes to which the laws do not provide a clear answer or where the courts have power to change the law. By the rule of precedent this exercise of discretion often amounts to the creation of new laws. The courts' discretion to decide unregulated disputes may be absolute or guided. They may be guided by law as to the manner in which discretion should be exercised. The law may, for example, direct judges to act on the rule that they think best for such cases, or to render a decision that would be the best from the point of view of the parties to the present dispute, or direct the courts to consult their conscience or the writings of moralists. Such instructions may be given in a statute, but they may also exist only in the practice of the courts. Very often, however, they are not ordinary precedents, but may instead derive their force from the continuing practice of the courts. When this happens, the legal system concerned contains two types of ultimate laws: laws of one type directing the courts which laws to apply, those of the other type guiding their discretion in deciding (partly) unregulated disputes. Laws of the first type are laws of recognition, laws of the second type are ultimate laws of discretion, and both impose duties on the courts. But laws of recognition oblige the courts to apply certain

[29] It is not clear whether Hart relies on this consideration, op. cit., pp. 92–3.

[30] It is the fact that a set of laws of recognition are maintained by the practice of the same law-applying organs that indicates that they are all part of one legal system.

laws, leaving them no choice which laws to apply. Laws of discretion, on the other hand, whether ultimate or not, merely guide the courts' discretion in the choice of laws to adopt and apply; they limit the courts' freedom of choice but do not deprive them of it.

Laws of recognition are thus deprived of part of their uniqueness. They are still the only ultimate laws that necessarily exist in every legal system, but they are not the only ultimate laws that can exist in a system. Moreover, the distinction between applying an existing law and applying a new one is seen to be more a difference of degree than of kind. This fact, together with the fact that in practice it is often difficult to decide whether in a particular case a new law was created or an old one applied, does not mean that the distinction cannot be drawn or that it is unimportant. Every legal system rests on its ultimate laws, which commonly means on a set of ultimate laws of recognition and discretion. The former provide the ultimate criteria of validity of the laws of the system, the latter guide the courts in the exercise of their powers to modify the system when deciding unregulated disputes and creating precedents for the future. The difference may be one of degree, but it is indispensable for the formulation of criteria of identity.[31]

C. The Relation of Law and State

If the theory of the rule of recognition is substantially correct, as I think it is, it forms part of the answer to the problem of identity. Although it sets necessary conditions for membership in a legal system, it does not provide all the sufficient conditions. Nothing is part of a legal system unless either it is a rule of recognition of the system, or the courts ought to recognize and apply it. To be a rule of recognition is sufficient to be counted as a law of the system, but to be a law that the courts are obliged to apply is not. Quite often the courts have an obligation to apply laws of other legal systems, rules of private associations, and so on, although these were not and do not become part of the legal system. Therefore, the rule of recognition provides

[31] In the next essay and in Essay 10 the test distinguishing between making and applying law is refined to explain how it is that a court is under an obligation to apply a law which it can, under certain conditions, revise.

no complete answer to the problem of the scope of a legal system—the problem of the identity of momentary legal systems.[32]

Nor does the rule of recognition solve the problem of the continuity of legal systems. That one legal system comes to an end and another takes its place manifests itself in a change of rule of recognition, for each legal system has a different rule of recognition. The rule of recognition, however, is a customary rule; hence it is constantly in a process of change. What changes are consistent with the continued existence of the same rule, and what changes compel the admission that a new rule has replaced the old one?[33] It is easy to bring examples for either situation, as well as examples of borderline cases. However, it is not the existence of borderline cases, which are inevitable, that is disturbing. The disturbing fact is that Hart's theory provides no clue as to *how* to draw the conceptual distinction. Even more disturbing is that this is no mere oversight on the part of Hart that can be easily remedied. He did not provide the answer because he did not ask the question to which the distinction is an answer. His theory provides substantially complete answers (whether or not they are correct) to the problems with which he was concerned: the role of the courts in a legal system, the truth in rule scepticism, the variety of laws and their interrelation, the relation of efficacy and existence. If his theory fails to provide a complete solution to the problem of identity it is because he overlooked not only part of the answer but also a whole question: that of the relation of law and state.[34]

The relation of law and state affects the two distinct aspects— scope and continuity—of the problem of identity. Every state— by which is meant a form of political system and not a juristic person—has one legal system that constitutes the law of that

[32] Hart has become aware of these problems. Cf. H. L. A. Hart, 'Kelsen's Doctrine of the Unity of Law', op. cit., pp. 195 f. The fact that a legal system may contain more than one rule of recognition is another reason for the need to revise Hart's doctrine of identity.

[33] See generally J. Finnis, 'Revolution and Continuity of Law' in A. W. B. Simpson, *Oxford Essays in Jurisprudence*, 2nd ser. (Oxford, 1973).

[34] In many legal systems the term 'state' or its equivalent is used to designate a certain legal person recognized in law as having certain duties, powers, and rights, and as acting through certain organs. This legal concept of the state should be clearly distinguished from the political concept of the state as a form of political system; only the latter is relevant to the problem of identity.

state, and every municipal legal system is the law of one state. Since, then, the identity of a legal system is bound up with that of the state the law of which it is, the relation between law and state necessarily affects the problem of scope. So too, since an end to the existence of a state is the end of its legal system, and since a law that is not a law of the state is not part of its legal system, the problem of continuity is similarly affected by the relation of state and law.

Two diametrically opposed views on the relation of law and state have been expressed by legal philosophers. Kelsen[35] claimed that the concept of the state can be explained only in legal terms. That is, the concept of a legal system must be explained first; from it naturally flows the explanation of the concept of a state, for a state is but a (municipal) legal system. No social facts, no social norms that are not relevant to the explanation of law have any relevance to the theory of the state. Bentham and Austin, on the other hand, held that law can only be explained after some theory of state has been established. First one must define the meaning of 'an independent political society'—'a state'. On the basis of this definition 'law' can be defined. Bentham's and Austin's definitions of 'an independent political society' are purely sociological, making use of no legal concepts, and the same is true of their definitions of sovereign and subject that are part of it.[36]

Bentham and Austin have the better of this controversy. Because Kelsen lacks the concept of the state as a political system, he fails to account for the identity of a legal system. He is driven to rely on constitutional continuity as a sole mark of identity, disregarding the fact that new states can be created and new legal systems established without any break in the constitutional continuity taking place.[37] A theory of law must be based, at least partly, on a theory of state, and denying this has been one of Kelsen's gravest mistakes. A theory of state, however, is partly based on a theory of law—the two are intimately interrelated.

Since I am concerned with the nature of the problem of

[35] H. Kelsen, *General Theory of Law and State*, pp. 181–207.

[36] Cf. J. Austin, *The Province of Jurisprudence Determined* (New York, 1954), pp. 192–215; J. Bentham, *A Fragment of Government* (Oxford, 1960), pp. 33–46.

[37] For a detailed criticism of Kelsen's theory of the identity of legal systems see J. Raz, *The Concept of a Legal System*, pp. 95–109.

identity rather than its solution, there is no need to discuss the concept of a state beyond mentioning some truisms. A state is the political organization of a society, it is a political system that is a subsystem of a more comprehensive social system. The social system includes, of course, many other subsystems and the political system interacts with most if not all of them, as well as interacting with other political systems. These social and political systems are normative systems; in other words, at least part of the pattern of interrelations constituting the systems is norm governed.

The legal system is only part of the norms constituting the political system; most political systems include numerous non-legal norms. Some of these non-legal norms apply to society in general: however much the system is resented and hated, if it is viable at all, it is based, among other things, on some norms of respect for at least some of the laws and some authorities on the part of some important sections in the society. Some non-legal political norms are more limited, of which Dicey's conventions of the constitution can serve as an example.[38]

It follows that since the continuity of a legal system is tied to the continuity of the political system, the former is affected by the fate of the non-legal norms that happen to form part of the political system concerned. However, emphasizing the importance of the fate of non-legal norms to the continuity of the legal system does not mean that these are the only factors affecting continuity. The substance of my contention is that whatever form one's ultimate account of continuity[39] takes, it must, in view of the relation of law and state, be based on the following two points: first, that continuity depends on the inter-action of legal and non-legal norms, and the extent and manner of their change; and secondly, that among the legal norms concerned some are more relevant than others. Since the continuity of the legal system is fundamentally a function of the continuity of the political system, political laws are more relevant than others. Constitutional and administrative laws are, therefore, more relevant than, for example, the law of contract or torts.

[38] See A. V. Dicey, *Introduction to the Study of the Law of the Constitution* (London, 1963).
[39] It may, for example, be based on the conception of change of system as a result of a short and intense period of fundamental change, or it may allow for a slow and gradual transformation of one system into another.

The problem of scope is similarly affected, and can be sub-divided into four sub-problems: first, that of the dividing line between political norms that are part of the legal system and those that are not; secondly, that of the dividing line between legal norms and social norms of the social system of which the political system is a subsystem; thirdly, that of the dividing line between the law and norms of other subsystems of the same society; and fourthly, that of the dividing line between one legal system and coexisting laws of other legal systems.

The first of these sub-problems of the problem of scope may be solved by insisting that the laws of a system are either the ultimate rules of its courts or the laws its courts ought to recognize and apply. Those political norms that are neither the courts' practice nor norms that the courts ought to apply are not part of the law of the state. The other three sub-problems, though each involving somewhat different considerations, have this much in common: sometimes the courts are under an obligation to apply norms because those norms belong to these other social or political systems. The courts ought to enforce private contracts, the rules of some private associations within the state, the laws of foreign countries, and so on. Some theorists have seen this as a reason for regarding those laws as part of the legal system, and Bentham maintained that all commands that are enforceable in law are laws of the sovereign.[40] Hart maintained in *The Concepts of Law* that all the rules that the courts have a duty to apply are laws of the system.

As indicated above, the backing of the state power is a defining characteristic of municipal law,[41] but it is not the only one. Also characteristic of the state system is that one of its main functions is to maintain and support other forms of social grouping; it is, therefore, characteristic of the law that it upholds and enforces contracts, agreements, rules, and customs of private persons and associations. To obscure the distinction between norms recognized as part of the law and norms that, although not part of the law, are recognized and enforced because it is the function of the law to support various social groupings is

---

[40] J. Bentham, *Of Laws in General* (London, 1970), pp. 22 ff.
[41] I have limited the discussion throughout to municipal law. Other types of legal systems are the law of other types of social organizations, be they tribes, churches, or the international community and they bear similar relations to those organizations.

to misunderstand the nature of the state and its relations to other social systems.

Admitting that not all the norms that the courts ought to apply are part of the law, where should one draw the line? This is not the place to attempt a solution.[42] I wish, however, to conclude with one last remark bearing on the problem. That a norm is identified as one the courts ought to apply by the fact that it is a norm of a certain society, association, or state is no indication whether or not it is part of the system. Legislation by reference is a familiar technique; for example, a statute passed in one country adopting by reference the civil code of another country. No other formal distinction will succeed in drawing a reasonable dividing line. The reasons for enforcing the norm, and the attitude of the courts and the legislature to its enforcement, are the crucial factors. Formal distinctions may give some indication as to the nature of the reasons for enforcing, but are never in themselves conclusive. Ultimately the problem turns on an accumulation of evidence justifying a judgment whether the norm is enforced on the grounds that it is part of the law's function to support other social systems or because it is part of the law itself.

[42] Cf. Essay 6 below.

6

THE INSTITUTIONAL NATURE
OF LAW*

INTRODUCTION

My purpose is to outline one view concerning the identifying features of municipal legal systems. Analytical jurisprudence deals with three main problem areas. One concerns the special features of the judicial process and of judicial reasoning. The second encompasses the discussion of legal concepts (e.g. rights, duties, ownership, legal person) and of types of legal standards (rules and principles, duty-imposing standards and power-conferring standards). The third range of problems revolves round the idea of a legal stystem and the features which distinguish such systems from other normative systems. It is with some of the problems belonging to this area that I shall be concerned.

It may be useful to begin by confessing to some of my prejudices and to make explicit a few of the assumptions underlying my reflections. One of them can be dubbed the assumption of the primacy of the social. We are familiar with the distinction between legal systems which are in force in a certain society and those which are not. There is a legal system in force now in Great Britain and there is one in force in Norway. But the legal system once in force in the Roman Republic is no longer in force, nor is the legal system proposed by a group of scholars for country X in fact in force in that country. Whether or not a system is in force in a society depends on its impact on the behaviour of people in the society. The precise nature of the criterion determining if a system is in force is a disputed issue with which I will not be concerned. But whatever it is, it concerns the attitudes and responses of all or certain sections in the society to the legal system: Do they know it, do they respect it, obey it?, etc. This seems to me to be a very significant fact. The reason is that whether or not a system is in force is not just another question about a legal system comparable with questions such as: Is it a Socialist or a Capitalist legal system?

* First published in *The Modern Law Review* (1975). The argument of this essay is further defended in sections 4.2, 4.3, 5.1, and 5.2 of *Practical Reason and Norms* which incorporate part of it.

Is it a Federal system or not?, etc. We identify the question of whether or not the system is in force with the question of its existence. A legal system exists if and only if it is in force. The significance of the point is that it brings out that normative systems are existing legal systems because of their impact on the behaviour of individuals, because of their role in the organization of social life. Consequently when we look at legal systems as systems of laws, when we consider their content and disregard the question of whether they are in fact in force, whether they exist, we should look for those features which enable them to fulfil a distinctive role in society. These will be the features which distinguish legal systems from other normative systems. This is the assumption of the primacy of the social. It does not mean that legal systems do not also have other characteristic features. They may, for example, have certain moral features. It may be a necessary truth that all legal systems conform to some moral values and that a system which violates those values cannot be a legal system. My claim is merely that if this is indeed the case then these necessary moral features of law are derivative characteristics of law. If all legal systems necessarily possess certain moral characteristics they possess them as a result of the fact that they have other properties which are necessary for them to fulfil their unique social role.

There are two other assumptions which I wish very briefly to mention. The first is the assumption of universality according to which it is a criterion of adequacy of a legal theory that it is true of all the intuitively clear instances of municipal legal systems. Since a legal theory must be true of all legal systems the identifying features by which it characterizes them must of necessity be very general and abstract. It must disregard those functions which some legal systems fulfil in some societies because of the special social, economic, or cultural conditions of those societies. It must fasten only on those features of legal systems which they must possess regardless of the special circumstances of the societies in which they are in force. This is the difference between legal philosophy and sociology of law. The latter is concerned with the contingent and with the particular, the former with the necessary and the universal. Sociology of law provides a wealth of detailed information and analysis of the functions of law in some particular societies. Legal philosophy has to be content with those few features which all legal systems necessarily possess.

My third assumption has already been incorporated into my second criterion of adequacy by restricting it to municipal legal systems. It can be called the assumption of the importance of municipal law. It reflects our, or at least my, intuitive perception that municipal legal systems are sufficiently important and sufficiently different from most other normative systems to deserve being studied for their own sake. They are, or are part of, a form of social organization which is both important and different from most others and which therefore should be made an object of a separate study. Obviously, in part the investigation of municipal systems is designed to compare and contrast them with other normative systems. Indeed it is to this part that the present essay is dedicated. In pursuing such investigations it may turn out that municipal systems are not unique, that all their essential features are shared by, say, international law or by church law. If this is indeed so, well and good. But it is not a requirement of adequacy of a legal theory that it should be so or indeed that it should not be so. It is, however, a criterion of adequacy that the theory will successfully illuminate the nature of municipal systems.

PRIMARY INSTITUTIONS

Many, if not all, legal philosophers have been agreed that one of the defining features of law is that it is an institutionalized normative system. Two types of institutions were singled out for special attention: norm-applying institutions such as courts, tribunals, the police, etc., and norm-creating institutions such as constitutional assemblies, parliaments, etc. I have argued elsewhere that the existence of norm-creating institutions though characteristic of modern legal systems is not a necessary feature of all legal systems, but that the existence of certain types of norm-applying institutions is. Let me try to say something about the nature of those institutions which are a necessary part of every legal system. What are the distinguishing marks of norm-applying organs? This is a notoriously difficult question. We have only to look at the debate concerning the nature of courts to become aware of the difficulties. Lawyers and sociologists have offered various incompatible explanations and the battle is still raging. Given this history of disagreement the first thing to note is that various theorists studying this question are really tackling a variety of problems. Lawyers studying the defining features of 'a court' or 'a tribunal' may be concerned with solving any one of a variety of legal problems arising under a specific legal system: a certain court in that system may have supervisory powers over all judicial determinations by judicial bodies. The law of evidence or some of its rules may apply to proceedings before every judicial body, etc. When a lawyer faces the question: 'What is a court?' he is usually concerned with one or more of the many problems which such laws give rise to. Is the body A a judicial body subject to the supervisory jurisdiction of the relevant court? Do the general principles of the law of evidence apply to proceedings before A?, etc. Social scientists have their own problems which are quite different, though usually indirectly related to those of the lawyer. They may be interested in the classification of different social methods of settling disputes, or the different channels for the articulation of demands, etc. Our purpose in looking for the identifying traits of norm-applying institutions is primarily to establish the nature of the kind of institutions the presence of which is a defining feature of legal systems. An adequate answer to our question need not be a satisfactory solution of the problems of the lawyer or of the sociologist, nor is it intended as an answer to their questions.

Some have attempted to define judicial and other norm-applying organs by the social functions they fulfil. Others have looked for an answer in the norms which establish these institutions. I shall follow the latter kind of approach. Norm-applying institutions are first and foremost normative institutions established by norms and it is to these we must turn for a clue to their identity. It may be true that they are established to serve some social functions, but it is likely that the same functions can be and are served by other means as well. Norm-applying institutions should, therefore, be identified by the way they fulfil their functions rather than by their functions themselves. This does not detract from the importance of studying the functions which the institutions serve, it merely means that the institutions have to be identified by other means.

Of legal systems it can be said that every act by a public

official which is the performance of a duty or an exercise of a regulative power is generally regarded as a law-applying act. A policeman arresting a suspect, an official granting a trader's licence, a court rendering judgment in which Doe is ordered to pay a sum of money to Roe—all these are commonly regarded as instances of the application of law by public officials. These cases differ from similar acts of private individuals who pay taxes, make contracts, give orders to their employees, etc., only in being the acts of public officials. Therefore, on the most general interpretation of 'norm-applying institutions' these are identical with public institutions (in one sense of the word 'public').

What are the identifying features of public officials? This is a problem which is both important and difficult. It is, however, a problem which it would be best to avoid here, for though we will find public officials in all legal systems, not all of them must exist in the system if it is to count as a legal system. Instead we should try to identify a subclass of norm-applying institutions, namely those the presence of which is necessary in all legal systems.

The terminological contrast between 'norm-creating' and 'norm-applying' draws attention to one important class of norm-applying institutions—those which apply norms not by making other norms but by physically implementing them. The courts apply the law by rendering judgments which are themselves norms. The prison service or public officials instructed to pull down a house against which a demolition order has been issued physically enforce the law. I shall call norm-applying institutions of this kind norm-enforcing institutions. There is no doubt that norm-enforcing institutions play an important role in all modern legal systems. Yet they cannot be regarded as the key to the identification of legal systems. Though all legal systems regulate the use of force and ultimately rely on force to ensure compliance with the law, not all of them need have law-enforcing institutions. There may be normative systems which share all the characteristics of legal systems and do not have law-enforcing machinery. Once a judgment is given its execution is left to the parties to the dispute. In such a system an individual is not allowed to use force to secure his rights whenever he likes. He is obliged to go to a court and obtain an authoritative declaration of his rights. But once he is in possession of a decision he is entitled to implement it using reasonable force and he may be entitled to authorize others to use force in his name for this purpose. Such a system is clearly a legal system. It does not have law-enforcing institutions, but it has other norm-applying institutions which warrant regarding it as a legal system.

We must, therefore, look elsewhere for the kind of norm-applying institutions which are crucial to our understanding of legal systems. I shall suggest that the type of institutions we are looking for are those which combine norm-making and norm-applying in a special way. Let us call these institutions primary (norm-applying) organs, to indicate their importance. Primary institutions are just one kind of norm-applying institution. Norm-enforcing organs are another kind of such institution and there are others as well. Norm-enforcing organs are concerned with the physical implementation of norms and this determines their character as norm-applying. Primary organs are concerned with the authoritative determination of normative situations in accordance with pre-existing norms. Consider judicial bodies. Courts and tribunals have power to determine the rights and duties of individuals. But cannot any person do the same? Cannot John determine whether he owes £100 to Alan or whether Paul owes money to Jack? He may be ignorant of the facts but like a court he may investigate them. He may be ignorant of the law but like a court he may study it. The difference between a court and a private individual is not merely that courts are provided with better facilities to determine the facts of the case and the law applying to them. Courts have power to make an *authoritative* determination of people's legal situation. Private individuals may express their opinion on the subject but their views are not binding.

The fact that a court may make a binding decision does not mean that it cannot err. It means that its decision is binding even if it is mistaken. My declaration of the legal situation is not binding at all because it is not binding if it is mistaken. To be a binding application of a norm means to be binding even if wrong, even if it is in fact a misapplication of the norm. This seemingly paradoxical formulation illuminates the nature and function of primary norm-applying organs.

The paradox is generated by the following problem: How can we say of a determination (decision or declaration) both that it applies a pre-existing norm and that it is binding? We may feel that we regard a determination as norm-applying if it merely determines which rights and duties individuals have in virtue of pre-existing norms, whereas we regard a determination as binding only if it changes the rights and duties of individuals. Only with regard to a new norm imposing duties on individuals or releasing them from their duties, investing them with rights or divesting them of their rights can we ask whether it is valid or not. If the determination purports merely to ascertain what rights and duties they already have and not to change them then the only question arising is whether the determination is correct or incorrect. The question of the binding force arises only with respect to creative determinations—those which change the normative situation. Creative determinations can be binding or not but cannot be either correct or incorrect. The reverse is true of applicative determinations.

On this view a determination cannot be both binding and norm-applying. This is, however, an over-restrictive view of the sense of 'binding'. A determination can be binding even if it does not change the normative situation, provided it would have been binding had it changed it. Consider a new piece of legislation which, though its authors may be unaware of this fact, merely repeats the content of an old but valid law. The new legislation can be judged to be either valid or invalid, even though it is clear that it does not change anybody's rights or duties. The point is that if valid it would have changed the legal situation had the old law no longer been in force. Put in another way—if valid it creates another basis for the rights and duties imposed by the old law. In the same sense a court's determination that Doe owes money to Roe is binding even though the debt existed by virtue of a pre-existing norm, provided that it is binding even if there would have been no debt but for the decision of the court—hence my original formulation that a norm-applying determination is binding only if binding even if mistaken.

Now we are in a position to describe the defining features of primary norm-applying organs: they are institutions with power to determine the normative situation of specified individuals, which are required to exercise these powers by applying existing norms, but whose decisions are binding even when wrong. A few comments on this characterization will be in place here:

(1) The definition attempts to identify one kind of institution. The nature of institutions in general is presupposed and is not explained in it. It is important to stress that we are concerned with primary *institutions*. Legal systems are not identified merely by the fact that they contain norms conferring powers to make binding applicative determinations. They must contain norms conferring such powers on institutions, i.e. on centralized bodies concentrating in their hands the authority to make binding applicative determinations.

(2) Courts, tribunals, and other judicial bodies are the most important example of primary organs. But other officials, such as police officers, may also be primary organs. There are obvious reasons to impose on primary organs a duty to follow judicial procedures, but this need not be always done. It does seem reasonable to suppose, however, that the notion of a primary institution provides a necessary step in any attempt to analyse the nature of judicial institutions.

(3) The definition of a primary organ may have to be further refined. As it stands it applies only to final and absolutely binding determinations. It has to be modified to allow for the possibility of appeal, re-trial, etc., and also for the possibility that the determination is binding for one purpose but not for others. In many legal systems there are applicative determinations which are binding only with respect to the cause of action whose litigation resulted in the determinations.

(4) The definition identifies primary organs by their power to make binding applicative determinations. This is compatible with the fact that the same institutions have other powers and functions. In particular, courts often have power to create precedent and lay down general rules, to issue orders to individuals to perform certain actions and authoritatively to determine the facts of the case (the *res judicata* doctrine). All these are either entirely different or, at best, overlap with the power to make binding applicative determinations. Applicative determinations are determinations of the rights or duties of individuals in concrete situations and are entirely different from the power

to create precedent or to issue orders instructing individuals to pay damages or fines or be gaoled, etc., because they disregarded their duties or the rights of others. Applicative determinations are most closely related to declaratory judgments. In fact the definition suggests that a declaratory judgment is an ingredient in many courts' decisions. This is part of the effect of the *res judicata* doctrine. But this doctrine is wider and applies also to purely factual findings, and not only to determinations of rights and duties in particular situations.

THE LIMITS OF LAW

My claim is that our common knowledge of intuitively clear instances of municipal systems confirms that they all contain primary institutions and that such institutions play a crucial role in our understanding of legal systems and their function in society. The analysis both of the existence conditions and of the identity of legal systems depends on the rules governing the working of their primary institutions and their actual behaviour. Furthermore, it seems reasonable to suppose that the law differs from any other methods of social control in providing machinery for the authoritative settlement of disputes. To explore these issues will take us beyond the scope of the present essay.

I would like, however, to point to one consequence of the necessary existence of primary institutions. We saw that their presence means that law provides a method for settling disputes. It is important to notice that this is a special method for settling disputes. Consider a normative system containing only rules instituting tribunals and regulating their operation. When a dispute is referred to a tribunal it will be authoritatively settled by its decision, for the system includes a rule to that effect. It contains a rule making it obligatory to observe the decisions of the courts and providing for their enforcement by a police force created for this purpose only. In such a system the courts can settle any dispute in any way they like. There are no legislated, customary, or any other standards which they have to apply. Nor do they have to follow their own precedents. The courts of this peculiar system are not entitled to decide in an arbitrary way. They are instructed by a rule of the system to make that decision which seems to them the best in the circumstances, taking account of all the considerations which seem to them relevant. Since the courts have to act on reasons and reasons are general, we could expect some regularity in the decisions of the courts. The same judge hearing two very similar cases on the same day is likely to reach the same decision in both. But cases will be heard by many different judges and judges may change their mind as well as forget complex and intricate arguments, etc. Consequently, the decisions of the courts over a period of time are unlikely to reflect any consistent line on any one issue. The degree of regularity will depend on contingent factors such as the number of judges, the degree of uniformity of their social background, etc.

It is unlikely that such a system has ever existed or will ever exist. I am conjuring up the image of a system of this nature simply because it resembles legal systems in having courts with powers to settle disputes. Therefore, by contrasting it with legal systems we can better observe what other features legal systems necessarily possess. Since its judges are not obliged to follow any common standards and can decide whatever they think best, the system does not provide any guidance to individuals as to how to behave in order to be entitled to a decision in their favour, should a dispute arise. Legal systems, on the other hand, do provide guidance to individuals. They contain laws determining the rights and duties of individuals. These are laws which the courts are bound to apply in settling disputes and it is because of this that they also provide an indication to individuals as to their rights and duties in litigation before the court.

Am I merely stating the obvious, namely, that legal systems must include laws, including some which are addressed to the general population? I think that two further consequences are contained in what I said, consequences which are far from being trivial. In the first place, law contains both norms guiding behaviour and institutions for evaluating and judging behaviour. The evaluation is based on the very same norms which guide behaviour. Indeed the test by which we determine whether a norm belongs to the system is, roughly speaking, that it is a norm which the courts ought to apply when judging and evaluating behaviour.[1] Thus the law can be said to possess its own internal system of evaluation. We can assess behaviour from

[1] One modification of this test is introduced in the next section.

the legal point of view and the legal point of view consists of the norms by which the courts are bound to evaluate behaviour which are the very same norms which are legally binding on the individual whose behaviour is evaluated.

The second important consequence of the difference between law and a system of absolute discretion described above is that legal systems contain, indeed consist of, laws which the courts are bound to apply regardless of their view of their merit. A more accurate formulation would be that legal systems consist of laws which the courts are bound to apply and are not at liberty to disregard whenever they find their application undesirable, all things considered. It does not follow that the courts are to be regarded as computing machines, always applying pre-existing rules regardless of their own views of which rules or which decisions are the right ones. But it does follow that they are to apply a certain body of laws regardless of their views on its merits and are allowed to act on their own views only to the extent that this is allowed by those laws. The law sometimes instructs judges to decide cases by whichever principle they find just or appropriate.[2] In many other cases the law requires the courts to render judgment in cases for which the body of laws they are bound to follow does not provide one correct answer. Because of the vagueness, open texture, and incompleteness of all legal systems there are many disputes for which the system does not provide a correct answer. Even if it rules out certain solutions as wrong, there are others which are neither wrong nor right in law. If the system requires, with respect to some such cases, as all legal systems in fact do, that the courts should not refuse to settle the dispute but should render judgment in it, then they are thereby required to determine the case in accordance with their own perception of what is right. Needless to say, even in such cases their discretion can be limited by general legal principles, but they will not eliminate the element of personal judgment of the merits.

It might be thought that there is one overwhelming objection to the view just expressed. In many legal systems, for example, in all common law jurisdictions, there are courts with power

---

[2] Such instructions are usually subject to various restrictions designed to preserve the coherence of purpose of the body of laws which governs cases similar to the one before the courts.

not only to settle at their discretion unsettled cases but actually to overrule established precedent. They are entitled, in fact, to repeal laws and replace them with rules which they judge to be better than the old ones. Does not that provide a counter-example to my claim that the law consists only of rules which the courts are bound to follow? It is possible, of course, to argue, indeed I wish to argue, that such courts derive their power to repeal or overrule settled law from laws of the very same system. But this is no answer to our problem. For even so how can it be said that the courts are bound to follow laws which they are at liberty to disregard? The answer is that this is quite impossible and yet the supposed counter-example fails for it misdescribes the situation.

A rule which the courts have complete liberty to disregard or change is not binding on them and is not part of the legal system. But the courts in common law jurisdictions do not have this power with respect to the binding common law rules. They cannot change them whenever they consider that on the balance of reasons it would be better to do so. They may change them only for certain kinds of reasons. They may change them, for example, for being unjust, for iniquitous discrimination, for being out of step with the court's conception of the purpose of the body of laws to which they belong, etc. But if the court finds that they are not the best rules because of some other reason, not included in the permissible list, it is nevertheless bound to follow the rules.

The situation is paralleled in other areas of practical reasoning. People have an obligation to keep their promises. This entails that they are not at liberty to break their promises whenever they find that, all things considered, it will be best to do so. But this does not mean that they ought to keep their promises come what may. The presence of reasons of a certain kind will justify breaking the promise. It follows that the fact that one is under an obligation is consistent with being at liberty to disregard it under certain conditions, provided that one is not at liberty to disregard it any time one finds that on the balance of reasons it would be best to do so. For this reason the purported counter-example fails. All it shows is that in common law jurisdictions there are courts which are sometimes at liberty to repeal some valid laws. Since they are entitled to do so only for certain specific types of reasons[3] and not whenever this is desirable all things considered, their liberty to use their power to repeal those laws is consistent with the fact that they are under an obligation to follow them.

These remarks are meant to establish the thesis that there are limits to law. If a legal system consists of a set of laws which can be identified by a certain test then it is meaningful to ask of rules and principles whether they are legal rules and principles or not. Law has limits and that is why we can refer to legal systems and to legal rights and duties which are not necessarily moral rights and duties, etc. The argument of the present section provides a partial answer to the question: why is it necessary that legal systems have limits? The answer is that the only alternative (for a system based on judicial institutions) is a system of absolute discretion. If the courts do not have absolute discretion to act on whichever standard seems to them best, this can only be because they are bound to follow some standards even if they do not regard them as best. That entails that they are bound to follow them even in preference to those standards which they regard as best. Thus the standards courts are bound to follow take precedence over other standards which they may on occasion be entitled to follow, and the two classes of standards are in principle distinguishable. That is the essence of the thesis of the limits of law.

THE UNIQUENESS OF LAW

It is a necessary feature of all legal systems (1) that they contain norms establishing primary institutions, (2) that a law belongs to them only if the primary institutions are under a duty to apply it and (3) that they have limits. These structural features of legal systems are not, however, sufficient to distinguish them from many normative systems which are clearly not municipal legal systems. I have in mind particularly the rules of voluntary associations such as universities, sports clubs or social clubs, trade unions, and political parties. Many of them have primary institutions and share all the mentioned structural features of

---

[3] The fact that their liberty is to act on reasons of types specified by the law does not negate the personal discretion of the court. They have discretion not only to establish whether the facts justify the conclusion that reasons of that type are present in the situation, but also a discretion to act on their personal view of what counts as a valid reason of that type: What is an unjust law, etc.

law. We could call normative systems sharing these character-istics institutionalized systems.

Legal systems differ from other institutionalized systems pri-marily by their relation to other institutionalized systems in force in the same society. I think that we feel that legal systems not only happen to be the most important institutionalized sys-tem governing human society, but that that is part of their nature. We would regard an institutionalized system as a legal one only if it is necessarily in some respect the most important institutionalized system which can exist in that society. My aim is to explain this feeling by attending to the spheres of human activity which all legal systems regulate or claim authority to regulate.

What is it for a normative system to regulate a certain sphere of behaviour? Every norm regulates that behaviour which is its norm-action, that is, the behaviour which the norm either requires or permits or which it turns into the exercise of a power. A normative system regulates all the acts regulated by its norms. A normative system claims authority to regulate all those acts which it regulates and which can be regulated by norms which can be enacted by the exercise of powers recognized by norms of the system.

The attempt to characterize legal systems by the spheres of activity which they regulate or claim authority to regulate cannot be a very precise one. The general traits which mark a system as a legal one are several and each of them admits, in principle, of various degrees. In typical instances of legal sys-tems all these traits are manifested to a very high degree. But it is possible to find systems in which all or some are present only to a lesser degree or in which one or two are absent altogether. It would be arbitrary and pointless to try to fix a precise borderline between normative systems which are legal systems and those which are not. When faced with borderline cases it is best to admit their problematic credentials, to enumerate their similarities and dissimilarities to the typical cases, and leave it at that.

Three features characterize legal systems:

1. Legal Systems are Comprehensive.   By this I mean that they claim authority to regulate any type of behaviour. In this they differ from most other institutionalized systems. These normally institute and govern the activities of organizations which are tied to some purpose or other. Sport associations, commercial companies, cultural organizations, political parties, etc., are all established in order to achieve certain limited goals and each claims authority over behaviour relevant to that goal only. Not so legal systems. They do not acknowledge any limitation of the spheres of behaviour which they claim authority to regulate. If legal systems are established for a definite purpose it is a purpose which does not entail a limitation over their claimed scope of competence.

We should be careful to see precisely the nature of this feature of comprehensiveness. It does not entail that legal systems *have* and other systems do not have authority to regulate every kind of behaviour. All it says is that legal systems *claim* such an authority whereas other systems do not claim it. Furthermore, legal systems do not necessarily *regulate* all forms of behaviour. All that this test means is that they *claim authority to regulate* all forms of behaviour, that is, that they either contain norms which regulate it or norms conferring powers to enact norms which if enacted would regulate it.

The authority which all legal systems claim is authority to regulate any form of behaviour of a certain community. They need not claim authority to regulate the behaviour of everybody. It should also be remembered that any action is regulated by a norm even if it is merely permitted by it. Furthermore, the test requires that every legal system claims authority to regulate behaviour in some way but not necessarily in every way. Therefore, the test is satisfied by those legal systems which contain, e.g., liberties granted by constitutional provisions which cannot be changed by any legal means. Such systems may not claim authority to regulate the permitted behaviour in any other way, but they regulate it in one way by permitting it.[4]

Finally, it should be remembered that this test sets at most a necessary condition and not a sufficient condition for a system

---

[4] A normative system does not, however, regulate behaviour which is merely weakly permitted by it. An act is weakly permitted if the system contains no norm prohibiting it. It is strongly permitted if the system contains a norm permitting it. See on the distinction my 'Permissions and Supererogation', *American Philosophical Quarterly* (April 1975). Explicit permissions (cf. p. 64 above) are also strong permissions.

to be a legal system. We should not be surprised, therefore, to find that some systems which are not legal systems meet this condition, though I do not think that there are many such cases. The laws of various churches qualify by this test, but then many of these meet the other conditions as well and are ordinary legal systems. If there are religious normative systems which meet this test but not the others, they would be borderline cases.

2. Legal Systems Claim to be Supreme.   This condition is entailed by the previous one and is merely an elaboration of one aspect of it. The condition means that every legal system claims authority to regulate the setting up and application of other institutionalized systems by its subject-community. In other words it claims authority to prohibit, permit, or impose conditions on the institution and operation of all the normative organizations to which members of its subject-community belong.

Once again this condition is a weak one in allowing for the possibility that a system claims only authority to permit the functioning of some such organizations. It seems to me, however, that this does not deprive these conditions of their importance since claimed authority to grant permission by a norm is a most significant feature of a normative system and is not to be compared with the mere existence of a weak permission because the system does not regulate the behaviour concerned and does not claim authority to regulate it.

Are legal systems necessarily incompatible? It is evident that two legal systems can coexist, can both be practised by one community. If they do not contain too many conflicting norms it is possible for the population to observe both and the institutions set by both systems could all be functioning. This would in most cases be an undesirable and an unstable situation, but it can exist and it need not always be undesirable or unstable. But in asking whether two legal systems can be compatible I am not asking whether they can coexist as a matter of fact but rather whether they can coexist as a matter of law. Can one legal system acknowledge that another legal system applies by right to the same community or must one legal system deny the right of others to apply to the same population? Of course, almost every legal system permits some normative systems to apply to its subject-community, but perhaps it does not permit this if the other system is also a legal system? There is no doubt that many legal systems are incompatible with each other, but there is no reason for assuming that this is necessarily true of all legal systems. Most legal systems are at least partly compatible—they recognize, for example, the extra-territorial validity of some norms of other systems. Cases of relatively stable and mutually recognized coexistence of secular and religious laws in various countries provide examples of different degrees of compatibility. All legal systems, however, are potentially incompatible at least to a certain extent. Since all legal systems claim to be supreme with respect to their subject-community, none can acknowledge any claim to supremacy over the same community which may be made by another legal system.

3. Legal Systems are Open Systems. A normative system is an open system to the extent that it contains norms the purpose of which is to give binding force within the system to norms which do not belong to it. The more 'alien' norms are 'adopted' by the system the more open it is. It is characteristic of legal systems that they maintain and support other forms of social grouping. Legal systems achieve this by upholding and enforcing contracts, agreements, rules, and customs of individuals and associations and by enforcing through their rules of conflict of laws the laws of other countries, etc.

Norms which are recognized for such reasons are not normally regarded as part of the legal system which gives them its sanction. They are, however, recognized and made binding in such systems by norms which require the courts to act on and enforce these norms. Therefore, we must modify the criterion of membership in an institutionalized system in order to exclude these norms. We want a test which will identify as belonging to a system all the norms which its norm-applying institutions are bound to apply (by norms which they practise) except for those norms which are merely 'adopted'. But how are we to characterize the adopted norms? How are we to define with greater precision the character of an open system?

Many have tried to find the distinguishing mark in the manner or technique of the adoption. It seems to me that this is a blind alley. These distinctions inevitably turn on formal and technical differences which bear no relation to the rationale of drawing the distinction and lead to counter-intuitive results. We must rely on the reasons for recognizing these norms as binding, for our purpose is to distinguish between norms which are recognized because they are part of the law and those which are recognized because of the law's function to support other social arrangements and groups.

Norms are 'adopted' by a system because it is an open system if and only if either (1) they are norms which belong to another normative system practised by its norm-subjects and which are recognized as long as they remain in force in such a system as applying to the same norm-subjects, provided they are recognized because the system intends to respect the way that the community regulates its activities, regardless of whether the same regulation would have been otherwise adopted, or (2) they are norms which were made by or with the consent of their norm-subjects by the use of powers conferred by the system in order to enable individuals to arrange their own affairs as they desire. The first half of the test applies to norms recognized by the rules of conflict of laws, etc. The second part of the test applies to contracts, the regulations of commercial companies, etc.

Norms which meet this test are recognized by a system but are not part of it. If a system recognizes such norms it is an open system and, as I said, all legal systems are open systems.[5] It is part of their function to sustain and encourage various other norms and organizations.

THE IMPORTANCE OF LAW

I have relied on our general knowledge of the law and human society in claiming that legal systems are institutionalized systems characterized by the combination of these three conditions. If my claim is right it is easy to see that they provide the beginning of an explanation of the importance of law. There can be human societies which are not governed by law at all. But if a society is subject to a legal system then that system is the most important institutionalized system to which it is subjected. The law provides the general framework within which

---

[5] Saying that all legal systems are open systems is not to commend them. They may 'adopt' the wrong norms and refuse to adopt those that should be 'adopted'.

social life takes place. It is a system for guiding behaviour and for settling disputes which claims supreme authority to interfere with any kind of activity. It also regularly either supports or restricts the creation and practice of other norms in the society. By making these claims the law claims to provide the general framework for the conduct of all aspects of social life and sets itself up as the supreme guardian of society.

7

KELSEN'S THEORY OF THE BASIC NORM*

Of all the various doctrines of Kelsen's legal philosophy it is his theory of the basic norm that has attracted most attention and captured the imagination. It has acquired enthusiastic devotees as well as confirmed opponents. Both admirers and critics owe much to the obscure way in which Kelsen explains his theory. The obscurity was criticized and led people to suspect that the whole theory is a myth; but it also provided admirers trading on ambiguities with an easy escape from criticism. In the following pages yet another attempt to demythologize the theory will be made. An explanation of the concept of the basic norm as Kelsen's attempt to provide an answer to some well-known jurisprudential problems will be offered. It will be further claimed that the attempt has not been altogether successful, but that its failure is illuminating. It sheds light on the intricacies of the problems involved and on their possible solutions.

Criticism will follow the exposition. The exposition, however, cannot be faithful to all the relevant texts. Some ambiguities and even contradictions cannot be eradicated by interpretation, however ingenious. Not wishing to trace the development of the theory or to present an exhaustive discussion of all the texts, the strategy I adopt will be always to prefer the more interesting of two conflicting interpretations, and to disregard the rest. The theory will be examined in relation to the problems it was designed to solve. It stands or falls according to its success in dealing with them. Kelsen regards the concept of the basic norm as essential to the explanation of all normative systems, moral as well as legal. Only his use of the concept in legal theory will be examined here.

1. EXPLAINING THE DOCTRINE

According to Kelsen's theory it is logically necessary that in every legal system there exist one basic norm. The basic norm

* First published in *The American Journal of Jurisprudence* (1974).

can be said to exist for Kelsen says that it is valid,[1] and validity is the mode of existence of norms.[2] This does not mean that all basic norms are identical in content. Indeed, no two basic norms can have the same content. They are all called basic norms not because of their content but because they all share the same structure, the same unique position each in its own system, and because they all perform the same functions.

Kelsen postulates the existence of basic norms because he regards them as necessary for the explanation of the unity and normativity of legal systems. A legal system is not a haphazard collection of norms. It is a system because its norms, as it were, belong together. They are interrelated in a special way. Kelsen accepts two propositions which he considers too self-evident to require any detailed justification. They can be regarded as axioms of his theory. The first says that two laws, one of which directly or indirectly authorizes the creation of the other, necessarily belong to the same legal system.[3] For example, a criminal law enacted by Parliament and a constitutional law authorizing Parliament to enact criminal laws belong to one legal system just because one of them authorizes the creation of the other. The second axiom says that all the laws of a legal system are authorized, directly or indirectly, by one law.

It follows from the second axiom that two laws, neither of which authorizes the creation of the other, do not belong to the same system if there is no law authorizing the creation of both. It follows from the first axiom that if one law authorizes the creation of another or if both are authorized by a third law then both belong to the same legal system. Thus the two axioms provide a criterion for the identity of legal systems and make it possible to determine with regard to any law whether it belongs to a certain legal system or not.[4]

Assuming, as I think one should, that Kelsen is trying to elucidate the common concept of the legal system and is not

[1] For example, *GT* 111, *PTL* 194. In referring to Kelsen's books the following abbreviations are used. *GT* for *The General Theory of Law and State* (New York, 1945); *PTL* for *The Pure Theory of Law*, 2nd ed. (Berkeley, 1967); *TP* for *Théorie Pure de Droit* (Paris, 1962) (this is the French translation of *PTL*); *WJ* for *What Is Justice?* (Berkeley, 1960).

[2] *GT* 30; *WJ* 214, 267.

[3] A law authorizes indirectly the creation of another if and only if there is a third law authorized, directly or indirectly, by the first and authorizing the second.

[4] For Kelsen's criterion of identity of legal systems see *GT* 111, *PTL* 195.

simply using the term to introduce a completely different concept, the second axiom looks on the face of it like an empirical generalization. To ascertain its truth one will have to examine all legal systems and find whether there is in each one a law authorizing the creation of the rest. Is there, for example, a law in Britain authorizing both Parliament and the common law? This problem is implicitly recognized by Kelsen in the following passage:

If a legal order has a written constitution which does not institute custom as a form of law creation, and if nevertheless the legal order contains customary law besides statutory law, then, in addition to the norms of the written constitution, there must exist unwritten norms of constitution, a customarily created norm according to which the general norms binding the law-applying organs can be created by custom. (*GT* 126.)

In such a legal system there will be no positive law authorizing all the rest. Some laws will be authorized by the customary constitution, whereas others will be authorized by the enacted constitution, and there will be no positive law authorizing both constitutional laws. Kelsen, therefore, is aware that as an empirical generalization his second axiom is false. He overcomes this problem by postulating that there is in every system one non-positive law—a law which authorizes all the fundamental constitutional laws and the existence of which does not depend on the chance action of any law-creating organ, but is a logical necessity. These laws are the basic norms of legal systems and their existence is necessary for the truth of the second axiom; they make it a logical truth. Since Kelsen's criterion of identity of legal systems depends on the truth of the second axiom it also depends on the theory of the basic norm.

This is one line of argument which Kelsen implicitly uses to prove the necessary existence of a basic norm in every legal system. Kelsen has a different and independent argument which he employs to reach the same conclusion. It aims to show that only the basic norm can explain the normativity of the law.

All laws are created by human actions, but human actions are facts and they belong to the realm of the 'is', whereas laws are norms and belong to the realm of the 'ought'. It is another of Kelsen's unquestioned beliefs that there is an unbridgeable gap between the 'is' and the 'ought'; that norms cannot derive their existence from facts. This can be regarded as a third axiom of his theory. He says: 'Nobody can assert that from the statement that something is, follows a statement that something ought to be' (*PTL* 6). Therefore, he concludes: '... the objective validity of a norm ... does not follow from the factual act, that is to say, from an *is*, but again from a norm authorizing this act, that is to say from an *ought* ...' (*PTL* 7–8).[5]

The principle of dichotomy, of the unbridgeable gap between the 'ought' and the 'is' entails the principle of the autonomy of norms. Norms exist only if authorized or entailed by other norms. In the law the autonomy of the legal norms is secured by the fact that they are all links in what may be called chains of validity. The term is not used by Kelsen, but the idea is essential to his philosophy. He explains it as follows:

To the question why this individual norm is valid as part of a definite legal order, the answer is: because it has been created in conformity with a criminal statute. This statute, finally, receives its validity from the constitution, since it has been established by the competent organ in the way the constitution prescribes. If we ask why the constitution is valid, perhaps we come upon an older constitution. Ultimately we reach some constitution that is the first historically and that was laid down by an individual usurper or by some kind of assembly. .... It is postulated that one ought to behave as the individual, or the individuals, who laid down the constitution have ordained. This is the basic norm of the legal order under consideration. (*GT* 115.)[6]

Thus, though every law is created by human action, it derives its validity not from the act, but from another law authorizing its creation. Ultimately all positive laws owe their validity to a non-positive law, a law not created by human action. Only a non-positive law can be the ultimate law of a legal system; only it does not presuppose another norm from which it derives its normativity. This non-positive law is the basic norm.

The idea of a chain of validity is central to Kelsen's solutions of the problems of normativity and unity of the legal system.

---

[5] This principle is often repeated by Kelsen; see 'Value Judgment' in *WJ* 218.

[6] Cf. *PTL* 199 f. On Kelsen's concept of chains of validity see further Raz, *The Concept of a Legal System* (Oxford, 1970), pp. 97–9. Two chains of validity linked together by a common link are regarded as parts of one chain.

Two laws belong to one chain of validity if one authorizes the other or if there is a third law authorizing both. The unity of the legal system consists in the fact that all its laws belong to one chain of validity and all the laws of a chain of validity are part of the same system. The normativity of laws is assured by the fact that each of the laws in a chain derives its validity from the one before it. The basic norm is essential to the solution of both problems. It provides the non-factual starting-point essential to the explanation of the normativity, and it guarantees that all the laws of one system belong to the same chain of validity.

The functions assigned to the basic norm explain its content and its special status. It must be a non-positive norm. Basic norms are not enacted, nor are they created in any other way. It is presupposed by legal consciousness, but Kelsen makes it clear that it is not created by being presupposed.[7] Nor is it created by the acts of enacting other laws,[8] or by the recognition by the population of a duty to obey the law,[9] as some commentators have assumed. It does not make sense with regard to any basic norm to ask when was it created, by whom or how. These categories simply do not apply to it. Nevertheless, they can be said to exist, for they are valid, and despite their uniqueness basic norms are part of the law, for they perform legally relevant functions.[10]

For them to explain the normativity and unity of a legal system, basic norms must authorize the creation of the laws of the various legal systems. Thus the functions of the basic norm account for its structure. It is an authorizing norm. It 'qualifies a certain event as the initial event in the creation of the various legal norms. It is the starting point of a norm creating process' (*GT* 114). 'The basic norm of any positive legal order confers legal authority only upon facts by which an order is created and applied which is on the whole effective' (*GT* 120). The basic norm is a power-conferring law. Kelsen, however, formulates it as duty-imposing: '. . . the basic norm . . . must be formulated as follows: Coercive acts ought to be performed under

[7] *PTL* 204.

[8] *TP* 271.

[9] *PTL* 218n.

[10] 'Professor Stone and the Pure Theory of Law', *Stanford Law Review* 17, Vol. 2 (1965), pp. 1128, 1141.

the conditions and in the manner which the historically first constitution, and the norms created according to it, prescribe. (In short: One ought to behave as the constitution prescribes.)' (*PTL* 200–1.) It is always possible to describe every law conferring legislative powers by saying that it imposes a duty to obey the laws made by the authorized organ.[11] This possibility should not obscure the nature of the law as power-conferring. The basic norm will, therefore, be regarded as conferring legislative power on the authors of the first constitution.

The formulation given by Kelsen in the quoted passage is not of any particular basic norm of any legal system. It merely exhibits the structure common to all basic norms. The content of basic norms varies according to the facts of the systems to which they belong. Kelsen explains that the content of a basic norm 'is determined by the facts through which an order is created and applied' (*GT* 120).

2. THE BASIC NORM AND THE UNITY OF LEGAL SYSTEMS

Kelsen's doctrine of the unity of legal systems fails for two independent reasons. As I have discussed them rather extensively elsewhere,[12] the following discussion will be brief. His doctrine depends on the first two axioms explained above. It is not difficult to see that both axioms must be rejected.

The first axiom asserts that all the laws belonging to one chain of validity are part of one and the same legal system. If this axiom were correct, certain ways of peacefully granting independence to new states would become impossible. Suppose that country A had a colony B, and that both countries were governed by the same legal system. Suppose further that A has granted independence to B by a law conferring exclusive and unlimited legislative powers over B to a representative assembly elected by the inhabitants of B. Finally, let it be assumed that this representative assembly has adopted a constitution which is generally recognized by the inhabitants of B, and according to which elections were held and further laws were made. The government, courts, and the population of B regard themselves as an independent state with an independent legal system. They are recognized by all other nations including A. The courts of

---

[11] See further on this subject *The Concept of a Legal System*, pp. 21, 23, 166 f.
[12] Ibid., pp. 100–9.

A regard the constitution and laws of B as a separate legal system distinct from their own. Despite all these facts it follows from Kelsen's first axiom that the constitution and laws of B are part of the legal system of A. For B's constitution and consequently all the laws made on its basis were authorized by the independence-granting law of A and consequently belong to the same chain of validity and to the same system.

Kelsen's mistake is in disregarding the facts and considering only the content of the laws. For his theory the only important feature is that the legal system of A has a law authorizing all the laws of B. That the courts and population of B do not consider this law as part of their own legal system is irrelevant. But the attitude of the population and the courts is of the utmost importance in deciding the identity and unity of a legal system in the sense in which this concept is commonly used.[13]

This criticism does not directly affect Kelsen's theory of the basic norm. However, if the doctrine of the unity of legal systems is rejected, one of the reasons for accepting the theory of the basic norm disappears. Kelsen's theory of the unity and identity of legal systems is vitiated by a second flaw which directly concerns the role of the basic norm.

The second axiom on which his theory of the identity and unity of the legal system depends says that all the laws of one system belong to one chain of validity. When discussing this axiom we saw that Kelsen admits, at least by implication, that disregarding the basic norm, all the positive laws of a system may belong to more than one validity chain. Some may owe their validity to a customary constitution while others derive their validity from an enacted constitution. It is only the basic norm that unites them in such a case in one chain of validity by authorizing both constitutions.[14]

A legally minded observer coming to such a country and wondering whether the enacted and the customary constitutions belong to the same legal system will be referred by a Kelsenite to the basic norm. It all depends, he will be told, whether

[13] The same point is made in H. L. A. Hart, 'Kelsen's Doctrine of the Unity of Law', published in H. E. Kiefer and M. K. Munitz (eds.), *Ethics and Social Justice* (New York, 1970).

[14] It should be noted that the basic norm in such cases is said to authorize several constitutional laws created by several norm-creating acts. It is not clear in what sense a basic norm doing this is itself one norm rather than a conjunction of several norms.

or not there is one basic norm authorizing both constitutions or whether each constitution is authorized by a different basic norm. Being told in answer to further questions that to know the content of the basic norm he should find out 'the facts through which an order is created and applied' (*GT* 120), for they determine it, he may very well be driven to despair. It seems that he can only identify the legal system with the help of the basic norm whereas the basic norm can be identified only after the identity of the legal system has been established. Even if our diligent observer succeeds in establishing that at least two sets of norms are effective in the society, one, a set of customary norms, the other, of enacted norms, there will be nothing a Kelsenite can say to help him decide whether or not they form one system or two. There is nothing in the theory to prevent two legal systems from applying to the same territory. Everything depends on the ability to identify the basic norm, but it cannot be identified before the identity of the legal system is known. Therefore, the basic norm cannot solve the problem of identity and unity of legal systems, and Kelsen has no other solution.

3. KELSEN ON NATURAL LAW THEORIES

If the previous criticism is correct the case for the basic norm must rest on its function in explaining the normativity of the law. It is with this problem that the rest of the essay will be concerned.

The role of the basic norm in explaining the normativity of law, and indeed Kelsen's explanation of that normativity, is closely connected with his critique of natural law theories. He conceived his own theory as an alternative, the only possible alternative to natural law. Kelsen even refers to the basic norm as a natural law.[15] This is not the place to examine in detail Kelsen's criticism of natural law theories, but a few remarks on some of the key ideas are essential to the understanding of his theory of the basic norm.

According to Kelsen's account, natural law theories claim that there is a set of norms, discoverable by reason, which have absolute and objective validity. They are completely and

---

[15] 'If one wishes to regard it [i.e. the basic norm—J.R.] as an element of a natural law doctrine ... very little objection can be raised.... What is involved is simply the minimum ... of natural law without which a cognition of law is impossible.' (*GT* 437.)

objectively just and good. Positive law, in so far as it is valid, derives its validity from natural law. It is valid to the extent that the natural law pronounces it just and good. Statutes, court decisions, etc., which are contrary to natural law are not valid and hence not laws at all. Kelsen correctly points out that according to natural law theories there is no specific notion of legal validity. The only concept of validity is validity according to natural law, i.e. moral validity. Natural lawyers can only judge a law as morally valid, that is, just, or morally invalid, i.e. wrong. They cannot say of a law that it is legally valid but morally wrong. If it is wrong and unjust, it is also invalid in the only sense of validity they recognize.[16]

Kelsen has four major reasons for rejecting all natural law theories. They are burdened with objectionable metaphysics, they are conceptually confused, they thrive on moral illusion, and they are unscientific.

(1) Natural law theories presuppose the dualistic metaphysics which has bedevilled the Western world since Plato.[17] They presuppose an ideal reality of completely just and good laws enjoying some form of objective existence independent of human acts or will which is contrasted with the imperfect social reality of man-made statutes, regulations, and decisions. The latter are imperfect and less real than the former, and whatever reality they have is due to the ideal reality. Only by imitating the ideal laws do human laws acquire validity. Kelsen is very much opposed to this kind of metaphysics and rejects it in favour of the anti-metaphysical flavour of Kant's critical philosophy. Rejecting this metaphysical dualism deprives natural law theories of their metaphysical foundation.

(2) Natural law theories are conceptually confused. They are of two varieties, one secular, and the other religious. The secular theories regard natural laws as rationally binding and self-evident in themselves. The religious theories regard them as the commands of God revealed to man through rational speculation about nature.[18] Both varieties commit the naturalistic fal-

---

[16] For example, *WJ* 144, 257 ff., 295.

[17] Cf. *GT* 419–33; *WJ* 198 ff. Kelsen is not rejecting the possibility of regarding laws as abstract entities provided they are given adequate interpretation relating them to human behaviour. Such a doctrine does not have the metaphysical implications of Platonism.

[18] For the explanation of the two types of natural law theories see, for example, *WJ* 285 ff.

lacy of deriving an 'is' from an 'ought'. Whatever is natural can only be a fact, and God's commands are also facts, even if divine facts, and from facts no norm is entailed. To avoid the naturalistic fallacy both types of natural law theories must be assumed to postulate a basic norm investing the facts with normative character.[19] The secular basic norm is that nature be obeyed, the religious basic norm dictates that God be obeyed.[20] The basic norms must be considered self-evident. They cannot be derived from any other norm, yet they are said to be objectively valid and binding. In this way Kelsen attempts to rectify the confusions committed by the proponents of the natural law.

(3) 'The doctrine is a typical illusion, due to an objectivation of subjective interests.' (*WJ* 228.) On Kelsen's analysis the natural law's claim to objective validity rests on the assumption that its basic norms are self-evident. Kelsen rejects all such claims as illusions. He is a moral relativist.[21] No moral position can be objectively proved and defended. There are no intuitively true moral beliefs.[22] Moral opinions are matters of personal preferences. By claiming objective validity, natural lawyers breed illusions and use them for various ideological purposes. Most commonly the natural law illusion has been used by conservative optimists to justify existing legal and political institutions. Occasionally the same illusion has been turned into a tool for promoting reform or revolution.[23]

Kelsen's relativism does not preclude the possibility or necessity of assessing the law by moral standards. He simply insists that every evaluation is valid only relative to the particular moral norm used which in itself has no objective validity. Consequently moral criticism or justification of the law is a matter of personal or political judgment. It is not an objective scientific matter and does not concern the science of law.[24]

(4) By condemning natural law theories as unscientific Kelsen means that they cannot be objectively confirmed. Therefore, Kelsen's desire to construct a scientific theory of law

[19] *WJ* 141.
[20] *WJ* 258, 260 f.
[21] Cf. *WJ* 141, 179 f., 228 f., 259, 295; *PTL* 64.
[22] *PTL* 221.
[23] Cf. *WJ* 297.
[24] Cf. *WJ* 295, 302; *GT* 436; *PTL* 68 f.

leads him to renounce the morality of the law as a subject of the theory. 'The problem of law as a scientific problem is the problem of social technique, not a problem of morals.' (*GT* 5.) Legal theory is and should be concerned with a special type of social technique for controlling human behaviour. Natural law theories, by distinguishing between just statutes which are law, and unjust ones which are not law, obscure the issue. For they thereby exclude some normative systems from being classified as legal, even though they are instances of the use of the same social technique.

4. THE BASIC NORM AND A VALUE-FREE STUDY OF LAW

To perform its task legal theory must be value-free. Consequently its explanation of the normativity of law must be independent of the moral value of the law. How is the notion of legal validity and normativity to be explained? Kelsen resorts to the conceptual framework of Kantian critical philosophy. Kant himself adopted a version of natural law theory only because he did not remain true to his own premisses.[25] His philosophy, however, provides the intellectual tools which Kelsen wishes to use.

A legal concept of validity and normativity is made possible only through the concept of the basic norm:

To interpret these acts of human beings as legal acts and their products as binding norms, and that means to interpret the empirical material which presents itself as law as such, is possible only on the condition that the basic norm is presupposed as a valid norm. The basic norm is only the necessary presupposition of any positivistic interpretation of the legal material. (*GT* 116.)

The basic norm is necessarily presupposed when people regard the law as normative, irrespective of its moral worth:

... the basic norm as represented by the science of law may be characterised as the transcendental-logical condition of this interpretation, if it is permissible to use by analogy a concept of Kant's epistemology. Kant asks: 'How is it possible to interpret without a metaphysical hypothesis, the facts perceived by our senses, in the laws of nature

---

[25] *GT* 444 f. Kelsen's interpretation of Kant can be disputed, but this need not concern us here.

formulated by natural science?' In the same way, the Pure Theory of Law asks: 'How is it possible to interpret without recourse to meta-legal authorities, like God or nature, the subjective meaning of certain facts as a system of objectively valid legal norms? ...' The epistemological answer of the Pure Theory of Law is: 'By presupposing the basic norm that one ought to behave as the constitution prescribes. ...' The function of this basic norm is to found the objective validity of a positive legal order. (*PTL* 202.)

The concept of the basic norm provides legal theory with an objective and value-free concept of legal normativity. 'The presupposition of the basic norm does not approve any value transcending positive law.' (*PTL* 201.) 'It does not perform an ethical political but only an epistemological function.' (*PTL* 218.)

Not performing a moral or political function the basic norm is objective:

To the norms of positive law there corresponds a certain social reality, but not so to the norms of justice.... Juristic value judgments are judgments that can be tested objectively by facts. Therefore they are admissible within a science of law. (*WJ* 227.)

The basic norm, therefore, is not the product of free invention. It is not presupposed arbitrarily in the sense that there is a choice between different basic norms when the subjective meaning of a constitution-creating act and the acts created according to this constitution are interpreted as their objective meaning. (*PTL* 201.)

With the aid of the concept of a basic norm Kelsen claims he has established a value-free legal theory using a specific legal concept of normativity:

The postulate to differentiate law and morals, jurisprudence and ethics, means this: from the standpoint of scientific cognition of positive law, its justification by a moral order different from the legal order, is irrelevant, because the task of the science of law is not to approve or disapprove its subject, but to know and describe it.... The postulate to separate law and morals, science of law and ethics means that the validity of positive legal norms does not depend on their conformity with the moral order; it means that from the standpoint of a cognition directed toward positive law a legal norm may be considered valid, even if it is at variance with the moral order. (*PTL* 68.)

5. KELSEN ON THE NATURE OF THE NORMATIVITY
OF LAW

Thus far it has been established that Kelsen regards the concept of a basic norm as necessary to the understanding of law as a normative system, and that he thinks that only by using this concept can legal theory be value-free and objective and avoid the blunders of natural law theories. Nothing has been said so far about the nature of the normativity accruing to the law by virtue of the basic norm. To this problem we must now turn.

Two conceptions of the normativity of law are current. I will call them justified and social normativity. According to the one view legal standards of behaviour are norms only if and in so far as they are justified. They may be justified by some objective and universally valid reasons. They may be intuitively perceived as binding or they may be accepted as justified by personal commitment. On the other view standards of behaviour can be considered as norms regardless of their merit. They are social norms in so far as they are socially upheld as binding standards and in so far as the society involved exerts pressure on people to whom the standards apply to conform to them. Natural law theorists characteristically endorse the first view, positivists usually maintain the second view. The most successful explanation of the normativity of law in terms of the concept of social normativity is Hart's analysis in *The Concept of Law*. Theorists using the concepts of justified normativity claim that a legal system can be regarded as normative only by people considering it as just and endorsing its norms by accepting them as part of their own moral views. Theorists using the concepts of social normativity maintain that everyone should regard legal systems as normative regardless of his judgment about their merits.

Much of the obscurity of Kelsen's theory stems from the difficulty in deciding which concept of normativity he is using. It will be claimed that:

(1) Kelsen uses only the concept of justified normativity.
(2) According to him an individual can consider a legal system as normative only if he endorses it as morally just and good.

(3) Legal theory considers legal systems as normative in the same sense of 'normative' but in a different sense of 'consider' which does not commit it to accepting the laws as just.

Let us consider the first statement first. Quite often Kelsen considers a concept of social normativity only to reject it as not being really a concept of normativity or at any rate as not being appropriate for legal theory. Thus he distinguishes between a subjective and an objective 'ought',[26] claiming that legal norms are objective norms, explained by the concept of an objective 'ought'. His subjective 'ought' is a variety of social normativity. Connected with this distinction is his comparison between objective and subjective value judgments. The latter are an explanation of one type of social normativity and are judged by him to be factual rather than normative judgments:

The value constituted by an objectively valid norm must be distinguished from the value that consists (not in the relation to a norm, but) in the relation of an object to a wish or will of an individual directed at this object. If the object is in accordance or not in accordance with the wish or will, it has a positive or negative value.... If the judgement describing the relation of an object to the wish or will of an individual, is designated as a value judgement ... then this value judgement is not different from a judgement about reality. For it describes only the relation between two facts, not the relation between a fact and an objectively valid norm.... The value that consists in the relation of an object ... to the wish or will of an individual can be designated as subjective value. (*PTL* 19–20.)

Describing laws as commands of a sovereign is, on this theory, describing them as subjective 'ought'. If one does not presuppose the basic norm, then judgments about the lawfulness of action, understood as judgments about their conformity to the commands of a sovereign, are merely subjective value judgments. Kelsen acknowledges that the law can consistently be interpreted in this way, but in this case it is not regarded as normative:

The fact that the basic norm of a positive legal order *may* but *need not* be presupposed means: the relevant interhuman relationship may

[26] For example, *PTL* 7. Here as elsewhere when Kelsen examines and rejects the concept of social normativity he considers only crude explanations of it. Social normativity cannot be explained in terms of efficacious commands.

be, but need not be, interpreted as 'normative', that is, as obligations, authorisations, rights, etc. constituted by objectively valid norms. It means further: they can be interpreted without such presupposition (i.e. without the basic norm) as power relations (i.e. relations between commanding and obeying or disobeying human beings)—in other words, they can be interpreted sociologically, not juristically. (*PTL* 218.)

This is a key passage. Kelsen claims in effect that the concept of social normativity is not a concept of normativity at all. It does not allow the interpretation of law as imposing obligations, granting powers, rights, etc. It makes the law indistinguishable from the commands of a group of gangsters terrorizing the population of a certain area.[27] Only by using the concept of justified normativity can one understand the true character of legal systems as normative systems.

Because Kelsen regards the concept of justified normativity as the only concept of normativity, he considers law as an ideology. For law is normative, i.e. justified and good for everyone who regards it as normative: 'This is the reason why it is possible to maintain that the idea of a norm, an "ought", is merely ideological. ... In this sense the law may be considered as the specific ideology of a certain historically given power.' (*WJ* 227.)

One should be careful to distinguish between the two senses in which legal norms are said by Kelsen to be objective. In the first sense they are objective for they reflect a social reality, i.e. because they are normative in the sense of social normativity. In the second sense they are objective for they are normative in the sense of justified normativity; they are an ideology. The two senses are manifested in the following passage: 'If we conceive of the law as a complex of norms and therefore as an ideology, this ideology differs from other, especially from metaphysical, ideologies so far as the former corresponds to certain facts of reality. ... If the system of legal norms is an ideology, it is an ideology that is parallel to a definite reality.' (*WJ* 227.)

In other words, it is normative in the sense of justified normativity (i.e. it is objective 'ought') but also normative in the sense of social normativity (i.e. corresponding to objectively ascertainable facts the meaning of which is the subjective 'ought').

[27] Kelsen uses this example for a different purpose in *PTL* 47.

This constant shift from one sense of objective to the other has not helped scholars to understand what concept of normativity Kelsen is using.

To anyone regarding the law as socially normative, the question 'why should the law be obeyed?' cannot be answered by pointing out that it is normative. The law is normative because of certain social facts. It should be obeyed, if at all, for moral reasons. The normativity of the law and the obligation to obey it are distinct notions. Not so to people who admit only the concept of justified normativity. For them to judge the law as normative is to judge it to be just and to admit that it ought to be obeyed. The concepts of the normativity of the law and of the obligation to obey it are analytically tied together. Kelsen, therefore, regards the law as valid, i.e. normative, only if one ought to obey it. 'By "validity", the binding force of the law—the idea that it ought to be obeyed by the people whose behaviour it regulates—is understood.' (*WJ* 257.) 'A norm referring to the behaviour of a human being is "valid" means that it is binding—that an individual ought to behave in the manner determined by the norm.' (*PTL* 193.) These statements are unavoidable for a theorist working with the concept of justified normativity. They are misleading if the normativity of the law is explained as social normativity only.

6. AN INDIVIDUAL'S 'POINT OF VIEW'

The normativity of the law is justified normativity; its reason is the basic norm which is, therefore, a justified norm. But it is not justified in any absolute sense. Kelsen believes in moral relativism. For him moral opinions are matters of personal preference which cannot be rationally confirmed or refuted. Hence he claims that the basic norm is presupposed, i.e. accepted, and the law is regarded as normative only by people who consider it to be just:

But there is no necessity to presuppose the basic norm.... The system of norms that we call 'legal order' is a possible but not a necessary scheme of interpretation. An anarchist will decline to speak of 'lawful' and 'unlawful' behaviour, of 'legal duties' and 'legal rights', or 'delicts'. He will understand social behaviour merely as a process whereby one forces the other to behave in conformity with his wishes or interests. . . . He will, in short, refuse to presuppose the basic norm. (*WJ* 226–7.)

. . . an anarchist, for instance, who denied the validity of the hypothetical basic norm of positive law . . . will view its positive regulation of human relationship . . . as mere power relations. (*GT* 413.)

A communist may indeed not admit that there is an essential difference between an organisation of gangsters and a capitalistic legal order. . . . For he does not presuppose—as do those who interpret the coercive order as an objectively valid normative order—the basic norm.[28]

For an individual to presuppose the basic norm is to interpret the legal system as normative, i.e. as just. For Kelsen all the values endorsed by one individual, all his moral opinions form necessarily one normative system based on one basic norm. One can speak of an individual's normative system, or of the normative system from the point of view of a certain individual. Regarded from one point of view every set of norms necessarily forms one consistent and unified normative order. The individual may think that some of the norms to which he subscribes conflict. But this is a psychological not a normative fact. He may feel torn between two opposing modes of action.[29] But it makes no sense to say that his normative system contains conflicting norms. It is of the essence of the concept of a normative system that it guides behaviour; it guides the behaviour of those persons who adopt the relevant point of view. But if conflicting norms are assumed to be valid from one point of view, then they do not guide behaviour for they point in opposing directions at the same time. Therefore all the norms held valid from one point of view necessarily form one consistent system:

It is logically not possible to assume that simultaneously valid norms belong to different, mutually independent systems. (*GT* 363.)

---

[28] 'Professor Stone and the Pure Theory of Law', op. cit., p. 1144.

[29] Cf. *GT* 375. In 'Derogation' published in *Essays in Jurisprudence in Honor of Roscoe Pound* (New York, 1962), and 'Law and Logic' published in *Philosophy and Christianity* (Amsterdam, 1965), Kelsen retracted his claim that valid norms are necessarily consistent. Unfortunately he did not discuss there the reasons that led him to accept this doctrine in the first place, nor did he modify those parts of his theory that depend on his previous doctrine, such as the relation of law and morality, municipal and international law, etc. Consequently his theory of the normativity of law is intelligible and consistent only on the assumption that valid norms are necessarily consistent.

If two different systems of norms are given, only one of them can be assumed to be valid from the point of view of a cognition which is concerned with the validity of norms. (*GT* 407.)

If one assumes that two systems of norms are considered as valid simultaneously from the same point of view, one must also assume a normative relation between them; one must assume the existence of a norm or order that regulates their mutual relations. Otherwise insoluble contradictions between the norms of each system are unavoidable. (*WJ* 284.)

All this is incomprehensible if it is assumed that Kelsen uses the concept of social normativity. It gains some plausibility if it is recognized that Kelsen is operating throughout with a concept of justified normativity. Then it is possible to appreciate Kelsen's reasons for maintaining that (1) for an individual to acknowledge that something is a norm is to accept it as just; (2) from an individual's point of view all his moral beliefs form one normative system; (3) all the norms held valid from one point of view must be consistent. For the normative interpretation of a person's belief is not a psychological but a rational enterprise intended to elucidate the direction in which his views guide him.

One rather surprising consequence of this analysis is that the concept of normative systems loses much of its importance. The most important concept is that of a point of view. It is logically true that from every point of view there is just one normative system, and therefore just one basic norm. An individual accepting the justice of his country's laws, but subscribing to further values not incorporated in the law, accepts not two normative systems but one. His country's laws are part of this system, though they can be viewed as a subsystem of his total normative system. To assert that all the norms held valid from one viewpoint constitute one system with one basic norm is, of course, to assert more than that they do not conflict. It is to claim that they all derive their validity from one basic norm. This is tacitly assumed rather than argued for by Kelsen. Granting, however, that the basic norm can confer validity on more than one norm renders this a rather technical matter of no great importance.[30]

[30] See footnote 14 above.

7. 'THE LEGAL POINT OF VIEW'

So far the notion of a point of view was considered only as apply-ing to particular individuals; only points of view adopted by individuals were discussed. But there are also more complex points of view. One can ascribe a point of view to a group of individuals, to a population, provided the population shares the same values. It is possible to consider hypothetical points of view, for example, to discuss what norms are adopted by indivi-duals who accept all and only the laws of their country as valid, without assuming that such individuals exist. One may call this particular example of a hypothetical point of view the point of view of *the legal man*. Throughout his work Kelsen uses the concept of a point of view of legal science. He talks about 'the basic norm of a positive legal order, the ultimate reason for its validity, seen from the point of view of a science of positive law'. (*WJ* 262.) He also says that the science of law presupposes the basic norm, but nevertheless is not committed to regard it as just.

There is, for Kelsen, a great difference between a personal point of view and the scientific point of view. Norms judged as valid from a personal point of view are those adopted as just. But legal theory is value-free and norms judged to be valid from its point of view are not thereby adopted as just. Any individual can discuss the law sometimes from his personal viewpoint, sometimes from the point of view of legal science. Adopting the latter 'even an anarchist, if he were a professor of law, could describe positive law as a system of valid norms, without having to approve of this law'. (*PTL* 218n.) At the same time the anarchist will reject the validity of the law when considering it from his personal point of view. What is the nature of the point of view of legal science? How can it be value-free, and at the same time regard the law as normative in the only sense admitted by Kelsen, i.e. that of justified normativity? One tempting explanation is that legal theory asserts that a legal system exists only if adopted, from the personal viewpoint, by the population to which it applies, and describes the law as seen from this point of view. Kelsen, however, rejects this interpreta-tion:

The doctrine of the basic norm is not a doctrine of recognition as is sometimes erroneously understood. According to the doctrine of recognition positive law is valid only if it is recognised by the individuals subject to it, which means: if these individuals agree that one ought to behave according to the norms of the positive law. This recognition, it is said actually takes place, and if this cannot be proved it is assumed, fictitiously as a tacit recognition. (*PTL* 218n.)

The Pure Theory of Law does not assert or assume any attitude of the population to the law. A legal system exists if it is effective and this does not entail acceptance as morally just.

An alternative interpretation would be that legal science describes not the population's point of view but the point of view of the hypothetical legal man, i.e. of a person accepting from a personal viewpoint all and only the legal norms, without assuming that such a person actually exists. Such an interpretation is supported by various passages like the following one:

The Pure Theory describes the positive law as an objectively valid normative order and states that this interpretation is possible only under the condition that a basic norm is presupposed. . . . The Pure Theory, thereby characterizes this interpretation as possible, not necessary, and presents the objective validity of positive law only as conditional—namely conditioned by the presupposed basic norm. (*PTL* 217–18.)

This interpretation comes very near the core of Kelsen's doctrine but it is not free from difficulties. On this interpretation the Pure Theory itself does not adopt any point of view; it does not presuppose any basic norm. It merely describes the point of view of the legal man and the basic norm he adopts. Is Kelsen mistaken when regarding legal science as having a point of view and presupposing a basic norm? Does he use these terms in a competely different sense when applied to legal science? Kelsen himself is unsure of his position on this crucial point, for occasionally he can be seen to waver.[31] The difficulty results from the fact that Kelsen does not distinguish between the science of law dealt with by jurists talking *about* the law, and the activities of lawyers and judges *using* the law. He considers both under the one title of juristic cognition. He wants to claim that:

[31] Compare his treatment of the anarchist in *PTL* 278n. with his discussion of the same problem in previous and subsequent publications. See also his explicit discussion of the question whether the Pure Theory presupposes the basic norm, *PTL* 204n.

By offering this theory of the basic norm, the Pure Theory of Law does not inaugurate a new method of legal cognition. It merely makes conscious what most *legal scientists* do, at least unconsciously, when they interpret the mentioned facts not as causally determined, but instead interpret their subjective meaning as objectively valid norms. . . . The Theory of the basic norm is merely the result of an analysis of the procedure which a positivistic *science* of law has always applied. (*PTL* 204–5.)

Kelsen, however, makes a similar claim not only about legal scientists, but also about legal practitioners. The following passage applies to lawyers as well as law professors:

That the basic norm really exists in the juristic consciousness is the result of simple analysis of actual juristic statements. The basic norm is the answer to the question: how—and that means under what condition—are all these juristic statements concerning legal norms, legal duties, legal rights, and so on. (*GT* 116–17.)

It can perhaps be claimed that legal scientists do not adopt a point of view; they do not regard the law as valid but simply describe what is considered valid from the point of view of some other person, i.e. the legal man. But legal practitioners do not describe what somebody else regards as valid but themselves consider the law as valid, refer to it as valid, and apply it to particular cases. They cannot be said merely to describe a point of view; they actually adopt one. Yet when acting professionally they need not express their personal point of view. An anarchist can be not only a law teacher, but also a lawyer. As a lawyer he adopts and expresses a professional point of view, the point of view of legal science, as Kelsen calls it, which does not commit him, and is understood not to commit him to the view that the law is just.

For Kelsen the legal scientist, as well as the legal practitioner, not only describes a point of view, but actually adopts one. Legal science regards the laws as valid and hence presupposes the basic norm. The point of view of legal science is that of the legal man. It is not merely described but actually adopted, and it is adopted in a special sense.

If a man were actually to adopt the point of view of the legal man he would adopt the law as his personal morality, and as exhausting all the norms he accepts as just. Legal science does not accept the point of view of the legal man in this sense. Legal science is not committed to regarding the law as just. It adopts this point of view in a special sense of 'adopt'. It is professional and uncommitted adoption. Legal science presupposes the basic norm not as individuals do—i.e. by accepting it as just—but in this special professional and uncommitted sense.

8. CONCLUSION

The analysis of Kelsen's theory of normativity and of the basic norm clarifies some of Kelsen's fundamental theses. It explains his insistence that the basic norm presupposed by legal science authorizes the first constitution and does not refer to any non-legal authority like God or nature. Individuals from their personal point of view are indeed unlikely to adopt this norm as their basic norm. They are likely to appeal to God or to nature or some other moral norm as their basic norm. But this is irrelevant to legal science which has a special point of view, that of the legal man, which it adopts in the special professional sense of adopting. Legal science, therefore, presupposes, in the special sense, this particular basic norm, for it is concerned as a science only with positive law.

On the present analysis Kelsen's position on the relation of law and morality is seen as entailed by the rest of his theory:

When positive law and morality are asserted to be two distinct mutually independent systems of norms, this means only that the jurist, in determining what is legal, does not take into consideration morality, and the moralist, in determining what is moral, pays no heed to the prescriptions of positive law. Positive law and morality can be regarded as two distinct and mutually independent systems of norms, because and to the extent that they are not conceived to be simultaneously valid from the same point of view. (*WJ* 284.)[32]

Kelsen is discussing here the professional points of view of the legal and moral scholar. He is not denying that a legal order can incorporate moral rules or that morality can incorporate the law and regard it as morally valid. Nor is he denying that an individual from his personal viewpoint can regard both legal and non-legal norms as valid. To the individual they will all form part of his personal normative system, based on his personal point of view. From the point of view of legal science,

[32] Compare also *GT* 374, 490.

however, only the law is valid, just as from the point of view of ethical theories only moral norms are valid.

Kelsen's insistence that from a single point of view there can be just one normative system and just one basic norm explains why his theory of normativity in itself entails that there is just one basic norm to every legal system. In so far as basic norms are necessary only to enable us to consider the law as normative, there is nothing to prevent one from postulating several basic norms relating to one system. One basic norm can make the criminal law normative, another will relate to the law of property, etc. However, on Kelsen's theory this will mean that there is no one point of view from which the legal system is considered but several, each corresponding to every one of the basic norms.

Furthermore, since there is one general science of law, it follows, on the Kelsenian premiss of the unity of a point of view, that all the laws form but one legal system. The ultimate reason for Kelsen's theory of the unity of national and international law is his theory of normativity. Since all the norms held valid from one point of view form one normative system, it follows without further argument that since both national and international law are considered valid from the point of view of one legal science, they are parts of one system. All that remains to do is to explain how they should be thus understood. 'The unity of national and international law is an epistemological postulate. A jurist who *accepts both* as sets of valid norms must try to comprehend them as parts of one harmonious system.' (*GT* 373.) 'Once it is conceded that national and international law are both positive laws, it is obvious that both must be valid *simultaneously from the same juristic point of view*. For this reason, they must belong to the same system.' (*WJ* 284.) 'If both systems are considered to be *simultaneously* valid orders of binding norms, it is inevitable to comprehend both as one system.' (*PTL* 332 emphasis added.)

This analysis of Kelsen's doctrine of the basic norm in its function in establishing the normativity of law is based on the claim that though Kelsen rejects natural law theories, he consistently uses the natural law concept of normativity, i.e. the concept of justified normativity. He is able to maintain that the science of law is value-free by claiming for it a special point of view, that of the legal man, and contending that legal science adopts this point of view; that it presupposes its basic norm in a special, professional, and uncommitted sense of presupposing. There is, after all, no legal sense of normativity, but there is a specifically legal way in which normativity can be considered.

This is the core of Kelsen's theory. To it he adds the further claim that all the norms held valid from one point of view must be considered as one consistent system. This further thesis can and should be criticized and rejected. It leads to a distorted view of the relations between the various values subscribed to by an individual. It also leads to a distortion of the common concept of a legal system. This is not the place to examine the inadequacies of Kelsen's view of personal morality. Kelsen's failure to account for the concept of a legal system is treated elsewhere.[33] It is, however, important to remember that it is possible to reject Kelsen's identification of the concepts of a normative system and a normative point of view while retaining the other basic tenets of Kelsen's theory of normativity and the basic norm.

It seems to me that Kelsen's theory is the best existing theory of positive law based on the concept of justified normativity. It is deficient in being bound up with other essentially independent as well as wrong doctrines and it is incomplete in not being supported by any semantic doctrine or doctrine of discourse capable of explaining the nature of discourse from the point of view of the legal man.

[33] Cf. section 2 above and Hart: 'Kelsen's Doctrine of the Unity of Law', op. cit.

8

LEGAL VALIDITY*

1. ITS NATURE

Rules, orders, contracts, wills, sales, marriages, and many other things can be legally valid or invalid.[1] The following discussion will be confined to the legal validity of rules but several of its conclusions apply with equal force to other cases of legal validity.

A rule which is not legally valid is not a legal rule at all. A valid law is a law, an invalid law is not. Similarly a valid rule is a rule and an invalid rule is not a rule at all. This last point is controversial. Many hold that an invalid rule is a rule which lacks the property of being valid (or is it that it has the property of being invalid?). This view is particularly appropriate if rules are identified with propositions or statements or some normative analogues of them, e.g. imperatives, prescriptions, or deontic propositions. On this view a legally binding rule such as 'Parents must support their children' is a deontic proposition which is accepted or endorsed within a certain legal system. Endorsement of a deontic proposition (or—in different theories—of imperatives) is conceived as being somehow analogous to belief with respect to ordinary propositions.

I do not wish to deny that persons (though perhaps not states or other organizations) may have attitudes to deontic propositions or to imperatives which are analogous to belief if not identical with it. But all this has nothing to do with rules. Rules, but not propositions, are reasons for action ('I did it because of the rule prohibiting so and so' but not 'I did it because of the deontic proposition (or the imperative) that so and so').[2]

* First published in *Archiv für Rechts- und Sozialphilosophie*, Bd. LXIII/3 (1977).

[1] Are all rules either legally valid or legally invalid? I shall assume so. Voidable rules are often valid until avoided—which is a special form of repeal. Sometimes when avoided they are repealed retroactively. On other occasions some of their consequences are maintained in order to protect the interests of people who have relied on them in good faith or for other reasons. I think that it is best to regard all such consequences as due to the operation of some further rules which apply to some of the cases of this special repeal through voidability.

[2] Strictly speaking it is not the rule but the fact that it exists, i.e. is valid, which is a reason.

Rules, but not propositions or imperatives, can be reasons for belief in or endorsement of some propositions or imperatives ('I believe that I ought to support my mother because of the rule (but not because of the deontic proposition) that children ought to respect their parents').

These considerations of the role of rules as reasons may suggest that rules if not propositions or imperatives are facts, since facts are reasons both for action and for belief. The existence of a rule is admittedly a fact. We can say 'It is a fact that there is a rule that ...' and if such a statement is true then it is a fact that there is such a rule. Yet even if every true or justified deontic statement states a fact ('the fact that one ought to ϕ', etc.) it does not follow that every such statement is a statement of a rule. On the contrary, this is clearly not the case. Consider the following three statements: (1) Everyone ought to keep his promises. (2) Women ought to keep their promises. (3) John ought to give me £5 (because he promised to). Clearly only the first statement states a rule (I am assuming that all three are true, correct, or justified). The other two are true in virtue of the rule stated by the first. They themselves do not state rules. They apply a rule to general or concrete situations.

It is not part of my purpose here to explain why some statements state rules and others do not.[3] For present purposes we can rely on our linguistic intuitions which tell us that only to some deontic sentences can we prefix 'it is a rule that' while preserving the truth value of the sentence.[4] In the case of the law we have perhaps a clearer grasp of the way to apply this distinction than with some other kinds of rules. The reason is that laws are normally the product of authoritative acts (either legislation or judicial law-making) and at the very least we feel that statements closely describing the product of one or more authoritative acts have a better claim to be regarded as state-

[3] In *Practical Reason and Norms*, ch. 2, I argued that not all statements of reasons for action are statements of rules on the ground that rules play a special role in practical reasoning which is significantly different from that of ordinary reasons. My present argument is more far-reaching and entails that not every statement of a rule-based reason is a statement of a rule. The clarification of this distinction is the function of the doctrine of the individuation of rules. I outlined a doctrine of the individuation of legal rules in *The Concept of a Legal System*, but its conclusions cannot be extended to all other rules.

[4] When discussing the law the relevant operator is 'there is a law that'—not 'it is the law that'.

ments of a rule than statements which apply the rule to particular circumstances. This test does not apply to non-institutionalized rules such as moral rules or customary rules where different considerations fulfil a similar role.

Rules, therefore, are not statements nor prescriptions, not even justified or true prescriptions or statements. They are things the content of which is described by some normative statements and such statements are true if the rules exist, i.e. are valid, and not true if the rules do not exist, i.e. are not valid. Hence our original observation that an invalid rule is not a rule: a non-existent stone is not a stone, though we can talk about such stones and describe some of their properties as we can do about invalid rules.

These remarks may lead one to conclude that explaining what is legal validity is neither more nor less than explaining what is law. This, however, is a mistake. The nature of law is explained primarily by explaining what are legal systems. Validity, on the other hand, pertains to the rules of the system. If we can say of the system itself that it is valid this is only in the sense that its rules are valid.[5] But now another proposition may suggest itself. Since it is clear that a legal system consists of legally valid rules[6] is it not the case that legal validity means simply membership in a legal system? When asking for the nature of legal validity we are, this suggestion goes, asking for the criteria of membership in a legal system.

Nevertheless, despite its initial attractiveness this suggestion must be rejected. Even if we assume that 'legally valid according to system S' and 'a law of system S' are necessarily co-extensive, we cannot conclude that they mean the same. The question is what is a reason for what. Is a rule part of a system because it is valid or is it valid because it is part of a legal system? It seems intuitively clear that there are two different answers to these questions. Those who want to explain validity as membership of a system would presumably maintain that despite our intuitions the two terms are identical in meaning and that

[5] Or that they are systemically valid namely, valid because they belong to such a system. See section 2 below.

[6] Here and throughout I use 'rules' to include principles and all other kinds of norms as well as non-normative laws. I am considering in this essay momentary legal systems only (cf. Essay 5 above). Obvious small adjustments are needed for the conclusions to apply to non-momentary legal systems.

both questions should be answered negatively. This is wrong if only for the simple reason that not every legally valid rule is part of the legal system according to which it is valid.

It is, of course, well known that most legal systems recognize and enforce many rules which are not part of the system. The rules of private international law of a legal system S are laws establishing the conditions under which foreign laws are to be held legally valid according to S. Legal systems often recognize the rights of various religious groups to regulate certain aspects of their members' life according to their religious laws. They recognize the right of various ethnic or tribal groups to be governed in certain respects by their customary ways. And they recognize the right of voluntary associations to make rules for the regulation of some activities of their own members. In all these cases the rules recognized and enforced in S are legally valid in accordance with S but are not thereby themselves part of the legal system S.[7]

Since validity according to law is broader than membership of the legal system, because though all laws are legally valid, not every legally valid rule is a law, it is clear that the notion of membership in a legal system cannot completely explain legal validity. The two notions though related are partly independent of each other.

The best route to the understanding of 'legally valid' is by attending to the fact that it is used interchangeably with 'legally binding'.[8] A valid rule is one which has normative effects. A legally valid rule is one which has legal effects.[9] To avoid misunderstanding, these statements should perhaps be augmented to read: A legally valid rule is one which has the normative effects (in law) which it claims to have. If it is a legal rule purporting to impose an obligation on X then X is under this obligation because this rule is a legal rule. If it is a rule purporting to confer a right or power on Y then Y has the right or power in virtue of the fact that the rule is a legal rule.

[7] See more on this point in *Practical Reason and Norms*, pp. 152–4.

[8] Outside the law 'binding' is used more extensively than 'valid'. We talk, for example, of morally binding rules rather than morally valid ones, of binding promises— not of valid ones. I will use 'valid' interchangeably with 'binding' and the analysis offered is meant to apply to both. The difference between 'binding' and 'valid' in all such contexts does not affect their normative significance.

[9] For the precise force of 'legally' in such contexts see the end of the next section.

It is evident that this conception of the nature of the validity of rules can easily be extended to explain the validity of contracts, sales, wills, marriages, etc. They are all valid if and only if they have the normative consequences they purport to have.

To those familiar with Kelsen's work it will be clear that I have so far simply adapted and explained his notion of validity. He identifies the validity of rules with their existence and he claims that to say of a rule that it is valid is to say that it ought to be obeyed. I have simply tried to explain and to generalize this by saying that the fact that a rule is valid means that it has the normative consequences it purports to have. But no sooner does one state this view than its inherent difficulties become apparent.

In the long-standing debate between natural lawyers and positivists the former adopted the view that 'a valid rule' means a justified one, a rule that one is justified, indeed required, to observe and endorse. Positivists on the other hand traditionally hold that the validity or at least the legal validity of a rule means not its justification but that it is recognized as enforceable by tests set down in an efficacious legal system, one which is in fact followed regardless of whether or not it should be. In following Kelsen we have adopted the natural law view on the meaning of 'validity'. This poses two questions: How could such a view be reconciled with the fact that law regulates its own validity, namely that it can and does set social and factual tests for validity quite unlike those determing the validity of moral rules? Secondly, how can it be that in stating what the law is we are not endorsing its moral merit?

2. SYSTEMIC VALIDITY

It seems reasonable to identify the moral validity of rules with their justification and identify justification with the existence of a moral rule. Moral validity is presumably established by argument and the way to argue that a rule is morally binding or valid is to show that it is justified, that the requirements and restraints it imposes ought to be observed. Here validity and justification seem particularly close. But law is different. The legal validity of a rule is established not by arguments concerning its value and justification but rather by showing that it conforms to tests of validity laid down by some other rules of the system which can be called rules of recognition. These tests normally concern the way the rule was enacted or laid down by a judicial authority. The legal validity of rules of recognition is determined in a similar way except for the validity of the ultimate rules of recognition which is a matter of social fact, namely those ultimate rules of recognition are binding which are actually practised and followed by the courts.[10]

In order to understand how the social and factual character of the law can be reconciled with the view of validity as justification, we must consider the sense in which law is a *social* system.

There is one obvious sense in which law is social. A legal system may be in force in a certain community or it may not. It is in force if it is effectively followed, observed, and enforced within the community. It is not pertinent to our purpose here to work out a test for determining when a legal system is in force in a certain community. Suffice it that all agree that its being in force is a matter of the efficacy of the law in that society. But so far as this consideration goes, the same is true of moral rules. They may be observed, followed, and enforced by a certain community (and I do not mean enforced by law), or they may be disregarded and violated more often than not. The precise test for the law being in force differs from that by which we judge whether a certain moral code is the moral code of a community. For one thing morality, unlike the law, does not rest on legislative and adjudicative institutions. But in essence, just as we can talk of the laws of England or Germany, so we can talk of the morality of the English or the Germans and the tests in either case are tests of the social efficacy of the rules.

There is, however, a second way in which law is a social fact: all laws have a source. The validity of every law is conditional on the existence of certain facts: certain Acts of Parliament or of a minister or of a town council, certain decisions of the courts, a general pattern of behaviour of the general population amounting to the existence of a custom, etc., these are law-creating facts. The existence of every law depends also on the non-existence of law-repealing facts. 'Law regulates its own

[10] I am here following Hart's doctrine of the rule of recognition in a slightly modified form. Cf. Hart, *The Concept of Law*, pp. 92–107, and my 'Legal Principles and the Limits of Law', *Yale Law Journal* (1972). See Essay 4 for an attempted conciliation between Kelsen's and Hart's views on ultimate legal rules.

creation' said Kelsen. The law itself determines which facts create laws and which abrogate them.

The view of law as a social fact, as a method of organization and regulation of social life, stands or falls with the two theses mentioned. At its core lie the theses that (1) the existence of a legal system is a function of its social efficacy, and that (2) every law has a source. The obvious importance of the first thesis should not obscure the equal importance of the second. It is vital for the conception of law, since it alone can guarantee that the content of law can be determined in an objective and value-neutral way. Since the validity of a law depends on its source, and since the source is an action or a series of actions, doubts and discussions about the validity of laws revolve on factual questions, on issues susceptible of objective determination to which one's moral or political views are essentially irrelevant.

Explaining the function and importance of the sources thesis does not, however, help to reconcile it with the view of validity as justification. It cannot be claimed that the justification view of validity entails the sources thesis. But it is clear that the two are compatible. When considering the validity of a law as a law one considers those reasons for adhering to the rule which depend on its being a law, i.e. part of a legal system in force in a certain community. The legal validity of the law prohibiting theft does not rest on arguments concerning the right to property and the wrong done in infringing it. It rests on the need to have effective law and the justified authority of those who make it.

Let us distinguish between the validity of a law or a rule, which means that it ought to be obeyed for some reason or other, and its systemic validity as a law, as a legal rule, which means that it ought to be obeyed because it is part of a legal system which is in force in the country concerned. While the direct (i.e. non-systemic) validity of a rule turns on the goals and values which it serves or harms, its legal, systemic, validity depends on the fact that it belongs to a given legal system and that it is justified as such. Hence proof that the law rests on a source which is recognized by the system is an essential part of the argument for its legal validity just as we expect it to be. Nor is the dependence of validity on a factual source unique to the law. A child ought to obey his parents' commands. Their commands addressed to him are valid. Some are directly valid, sometimes there are good reasons for behaving as one is commanded. But regardless of whether or not this is the case, all parents' commands are systemically valid, i.e. valid because issued by a legitimate authority, because they have a source and because there are reasons for following orders coming from that source.

To conclude: A rule of law is valid if and only if it has the normative consequences it purports to have. It is legally valid if and only if it is valid because it belongs to a legal system in force in a certain country or is enforceable in it, i.e. if it is systemically valid. Similarly an obligation is a legal obligation and a right is a legal right if and only if they are an obligation or a right in virtue of a rule which is legally valid. Validity presupposes membership and enforceability. Judgments of membership and of enforceability are judgments of social fact. Judgments of legal validity are normative judgments partly based on those facts.

3. STATEMENTS FROM A POINT OF VIEW

I have shown how the justification view of legal validity is compatible with the dependence of legal validity on factual sources. It remains to examine the other difficulty facing the justification view: the interpretation of detached legal statements.

A detached legal statement is a statement of law, of what legal rights or duties people have, not a statement about people's beliefs, attitudes, or actions, not even about their beliefs, attitudes, or actions about the law. Yet a detached normative statement does not carry the full normative force of an ordinary normative statement. Its utterance does not commit the speaker to the normative view it expresses. Lawyers' advice to their clients, law teachers' expositions in front of their students often belong to this category. I am not implying that lawyers or law teachers do not believe in the validity (i.e. justification) of the law with which they deal, only that often they do not commit themselves to such beliefs when acting in their professional capacity.

As we have already noted, the analysis of detached normative statements is a crucial test for every positivist theory of law. On the one hand their existence is a major source of strength.

It shows that normative language can be used without a full normative commitment or force. But on the other hand it is far from easy to explain what sense normative utterances have when they do not carry their full normative force. The Benthamite answer was to deny that they are normative utterances. 'X has a duty to ϕ' means 'X is liable to a sanction if he does not ϕ'. 'A law requires that X ϕ's' means 'a sovereign commanded X to ϕ'. Later positivists admitted that 'law', 'duty', 'a right', etc., have their normative uses but assumed that they carry a purely factual sense when qualified by the adjective 'legal' or prefaced by the operator 'it is the law that' and their equivalents. Thus qualified, they mean no more than that the rule or duty is recognized by a generally efficacious legal system. But this is essentially no more than a more sophisticated version of Bentham's view. Law is identified not necessarily as the product of legislation but as a practice of courts and other officials and it includes not only rules which are directly recognized by them, but also those they are implicitly committed to in view of their existing practices.

H. L. A. Hart recognized that even the sophisticated Benthamite view distorts the nature of many legal statements.[11] He called the statements to which this analysis applies external and insisted on the importance of internal statements to the analysis of law. Most ordinary statements about the law by citizens, the police, lawyers, judges, law teachers, and students are, according to Hart, internal statements. External statements about the law are statements about people's practices and actions, attitudes and beliefs concerning the law. Internal statements are those applying the law, using it as a standard by which to evaluate, guide, or criticize behaviour. Internal statements are thus full-blooded normative statements. Making internal statements is thus a sign of endorsement of the rule concerned. One endorses a rule if one uses it regularly in guiding, evaluating, and criticizing those actions to which the rule applies. Endorsement of a rule includes, therefore, a disposition to make internal statements.[12] It is crucial to the understanding of

[11] I am using 'legal statements' loosely to designate all kinds of statements about the law. Some such statements are properly analysed on the sophisticated Benthamite model.

[12] Though, of course, mere occasional resort to internal statements does not amount to endorsement.

Hart's position to understand that his notion of acceptance or endorsement of a rule does not entail *moral* approval of it. A man may hold a rule to be morally justified and he may endorse it for this reason. But equally a man may endorse and follow a rule for any other reason, or for no reason at all.

It seems to me that Hart is right in saying that judges and all other officials regularly involved in applying and enforcing the law do accept and follow it. They may have reservations concerning the moral justifiability of the law but nevertheless they accept and apply it for their own reasons (salary, social involvement, etc.) or for no reason at all.[13] Their legal statements normally reflect this attitude. They are internal, fully committed normative statements. When they state the legal validity of a rule they do mean to assert its binding force, though not necessarily its moral force.[14]

Hart's interest in internal statements was partly a result of his view that a legal system is in force in a certain community only if at least the officials of the system and normally many others in the community accept its laws and follow them, such acceptance being characteristically manifested by the use of internal statements. His dichotomy between external and internal statements tends, however, to obscure from sight the existence of a third category of statements. Their existence was realized by Kelsen for it is crucial to anyone holding his view on the meaning of 'validity' and rejecting natural law at the same time.[15]

If the internal statements are characteristic of the judge, and of the law-abiding citizens, this third kind of statement is characteristic of the lawyer and the law teacher (who of course often make internal and external statements as well) for they are not primarily concerned in applying the law to themselves or to others but in warning others of what they ought to do according to law. In an illuminating passage Kelsen contrasts

[13] It is important to distinguish (which in *Practical Reason and Norms* I failed to do) between one who fully endorses a rule, i.e. believes that its subjects ought to follow it, and one who weakly accepts it, i.e. believes that he should follow it himself. (The two coincide in the case of personal rules.) Hart maintains that judges at least weakly accept the rule of recognition. A judge who merely weakly accepts it must, it would seem, pretend that he fully endorses it. Hence his statements are fully normative.

[14] Cf. *The Concept of Law*, pp. 55–6, 86–8.

[15] A problem which Hart, because of his different account of 'validity', did not face.

the behaviour of the anarchist acting as a citizen making fully normative internal statements with the anarchist acting as a lawyer or scholar:

> In earlier publications I used as an example for the fact that the presupposition of the basic norm is possible but not necessary: An anarchist does not presuppose the basic norm. This example is misleading. The anarchist emotionally rejects the law as a coercive order; he objects to the law; he wants a community free of coercion, a community constituted without a coercive order. Anarchism is a political attitude, based on a certain wish. The sociological interpretation, which does not presuppose a basic norm, is a theoretical attitude. Even an anarchist, if he were a professor of law, could describe positive law as a system of valid norms, without having to approve of this law. Many textbooks in which the capitalist legal order is described as a system of norms constituting obligations, authorizations, rights, jurisdictions, are written by jurists who politically disapprove of this legal order.[16]

Legal scholars—and this includes ordinary practising lawyers—can use normative language when describing the law and make legal statements without thereby endorsing the law's moral authority. There is a special kind of legal statement which, though it is made by the use of ordinary normative terms, does not carry the same normative force of an ordinary legal statement. To examine its nature we should concentrate attention on the activities of lawyers. But it is a mistake to think that this kind of statement is unique to lawyers or to legal contexts. It is to be found whenever a person advises or informs another on his normative situation in contexts which make it clear that the advice or information is given from a point of view or on the basis of certain assumptions which are not necessarily shared by the speaker.

Imagine an orthodox but relatively ill-informed Jew who asks the advice of his friend who is Catholic but an expert in Rabbinical law. 'What should I do?' he asks, clearly meaning what should I do according to *my* religion, not yours. The friend tells him that he should do so and so. The point is that both know that this is not what the friend thinks that he really ought to do. The friend is simply stating how things are from the Jewish Orthodox point of view. It is important not to confuse such

[16] *The Pure Theory of Law*, 2nd ed., p. 218n.

statements from a point of view with statements about other people's beliefs. One reason is that there may be no one who has such a belief. The friend in our example may be expressing a very uncommon view on an obscure point of Rabbinical law. Indeed Rabbinical law may never have been endorsed or practised by anybody, not even the inquiring Jew. Nor can such statements be interpreted as conditionals: 'If you accept this point of view then you should etc.' Rather they assert what is the case from the relevant point of view as if it is valid or on the hypothesis that it is—as Kelsen expresses the point—but without actually endorsing it.

Much of the discourse about the law falls according to Kelsen into this category which I called statement from a point of view.[17] This is especially true of statements by legal practitioners and scholars acting in their professional capacity. The main differences between such contexts and the one of our imagined example is that the clear assumption that the Catholic does not share the point of view from which he speaks whereas the Jew does share it is missing. The lawyer—academic or practising—may or may not believe in the moral validity of the law. His reader or client may or may not share such beliefs. Such questions are irrelevant to the interpretation of such statements even though the answers to them—as in our example—may be known in some cases.

The analysis offered here of statements from a point of view is incomplete. Kelsen did not have a complete explanation of such statements. In fact what I have offered here is already an adaptation of Kelsen's position. We still await a full analysis of such statements. But Kelsen deserves the credit for drawing our attention to this most important class of statements. The discussion of the nature of normative discourse would have been saved from many confusions and mistakes had it not overlooked the prevalence of such statements.

4. VALIDITY AND POSITIVISM

If indeed statements from a point of view are a distinct type of statement then our view of the traditional controversy

[17] I am here presenting this view rather than defending it. For a more detailed defence of this interpretation of Kelsen and an examination of the way this doctrine is integrated in his general legal theory see Essay 7 above. For my own development of this theme see *Practical Reason and Norms*, pp. 170–7.

between natural lawyers and positivists is radically transformed. The main strength of the positivist's position is in its
insistence that law is essentially a form of social organization.
The main contention of the natural lawyer is that law is essentially moral. These formulations suggest that the two positions
are not necessarily mutually exclusive. The law may have
more than one essential property. There is no denying, however, that many of the proposed natural law theories are incompatible with positivism.[18] This impression of mutual incompatibility is enhanced by two semantic theses which are generally
endorsed by natural lawyers: First, that normative terms like
'a right', 'a duty', 'ought' are used in the same sense in legal,
moral, and other normative statements. Secondly, that legal
statements are moral statements. For example, when one states
'It is John's legal duty to repay the debt' one is asserting that
John has a (moral) duty to repay the debt arising out of the
law.

Positivists reject the second semantic thesis. Even if the law
is essentially moral—the cautious positivist would argue—it is
clear that establishing the moral merit of a law is a different
process relying on different considerations, from establishing its
existence as a social fact. To the positivist the identification of
the law and of the duties and rights it gives rise to is a matter
of social fact. The question of its value is a further and separate
question. Since one may know what the law is without knowing
if it is justified, there must be a possibility of making legal statements not involving commitment to its justification. The positivist need not deny that many legal statements do carry such
a commitment. First, it is admitted that whether or not the law
is in fact justified, if it is in force it is held to be so by some
of its subjects, and they are ready to make fully committed statements. Secondly, the law—unlike the threats of the highway-
man—claims to itself legitimacy. The law presents itself as justified and demands not only the obedience but the allegiance
of its subjects. The positivist need not deny that the primary
kind of legal statement is the committed statement—Hart's
internal statement—but he would want to allow, as we observed, for the possibility of non-committed detached state-

---

[18] In *Practical Reason and Norms*, pp. 162 ff., I tried to distinguish between two kinds
of natural law theories, those compatible with positivism and those not.

ments, i.e. ones which though not committed are nevertheless normative. Thus the positivist is bound to reject the natural lawyer's second semantic thesis.

It may be thought that this entails the rejection of the first thesis as well. For if normative terms are regularly used in their ordinary sense in legal contexts are not the statements made by their use always committed statements? But in fact my very arguments so far show that the first semantic thesis is not essentially a natural lawyer's thesis. It is one that positivists can and should adopt, for only through it and the doctrine of statements from a point of view can we understand the possibility of detached statements which are all the same normative and not merely statements about other people's actions or beliefs, etc. Admittedly, statements from a point of view are parasitic on the full-blooded normative statements. That is, there is normally no point in making statements from a point of view unless in relation to a society in which people are often ready to make the full-blooded statements. If there is nobody whose point of view it is, why should we be interested in it? This shows how the natural lawyer's second thesis is modified rather than rejected outright. If this is another pointer that the gulf between natural lawyers and positivists need not be as unbridgeable as is sometimes imagined, then it is welcome for this reason as well.

Part III

Internal Legal Values

9

THE FUNCTIONS OF LAW*

The concept of the functions of law is, quite obviously, of major importance to any theory of law which attempts a general explanation of the nature of law. Like so many other jurisprudential concepts, it is also relevant to a number of other disciplines concerned with the law. It is pertinent to the considerations of lawyers, judges, and officials faced with problems of the correct interpretation and application of the law. It is relevant to sociologists and political scientists wishing to explain the interaction of the law with other social norms and institutions. It is indispensable to moral and political theorists elaborating general principles to which the law should conform and for deviation from which it should be criticized. In a more indirect way the concept of the functions of law is also of interest to normative philosophy, for it bears on a more general explanation of the functions of norms, which is part of the elucidation of the nature of normative systems whether legal, moral, social, or other.

Bearing in mind the importance of the concept there is little wonder that statements relating to legal functions are often encountered in many discussions concerning the law. It is, however, surprising that legal theorists have paid so little attention to the elucidation of such an important notion. Not that legal theorists did not pronounce on the functions of law. Indeed, such pronouncements were often made. They were, however, too often made in an attempt to emphasize a particular way of viewing the law, which the philosopher concerned thought, quite often correctly, had been neglected. They were not meant to be comprehensive classifications of the functions of law.

Consider, for example, the following quotations:

For the purpose of understanding the law of today I am content

* First published in A. W. B. Simpson (ed.), *Oxford Essays in Jurisprudence*, 2nd series (Oxford, 1973).

with a picture of satisfying as much of the whole body of human wants as we may with the least sacrifice.[1]

Law is the enterprise of subjecting human conduct to the governance of rules.[2]

The norms of a legal order regulate human behaviour.[3]

What, then, is this law business about? It is about the fact that our society is honeycombed with disputes. Disputes actual and potential; disputes to be settled and disputes to be prevented.[4]

All these statements are correct and important, they all draw attention to important aspects of the law or illuminating ways of considering it. Yet it is curiously difficult to evaluate them, even to judge whether they are compatible or not. It would seem that this difficulty is not overcome by filling in more about the context in which these statements were made, for what all these philosophers fail to provide us with is a comprehensive reasoned scheme of classification of the functions of laws. It is the purpose of this article to contribute to the elaboration of such a general classification.[5]

Before undertaking this task, however, two further clarifications are in place.

Philosophers have occasion to refer to the functions of law in at least three different contexts. Some are concerned with the functions that all legal systems necessarily fulfil, thus regarding certain functions as part of the definition of a legal system, or as entailed by this definition and certain universal facts of human nature. (As the definition of a legal system should not be arbitrary but has to be justified, the contention that all legal systems necessarily fulfil certain functions is, if true, extremely important.) Similarly, the performance of certain functions might be a defining characteristic of certain branches of the law (e.g. the law of contract or the criminal law, etc.) On the other hand, theorists are often interested not in functions fulfilled by all legal systems but in those fulfilled by some or most; their enterprise may lie in comparing the degree to which these

---

[1] R. Pound, *Introduction to the Philosophy of Law* (New Haven, 1922, 1961), p. 47.
[2] Lon L. Fuller, *The Morality of Law*, revised ed. (New Haven, 1969), p. 106.
[3] H. Kelsen, *The Pure Theory of Law*, p. 31.
[4] K. N. Llewellyn, *The Bramble Bush* (New York, 1930, 1960), p. 12.
[5] It is not my purpose to discuss the concept of function itself.

functions are carried out and the techniques by which they are promoted in various legal systems. Finally, theorists are interested in claims that legal systems in general or under certain circumstances ought to fulfil certain functions in certain ways. Rather than putting forward any such claim, it is the aim of this essay to help in formulating a general classificatory scheme, by the use of which such claims can be made and evaluated.

Such a classificatory task can be carried out in great detail. Only the most general classifications will be proposed here, as only they are likely to prove of general interest. More detailed classification is bound to be made within the framework of the general categories. The exact way in which it is to be carried out depends, however, on the purpose at hand, which varies from one context to another.

1. SOCIAL FUNCTIONS OF THE LAW

The question of the social functions of law should be clearly distinguished from the question of classifying legal norms into distinct normative types. The normative character of a legal norm is a matter of its logical properties. It is a question of the logical implications of a statement stating that norm. The social functions on the other hand are the intended or actual social consequences of the law.

Distinguishing between different logical types of law is relatively easy. The classification is related to that of normative statements to which is added a doctrine of individuation.[6] It is possible to produce a reasoned and complete classificatory scheme of types of norms. The analysis of the social functions of the law is on much more slippery ground. No firm guide to the classification, comparable to the analysis of types of norms, is available. It is much more difficult to provide a classification with any claim to exhaust all the social functions that legal systems ever perform. It is even more risky to maintain that all legal systems necessarily perform some or all of these social functions to any extent. It is difficult to propose even a very general classification which would be more than an *ad hoc* device useful for very limited purposes, a classification which would serve as

---

[6] See further J. Raz, *The Concept of a Legal System*, pp. 73 f.

a firm basis for the further analysis of law by lawyers, philosophers, sociologists, and political scientists alike.

A special danger awaiting any analysis of the social functions of law is that it may be so closely tied to particular moral and political principles as to be of no use to anyone who does not completely and exclusively endorse them. Bentham's plan for the natural arrangement of the law is a good illustration of this danger. Bentham had the brilliant idea of arranging and expounding the law in a way which would not only facilitate the memory and make for easy retrieval of any relevant legal material by lawyers and laymen alike, but which would also enable everyone to see what the social effects of the law were, and would make the criticisms and reform of the law an easy matter. He thought he had discovered a single method of arranging the law which would achieve all these diverse purposes. Laws should be arranged on the basis of the actions they command or prohibit:

> With respect then to such actions in particular as are among the objects of the law, to point out to a man the *utility* of them or the mischievousness, is the only way to make him see *clearly* that property of them which every man is in search of.... From *utility* then we may denominate a *principle*, that may serve to preside over and govern, as it were, such arrangement as shall be made of the several institutions or combination of institutions that compose the matter of this science.... Governed in this matter by a principle that is recognized by all men, the same arrangement that would serve for the jurisprudence of any one country, would serve with little variation for that of any other. Yet more. The mischievousness of a bad Law would be detected, at least the utility of it would be rendered suspicious, by the difficulty of finding a place for it in such an arrangement.[7]

In proposing his scheme for a natural arrangement Bentham does not confuse the roles of the expositor and critic of the law. He does not confuse the law as it is with the law as it ought to be. But his method of expounding the law as it is is designed to serve the critic as well. This in itself is an admirable purpose, which should be served by every analysis. The trouble, however, is that the way Bentham conceived of the function of the

---

[7] *A Fragment on Government* (Oxford, 1960), pp. 24 f. See also on the same subject: *Introduction to the Principles of Morals and Legislation*, pp. 398–403, and *The Works of Jeremy Bentham*, ed. J. Bowring (1863), iii. 172, and elsewhere.

law was so closely tied to one particular way of evaluating it, namely his own, that his scheme for a natural arrangement is likely to be of little use for anybody but a utilitarian of the Benthamite brand. The aim of the analyst should be to propose a classification of the social functions of the law which is of use to the reformer, but is not too closely tied to any particular viewpoint.

It is my hope that the classification proposed below avoids all these pitfalls and successfully meets all the requirements mentioned. It seems to me that all legal systems necessarily perform, at least to a minimal degree, which I am unable to specify, social functions of all the types to be mentioned, and that these are all the main types of social functions they perform. These claims will not, however, be argued for here. Instead, the classification will be simply put forward and explained in general outline. It should be further clear that the price of making such claims is that only the most general and broad categories of social functions can be indicated. Apart from the need for justification the analysis proposed demands further elaboration and refinement.

It is possible to ascribe every legal norm to one normative category which explains its normative character. It is not possible to ascribe one distinct social function to every law or legal norm. Social functions are characteristically performed by legal institutions established and regulated by numerous laws. It is most common to inquire about the social functions of the banking system, ownership, the limited company, marriage, etc., rather than the function of any particular law involved in regulating these institutions, though occasionally it is useful to investigate the function of particular laws as well. Furthermore, one and the same legal institution, sometimes one law, often performs several social functions, though at the high level of generalization at which the present analysis is conducted it is easier to point out one type of function performed by each institution.

The social functions of the law can profitably be divided into direct and indirect functions. Direct functions are those the fulfilment of which is secured by the law being obeyed and applied. Indirect functions are those the fulfilment of which consists in attitudes, feelings, opinions, and modes of behaviour which are not obedience to laws or the application of laws, but which result from the knowledge of the existence of the laws or from compliance with and application of laws. The indirect functions which laws actually fulfil are the results of their existence or of following and applying them. It must be remembered, however, that the acts of following or applying the laws are themselves part of the direct, rather than the indirect, functions of the law. The intended indirect functions of laws are those results which it is the laws' intention to achieve, whether or not they are actually secured. The indirect functions are most commonly fulfilled not only as results of the laws' existence and application but also of their interaction with other factors such as people's attitudes to the law and the existence in the society concerned of other social norms and institutions. The direct functions of the law often depend for their fulfilment on similar factors, but this is not always the case. A person may conform to laws imposing obligations without knowing that they exist. He may exercise legal powers without realizing that his actions have any legal effects. Though such cases are relatively rare, it is quite common for people to perform their duties and exercise powers for reasons which have nothing to do with the law. When doing so they contribute to the fulfilment of the direct social functions of the law. For example, curtailing the use of violence is a direct function of the law for it is secured if the relevant provisions of the criminal law are obeyed. Inculcating certain moral values in the population is an indirect function, for its success consists in something more than mere conformity with the law.

Direct functions will be dealt with first. They can usefully be divided into primary and secondary functions. The primary functions are outward-looking, they affect the general population, and in them is to be found the reason and justification for the existence of the law. The secondary functions are the functions of the maintenance of the legal system. They make its existence and operation possible. They are to be judged by their success in facilitating the fulfilment of the primary functions by the law. Thus providing a national health service is a primary function. Regulating the operation of law-making organs is a secondary function.

2. PRIMARY FUNCTIONS

There are four primary functions:

(a) *Preventing Undesirable Behaviour and Securing Desirable Behaviour.* This function is mainly performed by parts of the criminal law and the law of torts. It is served by prohibitions on murder, assault, unlawful imprisonment, libel, certain forms of sexual behaviour, revealing official secrets, etc., as well as duties of care while engaging in dangerous activities, duties of parents and guardians, etc. It may be claimed that this function is the most basic and elementary the law performs. It has attracted much attention and there is no need to discuss it in any detail here. It should be obvious that by talking about undesirable behaviour it is not implied that the behaviour is really undesirable or that the majority of the population considers it undesirable. It is regarded so by the law. Such views are attributed to the law in a way similar to that by which intentions were attributed to it above. It may be regarded undesirable for any reason. But, and it is important to remember this, in so far as a mode of behaviour is prohibited because it is regarded as likely to affect adversely some other direct social function of the law it does not fall into this category. Though this function is mainly performed by duty-imposing laws, it sometimes involves power-conferring laws as well. Thus the law may confer certain powers and make it compulsory to use or refrain from using them under certain circumstances, because their use is deemed desirable or undesirable.

(b) *Providing Facilities for Private Arrangements between Individuals.* The main bulk of private law as well as large parts of the criminal law and the law of torts are concerned with this function. Most of the institutions of private law serve primarily this purpose. Contracts, negotiable instruments, private property, marriage, companies, co-operatives, banks, trade unions, and other forms of incorporation are all created to serve this function. They all form patterns of legal relations into which individuals enter of their own free will if and when they consider it will serve their ends or be to the good of somebody with whose well-being they are concerned.

In establishing and regulating such institutions both duty-imposing and power-conferring rules giving rise to rights under private law are involved. It is a mistake to think that only rights and powers have to do with this function. Rights and powers to conclude contracts, acquire and dispose of property, establish corporations, marry, etc., would be pointless and without effect but for the duties to perform contracts, respect property rights, etc. Duties imposed by the law of torts and the criminal law in respect of institutions designed for the performance of this function should, therefore, be regarded as contributing to its performance. Such duties include the provisions against trespass, theft, etc. The duty to avoid negligent harm is an instance of a duty serving both the first and the second functions. It serves the first function by protecting, e.g. people against bodily harm, and it serves the second function by protecting, e.g., property against negligent damage.

When fulfilling this second function the law sometimes provides ways of securing legal protection for arrangements that could be achieved by non-legal means. Often, however, it makes possible the achievement of ends that could not have been otherwise achieved in human societies. People can and often do reach agreements which are not legally binding. Men and women can and sometimes do establish lasting relations without marrying. The limited company, however, makes possible recruitment of capital from the general public to an extent that would not have been possible without some legal arrangements.

By prohibiting undesirable behaviour the law directs human activities in ways it finds appropriate. The law itself decides on ends which are desirable or undesirable and it limits individual choice to guarantee the achievement of the proper ends. By providing facilities for private arrangements between individuals the law helps individuals in pursuing ends of their choice. It does not impose its will on individuals but serves them in realizing their own will. The individual's freedom of choice is restricted only in consequence of his previous free decisions and actions.

While doing so the law makes the use of the facilities provided depend on observing various conditions. It does not allow individuals to invoke the protection of the law for any arrangement they may like. It creates frameworks within which individuals must make their arrangements and pursue their objectives if they are to enjoy legal protection. These restrictions are necessary to protect one party to an arrangement from being exploited by the other party, and to protect third parties from unfair consequences affecting them resulting from arrangements in which they did not participate. Hence the various restrictions on the freedom of contract, the limitations on the ways in which companies can be established and operate, etc. The more far-reaching the legal protection provided, the more it is likely to affect third parties and consequently the more severe will be the legal restrictions on the freedom of individuals to agree on the terms of their own arrangements. Thus, under the law of contract individuals have a wide freedom to decide the terms of their agreement, for they create rights *in personam* affecting only the parties to the agreement. But individuals have a very limited choice to decide the content of any rights *in rem* they may acquire. Basically it is a package deal. The law determines the consequences of the right and the individuals have to choose whether to take it or not and decide the price. Similarly, the less equal are the parties to an agreement likely to be the more the law will tend to restrict their freedom. These last remarks concern, of course, principles which should guide the law-makers. They do not pretend to reflect the way the law always operates.

(*c*) *The Provision of Services and the Redistribution of Goods.* This function has become of great importance in recent times, but as the following examples show it has always been performed by legal systems. The law performs it by making arrangements for defence against outside enemies (keeping internal order mainly belongs to the secondary functions discussed below), by providing for education, health service, road construction and maintenance, sewage and rubbish clearing, subsidizing industries or the arts, the payment of social security benefits, etc.

It is not generally possible to distinguish between redistribution of goods and the provision of services. When a law of agrarian reform is made, or when it is made compulsory to divide some of an industry's profits among its workers, or when a law stipulates a compulsory form of distributing the estate of deceased persons, it clearly provides for the redistribution of goods. Likewise, when a service is provided under the law against payment based on cost incurred as, for example, might be the case with a state-run railway service, this is a clear case of services rendered with no element of redistribution of goods. But many of the services stipulated by the law are paid completely or partly from the general budget. This means that they are largely paid out of taxes, and there is no guarantee that the amount of taxes paid by a man is proportionate to the benefit he derives from services provided by the law or to the cost of these services. Therefore, it is not possible to separate in general the provision of services from the redistribution of goods.

The previous remarks make also the well-known point that tax laws serve this social function. They also, of course, serve the secondary functions discussed below. Only the provision of services and the redistribution of goods by public bodies exercising public powers belong to this category. It does not include, for example, private gifts or voluntary labour contracts. Hence it is mainly the public law which is involved in the performance of this social function. Both laws conferring powers on officials and laws prescribing how these powers are to be exercised are involved as well as other duties. Quite often the law grants rights to these services to individuals enabling them to enforce the correlative duties on officials to provide the services.

(d) *Settling Unregulated Disputes.* It will be submitted here that laws regulating the operation of courts, tribunals, arbitrators, etc., fulfil both primary and secondary society functions. They fulfil a primary function inasmuch as they stipulate procedures for settling unregulated disputes. They fulfil a secondary function inasmuch as they stipulate procedures for settling regulated disputes, that is, cases where the law is clear and cannot be changed by the judicial organ. They fulfil both these functions when they apply to partly regulated disputes, that is, disputes governed by existing law which is either unclear, or can be changed by the judicial organ. (Normally I will take 'unregulated' to include the partly regulated.)

Both the distinction between regulated and unregulated disputes, and the corresponding distinction between the social functions of the law, are likely to raise many objections. The distinctions will, therefore, be explained at some length with the aid of three simplified models of different types of normative systems.

Type A. Let us imagine a normative system fulfilling all or some of the first three functions. It may or may not have norm-governed procedures for changing its norms. But it does not have any norms stipulating procedures by which disputes can be authoritatively settled. Such a normative system will guide behaviour, and in doing so will prevent many potential disputes. When a dispute does arise reference to the norms will often help in reaching an agreed solution. Two important features characterize such a system. (1) There will be no authoritative way of deciding what is the correct solution to disputes governed by the norms of the system, that is, regulated disputes. (2) There will always be disputes which cannot be solved simply by reference to the norms either because the case is not dealt with by the norms as they exist at the time it occurs or because the norms existing at that time are vague concerning the issue in dispute. These are disputes which are not completely regulated and the system does not help in settling them.

Type B. The second type of normative system is similar to the first except for the fact that its norms include some establishing authorities for settling disputes and regulating their operation. These authorities, however, have only power to settle questions of fact and pronounce about the correct application of existing norms to the case. Faced with cases not governed by existing norms, or cases with regard to which the existing norms are vague, the authorities will simply decline to make any decisions.[8] A system of this type has three distinctive features: first, such a system fulfils at least some of the first three social functions. Secondly, it provides for settling regulated disputes, but, thirdly, it does not provide any way for settling disputes which are not fully regulated.

Type C.[9] Normative systems of the third type are very different. They do not include any norms guiding the behaviour of ordinary people and performing any of the three first social

[8] Since there is no sharp line between regulated and unregulated disputes, systems of type B cannot exist. It is nevertheless useful to consider it as an intermediate stage between types A and C.

[9] This type is discussed by Hart: *The Concept of Law*, p. 139. See also R. M. Dworkin, 'Judicial Discretion', in *Journal of Philosophy* 60 (1963), p. 624.

functions. All their norms are concerned only with instituting organs for settling disputes and regulating their operation. Sometimes, they include norms making it a duty to bring disputes before the relevant organs.

When faced with a dispute the organ may decide it in any way it likes. It does not state its reasons and is not bound to reach similar decisions in similar cases.

This type of system can also be characterized by reference to three features: first, it does not fulfil any of the first three social functions, and does nothing to guide human behaviour in daily life. It does not help prevent potential disputes. Secondly, there are under it no regulated disputes;[10] thirdly, it provides procedures for settling all unregulated disputes.

Systems of type B differ from those of type A in having special organs improving the efficiency of the system. Their norms may be identical in content, affecting the same potential or actual disputes and performing the same primary functions. But in addition systems of type B provide recognized ways for official and authoritative settlement of disputes, which can be dealt with only informally under systems of type A. They fulfil an additional secondary function—they provide norm-applying organs, thus improving the efficient functioning of the system. Systems of type C, on the other hand, are not more efficient than those of type A. They differ not in their secondary but in their primary functions. They do not prevent undesirable behaviour, they provide neither facilities for private arrangement nor services to individuals. But they provide procedures for settling disputes whenever these occur. They perform only the fourth of the primary functions.

Legal systems are a combination of types B and C. They provide for the settlement of both regulated and unregulated disputes. (Though usually there are certain types of unregulated disputes with which legal systems will refuse to interfere.) Many legal systems by establishing some principle of *stare decisis* transform automatically every unregulated dispute once it is brought before the courts into a regulated or at least a partially regulated one. Therefore, legal systems perform both the primary function of providing ways for settling unregulated dis-

[10] I disregard disputes concerning the operation of the dispute-settling organs themselves.

putes and the secondary function of instituting law-applying organs for settling regulated disputes.

The distinction between the two functions is obscured by the fact that usually the same organs perform both. Furthermore, it is obscured by the fact that many disputes are partly regulated. To some extent this is inevitable and is due to the inherent vagueness of laws (both rules and principles). But to a large extent it is official policy of law-making organs to use very indeterminate terms (e.g. reasonable care) so as to leave much to the discretion of the courts. When dealing with a partly regulated dispute the courts, and therefore the laws regulating their operation, perform both primary and secondary functions.

3. SECONDARY AND INDIRECT FUNCTIONS

Secondary Functions

The law's secondary social functions have to do with the operation of the legal system itself. They provide for its adaptability, its efficacy, and its smooth and uninterrupted operation. There are two secondary functions: first, the determination of procedures for changing the law, and secondly, the regulation of the operation of law-applying organs. To adapt Kelsen's formulation: the law regulates its own creation and its own application.

The law regulates its own creation by instituting organs and procedures for changing the law. These include constitution-making bodies, parliaments, local authorities, administrative legislation, custom, judicial law-making, regulations made by independent public bodies, etc. The law regulates its own application by creating and regulating the operation of courts and tribunals, the police and the prison system, various executive and administrative bodies, etc. In the performance of these functions are involved laws securing the financial resources necessary for the maintenance of these organs, and laws arranging for the recruitment of the appropriate personnel. This is mainly the domain of public law, though an important role is played by criminal law in the performance of these functions. Both duty-imposing and power-conferring laws are involved.

The discussion makes clear the key position of the court system in all legal systems. They perform the primary function of settling unregulated disputes. They perform the two secondary functions of law-applying and law-making. They also perform important indirect functions. In many societies the courts are the most respected of legal institutions. They are often most directly connected in the public mind with the idea of the law and the rule of law. Consequently they play a vital role in promoting respect for the law and the values sustained by it.

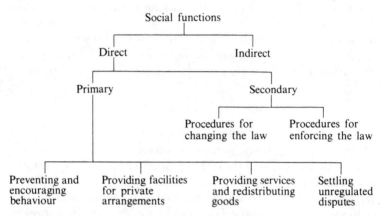

Throughout the preceding discussion it has repeatedly been pointed out that laws of all the normative types are involved in the performance of every social function. It was further emphasized that duty-imposing laws contribute to the performance of all legal functions. Duty-imposing laws, though not the only type of laws, are the ultimate basis of the law. Only because the other types of law have various logical relations to the duty-imposing laws, can they perform all the functions which they do perform.

Indirect Social Functions

The social effects of the law which come under this heading almost always depend for their achievement on non-legal factors, especially the general attitude to the law and its interaction with social norms and institutions. Some of these functions are performed by particular legal institutions, others by the existence of the legal system itself. The indirect social effects of the law are numerous and vary enormously in nature, extent, and importance. They may include such things as strengthening or weakening the respect given to certain moral values, for example, the sanctity of life, strengthening or weakening respect for authority in general, affecting the sense of national unity, etc. The law helps in creating and maintaining social stratification, it sometimes helps in creating a sense of participation in running the country, sometimes it contributes to a feeling of alienation. Some laws are created with the intention of securing indirect effects. For example, conferment of certain privileges on certain classes of people may be done with the intention of enhancing their status. Therefore, the distinction between intended and actual functions applies to the indirect functions as well. The previous example shows also that sometimes securing the indirect function is the main reason for enacting a law. Consider, for example, an exemption of university students from the draft as a measure of encouraging enrolment in the universities, or an employment-tax law as a means to increase efficiency in industry and commerce. These examples should make clear that the indirect effects of the law as conceived here are far from being relatively unimportant by-products of the law. They are part of its essential function in any society. Lawyers and legal theorists have paid little attention to the law's indirect functions. Sociologists and political scientists have great interest in them but found them a very elusive factor, difficult to pinpoint and quantify. There can be little doubt that our understanding of law will remain partial and deficient until the social sciences succeed in tackling more fully the problems involved in assessing the indirect functions of the law.

4. ON H. L. A. HART'S CLASSIFICATION OF LAWS

The classification of legal functions outlined above has not revealed any unknown functions of the law. It was not meant to do so. People have been thinking about the law long enough to have discovered all its main functions. But in discussing them they have often disregarded some and confused others. It has been my aim in this essay to attempt a comprehensive classification of the main legal functions, trying to distinguish between those functions which have often been confused and to separate various levels of analysis. Doing this is not solving the problems of the functions of laws, it is merely presenting them. In assessing the merits and failures of the proposed classification it may be useful to compare it with the ideas of other writers. I will conclude this essay with some remarks (no complete analysis is intended) on the classifications suggested by H. L. A. Hart.

Legal theorists of the positivist school, by concentrating on the criminal law, tended to emphasize the first primary function of prohibiting undesirable behaviour and to overlook the other functions. Bentham, for example, thought that in arranging the law:

> ... the penal code ought to precede the civil code and the constitutional code. In the first, the legislator exhibits himself to every individual, he permits, he commands, he prohibits, he traces for everyone the rules of his conduct.... In the other codes he has less to do with commandments than with regulations and explanations, which do not so clearly address themselves to everybody, and which are not generally interesting to those concerned...[11]

In *The Concept of Law* H. L. A. Hart has paid special attention to the second primary function, that of providing facilities for private arrangements, as well as to the secondary legal functions. The analysis proposed here is largely an elaboration of his ideas. Hart, however, did not clearly distinguish between normative types and social functions. Consequently, his theory suggests a simple relation between types of rules and social functions, according to which duty-imposing rules perform the first primary function whereas power-conferring rules perform the second primary function. In fact both rules have to do with each of these functions. Furthermore, this simplified picture of a one to one correlation between types of rules and types of functions obscures the fact that legal systems perform two more primary functions, those of providing services and settling unregulated disputes.

The confusion engendered by conflating normative types and social functions is increased when Hart turns to the examination of the secondary functions of the law. At this stage he again identifies types of rule with types of social function, but now with the distinction between primary and secondary functions. By doing this he obscures the distinction between the primary function of facilitating private arrangements and the secondary

---

[11] Bowring, iii. 161.

function of law-making. He also obscures the important role of duty-imposing laws in performing the secondary functions. Finally, the careless reader, who came to identify the distinction between primary and secondary rules with that between duty-imposing and power-conferring rules, may be misled into regarding the rule of recognition as power-conferring, whereas in fact it is a duty-imposing rule. All these confusions are caused by the fact that the classification of rules into primary and secondary is meant to serve two incompatible purposes. It is sometimes regarded as a distinction between normative types, sometimes as a distinction between social functions.

10

LAW AND VALUE IN ADJUDICATION*

1. THE PROBLEM

One constant source of objections to the view that all law derives exclusively from social sources[1] is the extent to which source-based and non-source-based considerations in adjudication are interwoven. This essay presents an outline of a positivist view of adjudication. The subject is inexhaustible and is perhaps the one aspect of jurisprudence which has more than any other affected judicial practices and judicial self-awareness. The purpose of the following remarks is more limited. They are confined to the examination of three or four problems concerning the interaction of law and value in adjudication.

Adjudicative institutions vary greatly from one country to another. Their practices are usually the product of informal traditions and slow evolution. It is more than likely that judicial institutions in modern industrial societies tend to develop similar practices, but in the absence of any evidence to that effect the following comments will be concerned with the English doctrine of precedent, though it may be hoped that parts of the analysis may be relevant to other legal systems as well. Of the local circumstances which contribute to the shape of the English doctrine of precedent three may briefly be mentioned. First, there is the custom of judges to write fairly long opinions or judgments justifying their view, regardless of whether they agree or disagree with other judges sitting in the same case. Not unnaturally, a large part of any judgment is usually dedicated to an analysis of the intention and meaning of judgments in previous cases. Second is the perhaps connected fact that English judges tend to pay little attention to the work of academic lawyers. Most debates are among and with judges. Finally, the English judiciary is small and highly centralized.

---

* I am indebted to P. S. Atiyah, A. M. Honoré, and C. McCrudden for helpful comments on an early draft of this essay.

[1] See on the sources thesis Essay 3 above. There the motivation for adopting the thesis was explained. Essay 4 established certain theoretical consequences of the thesis concerning the close interaction of law and morals in adjudication.

It is recruited exclusively from the Bar (itself small), comes from a more or less homogeneous social background, and is unified by strong professional and social ties into a relatively cohesive social group where personal authority often carries more weight than any formal rules of precedent.

It is this last fact which complicates and may well frustrate any attempt to provide a normative description of the rules and practices of precedent. My observations are meant to be faithful to the accepted theory of the practice rather than to the practice itself. Their aim is to explain the way judges and legal scholars regard the working of the doctrine of precedent. Only an empirical study going well beyond the examination of the law reports could reveal to what extent the actual practice conforms to these theories. My first aim is, therefore, descriptive: to highlight and improve our understanding of certain aspects of the doctrine of precedent in English law.[2] My second aim is practical, namely to comment on one or two aspects of the considerations which should guide judges in their law-making activities.[3]

One distinction is fundamental: that between regulated and unregulated cases or disputes. Regulated cases are those which fall under a common law or statutory rule which does not require judicial discretion for the determination of the dispute (rules referring to what is reasonable or just, etc., do require such discretion). A dispute is regulated if questions of the form: 'In this case should the court decide that p?' have a correct legal answer. It is unregulated if some of these questions do not have a correct legal answer, i.e. if there is a gap in the law applying to the case. Unregulated disputes, like regulated ones, are subject to laws applying to them and guiding the courts as to their solution. But since the law applying to unregulated disputes has gaps, no particular solution to the dispute is required by law, though the law may rule out several solutions as inappropriate and give some general guidance concerning the choice between some or all of the remaining possible solutions.[4]

[2] For a thorough and perceptive description of the doctrine cf. Prof. R. Cross, *Precedent in English Law*, 2nd ed. (Oxford, 1968), and Hodgson, *Consequences of Utilitarianism* (Oxford, 1967), chs. 5 and 6.

[3] All the moral arguments presented in this essay take the existence of the doctrine of precedent in its present general form as their starting-point. They are not meant to justify or criticize the existing doctrine itself.

[4] Cf. my 'Legal Principles and the Limits of Law', *Yale Law Journal* 81 (1972), 823

A regulated dispute may be governed by more than one rule, provided that in any case in which conflicting rules apply to a dispute, it is regulated only if a legally valid rule determines how the conflict is to be resolved. In short, a regulated dispute is one to which the law provides a solution. The judge can be seen here in his classical image: he identifies the law, determines the facts, and applies the law to the facts.[5] There is nothing mechanical about this. Regulated cases can be complex and more difficult to decide than unregulated cases. The difficulty in solving a complex tax problem according to law may be much greater than that of solving a natural justice problem according to moral principles. The difference between a regulated and an unregulated dispute is not that only the second calls for the exercise of judgment by the court. Nor is it that in regulated disputes the courts use their legal judgment to apply the law whereas in unregulated disputes they use moral judgment to make law.[6] The classical image mentioned above is misleading. The courts carry with them both their functions of applying pre-existing law and of making new ones into almost all cases (I do not mean they almost always make new laws, only that almost always they have to consider whether to do so). The difference between regulated and unregulated disputes is that because, by definition, in regulated disputes the law provides a solution to the case, the court cannot make new laws except by changing existing ones. Unregulated disputes are, as we shall see, partly regulated, hence the court has to apply existing law as well as to make new law. But since, by definition, in an unregulated dispute the law contains a gap, since it fails to provide a solution to the case, the court can make law without changing existing law. It makes law by filling in the gaps.[7]

---

at 838–42 and 846 on this aspect of judicial law-making in regulated disputes. See further Essay 4 above on the distinction between regulated and unregulated disputes. Partly regulated disputes are here treated as unregulated.

[5] This essay is not concerned with judicial fact-finding.

[6] My remarks presuppose the doctrine of precedent as it exists in English Law. According to it almost all decisions of the Supreme Court or the House of Lords in unregulated disputes create binding precedents. Needless to say, unregulated disputes exist and moral judgment is exercised even in legal systems where legal decisions are not a source of law.

[7] By doing so it will change the truth-value of some legal statements such as: 'The law on this question is unsettled'—if read as a timeless statement. Cf. Essay 4.

Here, then, is the problem this essay is about: To explain how the courts have both a law-applying and a law-creating role in regulated and unregulated disputes alike and how these respective functions differ in the different kinds of disputes. Finally, I shall show how the difference, though conceptually sharp, is gradual in application.

2. REGULATED DISPUTES—DISTINGUISHING

We may begin with a sketch of a simple case of following a binding rule. A reported decision, P, records that in that case where the facts were a, b, c, d, e, g, the decision was based on the rule that whenever A, B, C then X should be decided. (Lower-case letters stand for the particular circumstances of the case as recorded in the judgment—what is and what is not recorded will turn out to be important. Capital letters stand for general properties of facts so that a is an instance of A, etc.) The ruling in P, can be summarized as:

$$P: a, b, c, d, e, g/A, B, C \rightarrow X.$$

The novel case, N, is a case of a_1, b_1, c_1, $\bar{e}_1$ (i.e. not-e_1), f_1 and is thus governed by P, which, it is assumed, is binding on the court. If the court decides to follow P its ruling will be:

$$N: a_1, b_1, c_1, d_1, \bar{e}_1, f_1/A, B, C \rightarrow X.$$

The normal interpretation of the doctrine of precedent is, of course, that it is not up to the court to decide whether to follow a precedent; it is bound to do so (we are after all considering regulated disputes, namely, those governed by binding precedent). Admittedly, this common interpretation has always been difficult to reconcile with the considerable freedom of action experienced and exercised by courts (especially the courts of appeal and the House of Lords) even in the face of a binding precedent. Consequently, most commentators on the doctrine of precedent try to resolve the difficulty by assuming that it is very difficult to discover the *ratio decidendi* of a case. Until fairly recently most of the writings on precedent in English Law (and related systems) were preoccupied with devising ever more sophisticated tests for identifying the *ratio* of a case, which were designed to reconcile the binding force of precedents with the wide discretion judges often have when faced with them.[8] But there is something odd in the supposition that the identification of the *ratio* can be so difficult and mysterious. Essentially the *ratio* is the reason(s) by which the court justifies its decision. Establishing the *ratio* is partly a matter of the interpretation of a document: What is the reason on which a judge relied in reaching his decision as conveyed by his judgment?[9] (It may not have been his only reason. It may not have been his reason at all. But the doctrine of precedent includes the convention that one does not go beyond the written judgments of the courts.) Given that courts often consist of several judges who may disagree in their reasoning even when they agree on the result, the determination of the *ratio* must also rest on some relatively formal rules concerning the way the *ratio* of the court is to be extracted from the reasons on which the various judges rely. This includes the possibility that sometimes a decision will fail to issue in a binding *ratio*.[10] Sometimes these rules for determining the *ratio* may yield indeterminate results: it may be impossible to say what the *ratio* is or to say that there is none. Considerable problems may arise in the interpretation of statutes as well. In the main, however, the identification of the *ratio* of a case is reasonably straightforward. This, however, merely leads back to the question of the compatibility of the well-known and extensive judicial flexibility with the doctrine of precedent.[11]

[8] On the identification of the *ratio* I am following in general lines Prof. C. Cross's definition in *Precedent in English Law*, ibid. He also provides an excellent critical survey of previous attempts to define the concept. In 'The House of Lords and the Doctrine of Precedent', Hacker and Raz (eds.), *Law, Society and Morality* (Oxford, 1977), he showed that the doctrine of precedent does not itself rest on precedent. In English Law it is in fact part of the rule of recognition.

[9] It is sometimes assumed that only the direct and least general reasons of the court's judgment constitute its *ratio*, while more general reasons used to defend and justify the direct ones are mere *obiter*. Cf. Twining and Miers, *How To Do Things with Rules* (London, 1976), pp. 176–81. This view is a necessary result of adopting the tame doctrine of distinguishing which is criticized below. I assume that all the court's reasons of whatever generality are part of the *ratio*.

[10] Or at least none bearing on the main legal controversy in the case. *Haim v. D.P.P.* [1974] 2 All E.R. 41 and *Nissan v. A.-G.* [1970] A.C. 347 are, arguably, such examples. An illustration of the application of formal rules of precedent for deciding whose opinion represents the *ratio* is provided by *Harper v. N.C.B.* [1974] 2 All E.R. 441 at 446. The conclusion reached there was that no binding *ratio* is to be found in *Central Asbestos Co. Ltd. v. Dodd* [1972] 2 All E.R. 1135.

[11] Attempts to reconcile the two through complicated tests for identifying the *ratio* are bound to fail. They lead to the view that the doctrine of precedent is mere pretence

The solution to the problem lies in the role of 'distinguishing' in the working of the doctrine of precedent. Like many other rules moulded and remoulded in the hands of judges in every age and over many years its boundaries are far from fixed. They undergo continual change. There is nevertheless value in a theoretical systematization. There is what I shall call 'the tame view' of distinguishing according to which to distinguish a binding precedent is simply to determine that its *ratio* does not apply to the instant case. The rule laid down in the precedent is that a certain decision is to be rendered if operative facts *A*, *B*, *C* obtain, but the instant case is a case of a_2, b_2, *not-c_2* and therefore the precedent does not apply. On this interpretation there is no special rule of distinguishing in the common law. A rule which does not apply to the case does not apply to it. To distinguish is simply to discover that the rule does not apply. As against this there is another view of distinguishing according to which one distinguishes a rule by changing it so that a rule which did apply to the present case no longer applies to it in its modified form.[12] The rule laid down in *P* was when *A*, *B*, *C* then *X*. Since *N* is a case of a_1, b_1, c_1 the rule applies to it. But the court has a power to distinguish. It can change the rule into *A*, *B*, *C*, *E*, then *X*. This modified rule does not apply to *N*, which is a case of *not-e_1*. The rule in *P* was thus distinguished.

The English doctrine of precedent is that a precedent must be either followed or distinguished (though some courts also have power to overrule their own or other courts' decisions). It combines following precedent with considerable flexibility because it allows the courts, even those bound by precedent, to distinguish a previous decision rather than follow it. Since 'distinguishing' means changing the rule which is being distinguished, the power to distinguish is a power to develop the law even when deciding regulated cases and even by courts which have no power to overrule.

If distinguishing involves changing the rule distinguished

<hr>

to cover up for judicial creativity. J. Stone's *Legal System and Lawyers Reasoning* (London, 1964), is of this nature.

[12] My analysis of distinguishing was influenced by that of A. W. B. Simpson in 'The *Ratio Decidendi* of a Case and the Doctrine of Binding Precedent', Guest (ed.), *Oxford Essays in Jurisprudence*, 1st series (Oxford, 1963). On any view distinguishing differs from holding that a *ratio* is not binding because the decision is *per incuriam*. Only binding decisions can be distinguished.

how does it differ from overruling? Such a difference must exist for every court has the power to distinguish while only some have a power to overrule. Unless distinguishing differs from the general power to modify rules and to make new ones (as in over-ruling or in deciding unregulated disputes) my interpretation of distinguishing means, given the general power to distinguish, that precedents are never binding for the courts are always free to change them. Distinguishing, however, is a very restricted form of law-making. It is subject to two crucial conditions:

(1) The modified rule must be the rule laid down in the precedent restricted by the addition of a further condition for its application.
(2) The modified rule must be such as to justify the order made in the precedent.

The first condition means, first of all, that in distinguishing courts can only narrow down rules. They cannot extend them. (Their power to extend rules will be discussed in section 9 below.) This is a direct consequence of the very function of distinguishing, i.e. modifying a rule to avoid its application to a case to which it does apply as it stands. This, in a precedent-based system, can only be done by restricting the application of the rule through adding to its conditions of application so that the modified rule no longer applies to the instant case. Furthermore, in distinguishing the court cannot replace the previous rule with any rule it may like even if it is narrower in application. The new rule must be based on the old one and contain all the conditions which the old one contains together with the new restricting condition. A, B, C then X is transformed into A, B, C, E then X. The previous conditions are preserved and become the foundation of the new rule.

The second condition restricts the power of the court still further. It limits its choice of the new restricting conditions. It must be such that the modified rule would be a possible alternative basis for the original decision. In our example the original decision was $P: a, b, c, d, e, g/A, B, C \rightarrow X$. Given that the new case is one of $a_1, b_1, c_1, d_1, \bar{e}_1, f_1$ the court will comply with the first condition of distinguishing equally by adopting $A, B, C,$ not-D then X as by adopting A, B, C, E then X. Both are restrictive modifications of the rule in P. But only the second of these satisfies the second condition. A, B, C, *not-D* then X would not in itself justify the order made in P, namely X. Note that the second condition is strong in that it does not merely require that the modified rule will be compatible with the earlier order. A, B, C, *not-D* then X is compatible with the order of X in P, for it does not require a contrary decision. It merely fails to justify the order in P.[13] But that it must do to meet the second condition.

In another respect the second condition is weak or at least ambiguous. Like other aspects of the doctrine of precedent it is concerned not with the actual facts of the case but with their public record. It seems to me that most of the time the doctrine is interpreted as allowing the court to distinguish P by adding the condition that *not-F*. The modified rule A, B, C, *not-F* then X may justify the order in P. There is no record whether it was a case of F or of *not-F* and the latter court is normally allowed the benefit of the doubt in such cases.

There is an indefinite number of different modifications of every rule conforming to the two conditions spelt out above. The court's obligation, however, is to adopt only that modification which will best improve the rule. Hence its real problem is usually limited to a judgment on the relative merits of but a few modifications. Often none will be accepted and the court will have to follow the rule. This will be the case not only when the court is perfectly happy with the rule but also when it would have preferred a different rule altogether but finds no improvement in the modifications it is allowed to make within the narrow boundaries of the rule of distinguishing.

A proper understanding of the substantial limitations the rule imposes on the court's creativity explains how it is possible and reasonable to allow a court that room for flexibility even when it is bound by a precedent. A modified rule can usually be justified only by reasoning very similar to that justifying the original rule. Not only will its justification show the reason for applying the ruling to a subclass of the cases to which it was originally applicable, it will also show the relevance of all the operative

---

[13] All *rationes* can be formulated as setting sufficient conditions. A decision that the absence of A is sufficient to show that the action must be dismissed establishes that A is a necessary condition for such an action to succeed.

conditions set out by the original rule. The second condition above makes it tempting to say that the modified rule was really the rule the original court had in mind but which it failed to articulate clearly. Often enough this may indeed be the case. It may be that the court in *P* was influenced by the fact that the case was one of *E*, but somehow perhaps they took this feature too much for granted, they failed to specify its existence among the operative conditions of their *ratio*. Yet this is not always so and often there is no evidence either way. Nevertheless this feature may hold the key to our understanding of the rationale of giving the court the power to distinguish: courts may be and often are a little careless in formulating rules. They approach the question through the example of one case (or several cases recorded in the law reports) and they do not enjoy the research and drafting facilities generally available to legislators. As a result it is unreasonable to attribute great weight to the actual formulation of the rule in the hands of the court. Statutory interpretation turns sometimes on the employment of one word rather than another. Not so the interpretation of precedent. Another result is that it is reasonable to read the rule in its context (i.e. the facts of the case as recorded) rather than in the abstract as one does a statute or a regulation.[14] The power to distinguish reflects this dependence on context. The *ratio* is binding in its basic rationale and as applying to its original context. Courts can, however, modify its application to different contexts so long as they preserve its fundamental rationale.

It is time to sum up the argument. The simple and initially attractive view that statutory and common law rules bind the courts in the same way (subject to the power to overrule) is hard to reconcile with the considerable flexibility exercised by the courts. This problem led to the mystical view of the identification of the *ratio* as a great occult art of tremendous difficulty, or the view that there is no *ratio* binding on future courts. They are free to invent one and attribute it to the original court (provided they observe some restraints). These mystical views made possible the tame view of distinguishing: to distinguish is to show that the *ratio* does not apply to the present case, a proof made possible by the magical art of interpreting the *ratio*.

[14] Generally at least. Interpreting a statute by the mischief rule comes sometimes close to distinguishing.

Instead, I have argued that common law rules are 'less binding' than statutory ones for the courts have power to modify them through the rule of distinguishing. They are binding in their essential rationale and as applied to their context. But the courts have power to impose further restrictions on their application to avoid having to follow them, so long as they observe the two conditions analysed above. This difference in the binding force of statutory and common law rules is reasonable given the difference in the circumstances in which the two kinds of rules are made. This view of the doctrine of precedent enables one to adopt a simple and straightforward view of the identification of the *ratio*, but it presupposes a 'strong' interpretation of distinguishing, regarding it as a limited form of law-making.

3. REGULATED DISPUTES—OVERRULING

Like distinguishing, overruling is changing a common law rule established by precedent. Unlike the power to distinguish which is vested in all courts and which is frequently used, the power to overrule is more selectively distributed and is used more sparingly. On the other hand, its use is free of the restrictions attached to distinguishing. A court with the appropriate power can overrule a previous decision root and branch and substitute a completely different rule, even a diametrically conflicting one, in its place.

There are two kinds of cases of overruling: first, when a superior court overrules a rule laid down by an inferior court; second, when a court overrules its own previous decision (or one by another court of equal authority). Common to both is the fact that the overruled decision was binding in law until overruled. Since decisions of the courts of appeal are legally binding (and in fact much of the common law rests on no higher authority) a decision by the House of Lords overruling the court of appeal is an instance of the first kind of case, whereas the House of Lords overruling itself is an instance of the second.

In a system based on precedent the power to overrule is necessarily limited. If every court is entitled to overrule any decision of any other court which applies to the case before it whenever it thinks it best to do so, then the legal system does not recognize

the binding force of precedents. Precedents are binding only
when the courts are not free to overrule them whenever they
wish.[15] The restrictions on the power of the courts to deviate
from previous decisions are of three kinds: (1) Restriction on
the kind of rule they may substitute for the existing one; (2)
Conditions which must obtain for them to have the power to
introduce a new rule; (3) Conditions which must obtain before
they may use their power to make a new rule. In the previous
section I argued that restrictions of the first kind (and the first
kind only) characterize the rule about distinguishing. No such
restrictions apply to the power to introduce new rules when the
court has power to overrule. Any new rule which will form the
ratio of the case will become legally binding. In this respect overruling is like a decision in an unregulated dispute and unlike
distinguishing. But the courts' right to overrule is limited by
conditions of the remaining two kinds.

The precise nature of many restrictions is difficult to determine. On occasion it is undetermined in English Law today.
For example, it seems that a decision of the court of appeal purporting to lay down a rule which overrules a rule by the House
of Lords is not legally binding. The court has no power to overrule. But is the same true of a decision by the court of appeal
overruling itself? Or does the latter decision bind despite the
fact that the court should not have reached it? (*Davis v. Johnson*
[1978] 1 All E.R. 1132 is ambiguous on this point.) A restriction
which definitely belongs to the third kind is that a court should
not overrule unless it is certain that the new rule is an improvement compared with the old. Here it is clear that if a court
overrules because it thinks it likely (though it is not certain)
that the new rule is an improvement, its decision is binding de-

---

[15] Cf. the analysis in *Practical Reason and Norms*, section 4.3. The following observations
modify and expand the point made there on pp. 140–1. The attitude of the courts
to overruling was expressed in an extreme form by Lord Reid in *Knuller v. D.P.P.* [1972]
2 All E.R. 898 at 903: 'I dissented in Shaw's case. On reconsideration I still think
that the decision was wrong and I see no reason to alter anything which I said in my
speech. But it does not follow that I should now support a motion to reconsider the
decision. I have said more than once in recent cases that our change of practice in
no longer regarding previous decisions of this House as absolutely binding does not
mean that whenever we think that a previous decision was wrong we should reverse
it. In the general interest of certainty in the law we must be sure that there is some
very good reason before we so act. I think that however wrong or anomalous the decision may be it must stand and apply to cases reasonably analogous unless or until
it is altered by Parliament.'

spite the fact that it acted improperly.[16] As we will see below
(section 7) there is a general reason for courts to observe such
a restraint of caution in almost all their law-creating activities.
It applies with particular force to overruling, for it (unlike decisions in unregulated disputes) upsets established legal rules
and (unlike distinguishing) substitutes a rule which differs substantially from the old one. In such cases the arguments discussed in section 7 apply with greater force. They have also
acquired legal force (whereas in other law-creating activity
they have no more than their inherent moral force). This at
least seems to me the best interpretation of the repeated judicial
self-exhortations to exercise the power to overrule with great
caution (particularly when the House of Lords intends to overrule its own decisions). It is unreasonable to regard these as
implying that a rule should not be replaced by a new one
unless the substitution will be a great improvement. Why not
bring about small improvements? The exhortations obviously
do mean that the court should be very careful to take notice
of the possible bad effects of the very process of changing the
law on the social and economic activities dependent on it. But
beyond that the exhortations seem to reflect an awareness of
the disadvantages under which the courts labour in trying to
assess the different social and economic consequences of different legal arrangements. Hence the need to avoid acting unless one is certain that the change is an improvement, however
small it may be.

   There are no doubt other judicial conventions imposing
other restrictions on the power and right to overrule. Most of
these will be specific to particular legal areas (e.g. the criminal
law). Their exploration will, however, involve a much closer
examination of the details of the English doctrine of precedent
than is appropriate here. The purpose of this essay is to examine
the kinds of cases in which English courts exercise law-making
powers and compare their activities in such cases to their law-
applying activities. Distinguishing and overruling are the two
kinds of powers to change existing common law rules which
the courts have. They also have a more limited power to change
statutory law. This power also will not be examined here. To

---

[16] On the difference between lack of power and a duty not to exercise a power cf.
Practical Reason and Norms, p. 111.

do so will take one deep into the doctrines of statutory interpretation. Suffice it to say that the power is exercised to 'update'
old statutes and adjust their application to contemporary conditions and also to narrow down the application of a statutory
rule where this is desirable and the case is one of open texture.
In both situations the power is very limited, even more than
in distinguishing, though the limitations are different.

4. REGULATED DISPUTES—CLOSURE RULES

One special case of law-making in regulated disputes should
be briefly mentioned. It was pointed out in Essay 4 above that
a dispute may be a regulated one not in virtue of a law governing its solution but because in the absence of any law applying
to it a closure rule comes into operation. For example, since
one of the disputants claims a right to a service from the other
and since no law gives him such a right, he does not have it
and the dispute should be settled in favour of the other party.
In a precedent-based system a court's decision that in certain
cases persons do not have a right against others is itself an
explicit permission and, for the reasons described in Essay 4,
thereafter the case is usually treated for practical purposes
as governed by the explicit permission and is thus subject to
the usual rules of precedent. But so long as the case is governed
by the closure rule alone the doctrine of precedent does not
apply—it does not rest on precedent. Hence though the court
may be able in such a case to change the law (e.g. by granting
a right to the relevant litigant) it will not be distinguishing or
overruling any decision in doing so for by definition there is
none.

It is sometimes assumed that all courts have complete freedom to change the law when it rests on nothing more than
silence, i.e. absence of sources. But this is a mistake. After all
silence may speak louder than words, and a change in the law
is a change in the law, regardless of the way the legal situation
came to be. People rely on the law when it is based on silence
as much as on the common law. The limitations of the courts'
ability to improve the law are not much affected by the basis
of the law they are trying to improve. Thus it is now generally
accepted that the courts have no power or only a very limited
power to create new criminal offences (to do so is often to

change the law in cases now governed by the closure rule that what is not prohibited is permitted). It is true that in other areas the limitations on judicial powers and rights to make law are less restrictive and in some areas their right extends further than under either distinguishing or overruling. The boundaries of the courts' law-making activities in closure rule cases are indeterminate (like so many aspects of the doctrine of precedent). But it is likely that a detailed study will reveal much more than meets the superficial glance.

5. UNREGULATED DISPUTES

All unregulated disputes are due to intended or unintended indeterminacy of language and intention. The most simple kind comprises all the cases which fall within the vague borderlines of various descriptive concepts. Such are cases where it is unclear whether the instrument in question is an electrical appliance for the purpose of VAT, whether a person is domiciled in England, or whether a building is used for dwelling. In these cases the indeterminacy arises because of the vagueness in the criterion for the application of the concept or because the several criteria for its application yield, in the case under consideration, conflicting indications. Not all cases which fall within the borderline area of a legally relevant concept are unregulated. They may fall under a different rule as well and it may resolve the indeterminacy. But many cases are indeterminate for these reasons and appeal to legislative intention is often of no avail, for that intention, even when ascertained, is often itself indeterminate.

Slightly different is the indeterminacy of the cases falling under two conflicting rules, which is due to the absence of an appropriate conflict-resolving rule in the system. Here the verdict of each rule on the case is clear, but the system does not determine which rule is to be followed. It may lack an appropriate conflict-resolving rule altogether or it may include one which is indeterminate in its application to the present case.

It is true that the existence of unregulated disputes is an inevitable result of the indeterminacy of language and intention. Yet not all the existing unregulated disputes are inevitable. Very often legislators and courts when making laws prefer to use less rather than more determinate expressions in their formulation. They prefer to leave unregulated cases whose fate will be determined by the courts in due course, using their discretion within the limits allowed by the law. In such cases the law determines the general legal framework, leaving it to the courts to fill in the gaps which exist in all but the clearest of cases. Rules referring to 'reasonable care', 'good behaviour', 'just cause', 'material change in the use of the premises', 'offensive or abusive behaviour', 'obscene language', 'behaviour likely to lead to breach of the peace', or 'likely to offend religious feelings' are all examples of such deliberately underdetermined rules.

The common law divides such cases into two categories: those in which the gap in each case is filled by the judge, whose opinion becomes a precedent (so that in a sense the gaps narrow with every decision in an unregulated case), and those in which the decision is left to the jury, whose decisions are not explained and therefore not binding precedents. The distinction is tied up with the technical legal distinctions between law and fact and between terms used in a special legal signification to be explained by the court and terms used in their plain, ordinary meaning which the court may not explain but must leave it to the jury to apply. But in substance the decision in each case is a combination of two issues of legal principle. First, whether to regard the underdetermined law as a framework for further legal development filling in the gaps and charting out more and more detailed legal guidelines, or whether to hold that the law should remain underdetermined, the decision being left to the court to take afresh in every case. Second, whether to entrust the decision to judge or jury. The common law holds that generally when it is best to develop the law progressively the job is best done by judges, whereas where it is best to let full discretion reign in each new case the matter is to be entrusted to the jury to inform its decision with the shifting views and attitudes prevailing in society.

6. JUDICIAL LAW-MAKING AND LEGISLATION

In the previous sections the powers of the courts to make law both in regulated disputes (through distinguishing, overruling, and changing law governed by closure rules) and in unregulated ones (underdetermined by law, where the decision is assigned to a judge whose ruling creates a precedent) were described. The description intimated how extensive these law-making powers are. There is hardly a case of importance in which they cannot be used and often they are used. At the same time the description indicates the degree to which the use of these powers is limited and regulated by law. There are no pure law-creating cases. In every case in which the court makes law it also applies laws restricting and guiding its law-creating activities. Unregulated cases are partly, not wholly, unregulated, and distinguishing and overruling are circumscribed and hedged by legal limitations.

These limitations go a long way towards explaining the difference between judicial law-making and legislation. Yet the main conceptual difference is in the constant possibility of distinguishing judge-made law. This means that judge-made law has a different status from legislated law. Strictly speaking judge-made law is binding and valid, just as much as enacted law. But judge-made law is unique in the ample powers the courts have to change it by overruling and distinguishing. The importance of the point is not merely the existence of more numerous repeal powers, but rather in the occasion for their exercise. Judge-made law is constantly subject to potential (though modest) revision on all occasions on which its application is litigated (and it can be litigated in almost all cases to which the law applies). In this respect it can be metaphorically said that judge-made law is less 'binding' than enacted law,

This special revisability of judge-made law is of crucial importance in understanding the difference between enacted law and the common law and also the difference between the law-making function of courts and legislators. It accounts for the sense of organic growth which is so characteristic of the common law. It is typical of common law rules to be moulded and remoulded in the hands of successive courts using explicitly or unconsciously their powers of reformulating and modifying the rules concerned. Hence the reason for the judicial habit of citing the most recent important authorities dealing with a rule in addition to, or even instead of, those cases where the rule was first laid down.

Several further features of the doctrine of precedent help to explain the appropriateness of applying metaphors of organic growth to the common law. Judicial law-making tends to be by way of piecemeal reform. The ability of the courts radically to reshape a substantial area of the law by a single decision is very limited. This is partly due to the power to distinguish itself. It has the result that the wider the principle enunciated by a court the easier it is to distinguish it, to whittle it down. Consequently, judges often avoid pronouncing new general principles and prefer to trim their rulings to fit closely the case at hand. Needless to say, the fact that the bulk of judicial law-making is by way of filling in gaps in unregulated disputes and of distinguishing in regulated ones does in itself limit the opportunities for laying down radically new broad principles. Finally, there is the basic rule that only the *ratio* of the case is binding. Courts can never promulgate a code governing a whole area of law. They are basically limited to laying down single rules or principles. If they pronounce a view in favour of a whole set of principles this view is *obiter* except in so far as it concerns the principle on which the actual decision in the cases rests.

These explanations of the piecemeal progress of the common law are not meant to deny that over the years the common law may undergo radical transformation. Nor do they diminish the important contributions of single judgments by great judges to such developments. The very knowledge that one's pronouncements from the Bench can later be revised and moderated, while acting to restrain many judges from departing too far from existing doctrine, does on occasion encourage bold spirits to experiment. A judge may voice far-reaching innovative ideas hoping that they will bear fruits while enjoying the assurance that if they fall on unreceptive ground, or prove to be barren, the way of retreat is always open. This too is an important feature of the common law, but it exists against the more usual background of a succession of small-scale accumulating changes.

It is easy to see that this major difference between judicial law-making and legislation is not without justification. It is just what one would expect given the lack of special qualification in the Bench to carry out major law-reform. The judges' training and practice familiarize them with the detailed problems arising from the application of existing legal doctrines. It reveals to them opportunities and needs to extend or to attenuate the operation of those doctrines or to resolve conflicts or anomalies in their application. But nothing prepares them to rethink radically the fundamental assumptions on which the law is based. Similar observations apply to the submissions before the courts by the attorneys of the litigants.

7. CONSERVATIVE RESTRAINTS

The previous section explains the difference between judicial law-making and legislation in terms of the more limited powers (in cases of distinguishing and of filling in gaps) and effects of the former. Such an account assumes that it is possible to distinguish between the roles of the courts in applying and making law. The concomitant of this view is the conclusion that within the admitted boundaries of their law-making powers courts act and should act just as legislators do, namely, they should adopt those rules which they judge best. This is their only remaining legal duty. That it is a legal duty follows directly from the fact that by law the courts are not allowed to act arbitrarily; not even when making new law. They must exercise their judgment in order to reach the best solution. The difference between judicial law-applying and law-making is not that between reasoned and arbitrary judgment. It is the difference between rules imposed by authority which the courts are bound to apply (subject to the qualifications noted in sections 2 and 3 above) whether they like them or not and rules which they follow because they judge them to be suitable.

The last point must be somewhat qualified. The limitation on the law-making power of the courts and the existence of legal duties which they are bound to observe in exercising such powers may prevent the courts from adopting the best rule and may force them on occasion to settle for the second best. (It should be remembered that no attempt is here made to survey all such limits and duties—my aim is merely to outline the framework of the common law doctrine of precedent.) Yet essentially it is true that in the exercise of their law-making power the courts should—within the legally imposed restrictions—act as one expects Parliament to act, i.e. by adopting the best rules they can find.

This last statement has often been criticized. Much of the criticism is confused. It is sometimes said that courts do not have law-making powers for they are not democratically elected. Quite apart from the fact that, given the supremacy of Parliament, judge-made law is no more undemocratic than much delegated legislation,[17] the objection is at best a criticism of the existence of judicial law-making powers. It provides no evidence that they do not exist. The same is true of the objection that such powers mean that judge-made law is retroactively applied (to the instant case and all cases litigated after the precedent was laid down but where the cause of action occurred before it). It may be worth noting that the objection to retroactive law-making is based on the frustration of justified expectations. Such an objection to judicial law-making has no force at all when unregulated disputes or any hard and controversial legal case is concerned since no justifiable expectations can arise in such cases. The force of the retroactivity objection is confined to clear instances of distinguishing and is particularly acute in cases of overruling, where it accounts for the courts' great reluctance to overrule on any but the clearest grounds (cf. section 3 above).[18]

The view that the courts in making law are, subject occasionally to specific legal restraint imposed on their powers (cf. footnote 4 above), to act just as legislators do can be supported by many quotations from the Bench. Two references will have to do here. This view is supported by Lord Wilberforce in *Milliangos v. George Frank (Textile) Ltd*. [1975] 3 All E.R. at p. 812 (opposite the letter g) and by Lord Reid in *British Railways Bd. v. Herrington* [1972] 1 All E.R. at p. 757 where he said:

The question, then, is to what extent this House sitting in its judicial capacity can do what Parliament failed to do in 1957. I dislike usurping the functions of Parliament. But it appears to me that we are confronted with the choice of following Addie and putting the clock back or drastically modifying the Addie rules. It is suggested that such a modification can be achieved by developing the law as laid down in

[17] The situation is different in countries—like the U.S.A.—in which judicial decisions in certain constitutional cases cannot be reversed by the democratic legislature. The justification of such powers is bound up with the justification of having a constitution limiting the power of the majority.

[18] Judges often anticipate major overrulings with several *obiters* or off-the-Bench pronouncements, thus indicating the vulnerability of that branch of the law to revision. The law is still formally settled but people are put on notice not to rely on it. The 'vice' of retroactivity is here avoided. Instead we have the disadvantages of uncertainty which apply to all unregulated disputes.

Addie's case without actually overruling any part of the decision. I do not think that that is possible. It can properly be said that one is developing the law laid down in a leading case so long but only so long as the 'development' does not require us to say that the original case was wrongly decided. But it appears to me that any acceptable 'development' of Addie's case must mean that Addie's case if it arose today would be decided the other way. The case for the pursuer in Addie's case was stronger on the facts than the case for the present respondent and I do not think that we could dismiss this appeal without holding or at least necessarily implying that Addie's case was wrongly decided.

Thus clearly asserting his right to 'do what Parliament failed to do in 1957'.

The great number of similar judicial utterances does not, however, resolve the remaining doubts whether within the legally imposed bounds the courts are indeed completely free to act on their own judgment as to which is the best rule to be adopted. It is sometimes felt that judges are never free to follow their own judgment, that the body of existing legal doctrine should always determine their decision. Even unregulated disputes are, it is said, so determined by arguments of analogy which extend the force of existing rules beyond their direct range of application. I shall argue that whatever truth there is in such views is consistent—once it is purified of the exaggerations involved in their traditional statements—with the thesis that in their law-making judges do rely and should rely on their own moral judgment.

The simple but basic truth which is the clue to our problem is that the mere fact that two people act on their moral judgment is no guarantee—even if they share the same moral views and the same information—that they will decide on the same action. Because of differences in their circumstances and in their abilities they may correctly conclude that different courses of action are appropriate to each of them. In other words, though both courts and legislators act, in making law, on their own best judgment there is a perceivable difference in their law-making actions (not in every single case but in their general pattern) which is totally explicable by the difference in their circumstances and powers.

The circumstances under which the courts operate impose

certain moral requirements on them which do not apply (at least not to the same degree) to legislators. The circumstances referred to are none other than those analysed above, namely, the piecemeal nature of judicial law-making resulting from the fact that so much of it concerns filling in gaps within existing legal frameworks in unregulated disputes and with modifying rules while preserving the main part of their rationale through distinguishing. Most law-making decisions are concerned with extending existing doctrines, successively adjusting them to gradually changing technological, economic, or social conditions and introducing small alterations to avoid the undesirable and unintended consequences of applying rules to circumstances which were not foreseen when those rules were laid down. Such maintenance, repair, and conservation are the function of much legislated law as well. In this respect there is no substantial difference between precedent and legislation. But there is here already a difference in the public image of the institutions. In thinking of legislation one tends to think more of its innovative, reforming role than of its conserving role, which is more prominent in our image of the courts' law-making role.

The real morally relevant difference lies in the conditions for introducing far-reaching reforms. The law affects social and economic conditions through the complex interaction of many legal provisions with various social and economic conditions which are usually at least partly unknown and invariably complex. It is a well-known truism that changes in the law do not always achieve their 'obvious' effects: the legally imposed duty to equalize women's pay may lead to women's unemployment, etc. A major reform in property law may necessitate changes in Torts, criminal law, family law, and planning law to make sure that its objectives are achieved.

For all the reasons explained above it is usually impossible for the courts to introduce in one decision all the changes necessary for the effective implementation of a radical reform in any aspect of the law. The choice a court will face is one between taking a first step towards reform in the hope that with time the work will be completed by other decisions (or by legislation) or to remain faithful to existing doctrines. Such a choice is often very hard since partial measures not only fall short of producing the good which a complete reform may bring, but they often have bad consequences. Partial reform introduces a new discordant element into an existing doctrine. It means that the law will now include provisions reflecting and pursuing different and inconsistent social goals. It incorporates pragmatically conflicting provisions. Normative conflict exists when two valid requirements cannot both be complied with. Pragmatic conflict is a wider concept. Laws conflict pragmatically if one is designed to promote or sustain a state of affairs which cannot coexist with that which the other is designed to promote or sustain. A law sustains or promotes a state of affairs not only through compliance with its requirements but also through actions using rights, powers, or permissions it grants and through the social and economic consequences of such behaviour. Partial reform does not involve normative conflict but it invariably introduces pragmatic conflict into the law.

Parliament does not normally have to choose between partial reform and conservatism. It can opt for radical reform (though for a variety of reasons this is not always a practical option). The courts are invariably presented with this choice. The adverse consequences of partial reform with its attendant pragmatic discord leads the courts very often to opt for a conservative policy. Such a preference is justified in many cases. But not always do the courts choose the conservative route nor is it always justified. The pragmatic discord may quickly be resolved if the remaining reforming measures follow within a short period of time. The evils of the existing doctrine may be grave enough to justify even partial reform with its undesirable by-products. These and similar considerations may frequently justify the courts in taking bold steps, however incomplete they may be.

8. ANALOGICAL REASONING

In the previous section I have tried to explain why it is that even though, within certain limits, the courts, just as legislators, are required to act on their own judgment, they will often, if acting rationally, reach different conclusions from those which legislators should rationally arrive at. The difference derives from the systematic difference in the circumstances in which they operate. Without justifying any particular judicial decisions and without approving of the over-all balance between conservatism and reform struck by English judges in recent times, it is evident that they are aware of the problems inherent in partial reform as outlined in the previous section. This awareness is manifested in the widespread use of argument by analogy.

A court relies on analogy whenever it draws on similarities or dissimilarities between the present case and previous cases which are not binding precedents applying to the present case. Take our example of the ruling in P:

$$P: a, b, c, d, e, g/A, B, C \to X.$$

If the facts in the new case N_1 include a_1, b_1, and c_1, there is no room for argument by analogy with P. N_1 falls directly under the rule in P which is, it is being assumed, binding on the court in N_1. Suppose, however, that the new case is N_2 which is a case of a_2, b_2, $\bar{c}_2$, d_2, $\bar{e}_2$. The ruling in P does not apply to the facts of N_2. Yet the two cases are similar in some respects. They are both cases of A, B, D. That analogy is *not* binding on the court. There is, by hypothesis, no binding rule of law to the effect that A, $B \to X$, or A, B, $D \to X$. In other words argument by analogy is not a method of discovering which rules are legally binding because of the doctrine of precedent. That discovery requires nothing more than an interpretation of the precedent to establish its *ratio*. Analogical argument is a form of justification of new rules laid down by the courts in the exercise of their law-making discretion. As such it succeeds when it helps to establish that the rule adopted by the court is the best it can adopt.

What are the conditions which a successful argument by analogy must meet? One talks of argument by analogy whenever the court relies on the existence of similarities with previous decisions, but naturally not all such reliance is justified. How is one to judge? Two major difficulties hinder a clear analysis of analogical argument. The first is the difficulty of providing a general test for relevance of similarities. The second difficulty, which compounds the first, is the problem of explaining how analogical arguments can be forceful and non-binding at the same time.

Compare P and N_2: they resemble each other with respect to *A* and *B* which were thought relevant in *P* and also in respect of *D* which was not thought relevant. They are dissimilar regarding *C* (relevant) and *E* (not relevant to the rule in *P*). Clearly it is not the number of the differences but their importance which counts. What, however, is the test of that importance?

The answer lies in the rationale of the rule in *P*—the reasons for having it, the purpose it serves. It is this which explains the role and importance of the conditions laid down in it. By its very nature the justification of a rule is more abstract and more general than the rule it justifies. Therefore just as it justifies this rule it could justify another. If this rule is justified as a way of achieving a certain purpose, or of protecting a certain value, so might other rules be if they promote the same purpose or protect the same value in different ways or under different circumstances. One example will have to do here: in *D v. NSPCC* [1977] 1 All E.R. 589) the House of Lords had to decide whether the NSPCC is entitled to refuse to disclose the identity of one of their informers despite the fact that his identity is relevant to an action for negligence against the NSPCC. Existing rules compel the NSPCC to produce the information. There is, however, a rule allowing departments of the government to withhold relevant evidence when its production will harm the public interest in the proper and efficient functioning of the government. This rule does not cover the NSPCC, which is not a government department. The Lords, however, found sufficient similarity between cases governed by this rule and the present case to justify changing the law and extending the rule to protect the anonymity of NSPCC informers. The similarity is in the statutory *functions* which the NSPCC fulfils and those of various government agencies (police, social services, etc.). This similarity is sufficient because the purpose of the original rule is to secure the efficient exercise of powers of a certain character. One way of doing this is by providing protection to government departments. But the same purpose equally justifies extending the protection to other bodies fulfilling similar functions.

This is a brief and crude summary of a long and subtle judgment. The case itself is simple since the analogy drawn is just between one rule and the new case. Often analogies to a number of rules are invoked. But the case illustrates the general technique of analogical arguments—reliance on partial similarities to extend a rule (A, B, $C \rightarrow X$ in P may simply be extended in N_2 by dropping a condition to yield A, $B \rightarrow X$) or to create another rule leading to the same result (N_2 may lay down the new rule A, B, $D \rightarrow X$ which will coexist with the old one in P) when such a change in the law is justified by the same purpose or value which justifies the original rule on which the analogy is based (namely A, B, $C \rightarrow X$).

This then is the answer to the first difficulty: the test of relevance for similarities is the underlying justification of the rule which forms the basis of the analogy. Argument by analogy is essentially an argument to the effect that if a certain reason is good enough to justify one rule then it is equally good to justify another which similarly follows from it.

These remarks implicitly contain the solution to the second difficulty in the explanation of analogical argument: if analogical argument has any force at all how can it fail to be absolutely binding? Why is it only one guide for the courts' exercise of their law-making discretion? The first thing to note is that argument by analogy does not in itself justify the new rule supposedly based on it. All it shows is that if the old rule is justified so is the new one. But then, it may be contended, analogical arguments are themselves without any force: if the old rule is a bad one and its supposed justification is faulty then it should not be relied on to generate a new rule. If, on the other hand, the justification is valid and good it can be relied upon to generate a new rule regardless of whether or not it is also the justification of an existing rule. Either way there is no force in the analogy as such. There is some truth in this argument, but ultimately it fails through overlooking the predicament of partial reform as described in the previous section. That predicament stems from the objection to partial reform based on its alleged bad by-products resulting from the introduction of pragmatic conflicts into the law. Argument by analogy shows that the new rule is a conservative one, that it does not introduce new discordant and conflicting purposes or value into the law, that its purpose and the values it promotes are already served by existing rules.

This is the force of the analogical argument, but this is also its limitation. As was noted in the previous section, though there is reason to avoid pragmatic conflicts, that reason is overridden if the conflict is likely to be short-lived or if, for any other reason, its undesirable consequences are less undesirable than the consequences of perpetuating and extending the scope of bad legal rules and doctrines. This is why analogical arguments have some force but are not conclusive. They establish coherence of purpose with certain parts of the law. This is a relevant consideration, but there are others.

It is often felt that analogical arguments are inconclusive because there are many incompatible analogies which can be drawn and the courts choose which ones to draw on other independent grounds. This is a valid point, but its significance is misunderstood if it is supposed that it shows that analogical argument is a mere window-dressing. The point is valid to the extent that the law already contains pragmatic conflicts. When rules P_1 and P_2 promote conflicting social goals, the court will have to choose whether to introduce a new rule N_1 promoting the same goal as P_1 or N_2 which promotes the goal of P_2. That choice will not be based on analogy (except where it relies on one of the existing rules being deviant and out of step with the goals of the bulk of the law). But the fact that whichever rule the court adopts is analogical to some existing rule is still relevant in showing that the court is not introducing a new pragmatic conflict but is supporting one side in an existing dispute, so to speak.

One controversy among students of judicial reasoning in England and elsewhere (much the same problems arise concerning the use of analogy by courts in a number of countries) concerns the status of analogical argument. Some, noting the possibility of drawing different analogies leading to different conclusions in many cases and the fact that other considerations may justify refusing the conclusion, have concluded that analogical argument is mere window-dressing, a form of argument without legal or other force resorted to for cosmetic reasons. Others regard it as a powerful tool which is legally binding and is the only route to the correct solution of all hard cases.[19] The analysis offered above is yet another attempt to

---

[19] Professor Dworkin's theory of adjudication is the most extreme case of total faith in analogical arguments. In 'Hard Cases', *Harvard Law Review* (1975), p. 1057, reprinted

steer a middle course. It explains why analogical arguments are always morally relevant to the question whether and how should the courts use their law-making powers. It also explains why analogical arguments can point in different directions and why they are only one of a myriad considerations the courts should (morally) bear in mind.

The relevance of analogical argument is appreciated by the judiciary even though the reasons for it may sometimes be misunderstood. Despite this there is no point in saying that judges are *legally* obliged to use analogical arguments. There are no legally agreed standards on how such arguments should be used beyond the general advice that they should be used to establish harmony of purpose between the proposed and established rules and that they should be assigned the weight which it is morally right to give them. Analogical arguments are and should be used according to their inherent moral relevance. There are no special legal requirements concerning their use.

9. THE CONTINUITY OF APPLYING AND MAKING LAW

The analysis of judicial reasoning in this essay is inevitably simplified and one-sided. It is simplified for it attempts to isolate the elementary steps in judicial reasoning. Decisions in important cases involve reference to many rules of law, some of which are followed, some distinguished, while others provide the basis for various analogies. This complexity is not represented in the analysis here presented. The analysis provides, however, the means for understanding complex judicial arguments. The discussion above was also one-sided. It concentrated on the relations between law and value in judicial reasoning and neglected other questions. The judicial method

---

in *Taking Rights Seriously* (London, 1977), he propounded a view according to which judges are obliged to solve all legal cases on the basis of a total analogy—to all the existing statutory and common law rules. Such a total analogy is necessary to yield the best theory of political morality which best justifies all existing statutory and common law rules and which entails a legally binding correct solution to all hard cases.

Professor Dworkin has thus opted for the most conservative interpretation of the judicial role: Judges are neither legally nor morally entitled to assume a reforming role. They must rely only on analogical arguments which perpetuate and extend the existing legal ideology. For a criticism of Professor Dworkin's views see my 'Professor Dworkin's Theory of Rights', *Political Studies* (1978), p. 123.

of restricting previous rules by distinguishing them was analysed at length, but little was said, for example, about ways of
extending the scope of rules. The reason is simple. There are
no formal legal rules about how courts may extend rules. (Nor
are all the cases of restricting rules governed by the rule of distinguishing. Whenever a court overrules it may narrow the scope
of the overturned rule.) Sometimes one extends one rule by distinguishing and thus narrowing the scope of another rule which
creates an exception to the first. Sometimes various separate
rules are united into a new and wider doctrine which in effect
extends the scope of the old rules. Analogical arguments are
often used to support the case for new and independent rules
by showing that they serve the same broad aims as existing ones.
Equally often they are used to support the case for replacing
a narrow rule by a more comprehensive one which, by stipulating that the legal result which the original rule provided for
should apply to the original and to other circumstances, extends
the scope of the old rule. These and other facets of judicial
reasoning remain to be explored. Their exploration would be
based on the foundations laid in the analysis above.

One remaining problem should be confronted now. The view
defended above is that the courts make law in unregulated disputes. They do so regardless of whether they are aware of the
fact that they do. This makes for an important conceptual difference between legislative and judicial law-making. A legislative action is an action intentionally changing the law. Judicial
law-making need not be intentional. A judge may make a new
rule in a decision which he thinks is a purely law-applying decision. Nowadays judges are for the most part fully aware of
their law-making powers. Yet this conceptual distinction has
not lost its importance. Even though judges know that they
often make law, they do not always judge correctly whether
a particular point made in a judgment is innovative or applicative. It is naturally of crucial importance to the proper functioning of the administration of justice that judicial decisions are
valid regardless of whether the court correctly identified their
character as innovative or applicative.

Notwithstanding all these facts it may be surprising that the
courts do not take more trouble to identify the exact borderline
between the parts of their judgements concerned with applying

and creating law. Since the two are radically different one would have expected—it is sometimes said—that the courts will divide their judgment into clearly defined parts employing radically different reasons to justify their law-applying and law-creating conclusions. This, of course, does not happen. Though the courts often indicate their awareness that different kinds of arguments are appropriate when they consider using law-making powers, they often also mover imperceptibly from one function to the other. Nor will anyone who accepts the analysis offered in this article be surprised by the existence of strong continuity between law-applying and law-making.

The continuity is not uniform in all types of cases. Overruling is normally clearly identified and moral, economic, etc., arguments are on the whole freely used. By and large this is also true of distinguishing, though here the confusion over what counts as *ratio* and the limited scope for reform often tend to blur the border between following and distinguishing a precedent.[20] In cases of indeterminacy there is often no clear divide between application and innovation. Whether or not a case falls within the vague, indeterminate borderline area of a descriptive concept is often itself an indeterminate issue. In such decisions the continuity is complete.

The really important point to bear in mind, however, is that on most occasions the reasoning justifying law-making decisions is similar to and continuous with decisions interpreting and applying law. This is so in all cases of small-scale or conservative judicial law-making. Argument by analogy, used in law-making, involves interpreting the purpose and rationale of existing legal rules; these are equally essential for a correct interpretation and application of the law. Analogy is used in law-making to show harmony of purpose between existing laws and a new one. It is also used in interpretation through the assumption that the law-maker wished to preserve harmony of objectives and his Acts should be interpreted as designed to pursue goals compatible with those of related rules. The use of analogy both for law-making and for interpretation is merely an example of the fact that in general the same or very similar

---

[20] Often the courts minimize the extent to which a decision is innovative in order to avoid the need to bear full responsibility for it or to avoid having to justify it by long and explicit arguments.

types of argument are relevant for both purposes. In most cases of interpreting relatively modern law it can be assumed, other things being equal, that the intention and purpose of the law-maker was to promote reasonable goals. Thus indirectly interpretation no less than law-making, involves evaluating different goals.

The fact that the same kind of arguments are used in applying and creating laws does not show that there is no difference between the two activities. The arguments are used under different assumptions and are assigned different roles and weights. But the occurrence of the same type of arguments in both kinds of judicial reasoning explains why the courts often do not bother to define explicitly which function they are fulfilling at any given stage in their reasoning. As we saw, for the most part such continuity of argument exists where it is inevitable, namely, in un-regulated disputes where the indeterminacy does not allow sharp distinctions between applying and making law. It is not by chance that in such cases in particular very similar arguments are normally appropriate for either activity. It is perhaps apt to end on the theme of continuity of argument between law-applying and law-making for it has been the main objective of this article to demonstrate the intricate interconnection between these two judicial activities while maintaining that despite this intricacy the two are conceptually distinct and mutually present in the working of the English courts.

11

THE RULE OF LAW AND ITS VIRTUE*

F. A. Hayek has provided one of the clearest and most powerful formulations of the ideal of the rule of law: 'stripped of all technicalities this means that government in all its actions is bound by rules fixed and announced beforehand—rules which make it possible to foresee with fair certainty how the authority will use its coercive powers in given circumstances, and to plan one's individual affairs on the basis of this knowledge'.[1] At the same time the way he draws certain conclusions from this ideal illustrates one of the two main fallacies in the contemporary treatment of the doctrine of the rule of law: the assumption of its overriding importance. My purpose is to analyse the ideal of the rule of law in the spirit of Hayek's quoted statement of it and to show why some of the conclusions which he drew from it cannot be thus supported. But first we must be put on our guard against the other common fallacy concerning the rule of law.

Not uncommonly when a political ideal captures the imagination of large numbers of people its name becomes a slogan used by supporters of ideals which bear little or no relation to the one it originally designated. The fate of 'democracy' not long ago and of 'privacy' today are just two examples of this familiar process. In 1959 the International Congress of Jurists meeting in New Delhi gave official blessing to a similar perversion of the doctrine of the rule of law.

The function of the legislature in a free society under the Rule of Law is to create and maintain the conditions which will uphold the dignity of man as an individual. This dignity requires not only the recognition of his civil and political rights but also the establishment of the social,

---

* First published in *The Law Quarterly Review* (1977). A draft of this paper was presented to a conference sponsored by the Liberty Fund and the University of San Francisco. I am grateful to Rolf Sartorius, Douglas Hutchinson, and David Libling for useful suggestions on ways to improve an early draft of the paper.
[1] *The Road to Serfdom* (London, 1944), p. 54.

economic, educational and cultural conditions which are essential to the full development of his personality.[2]

The report goes on to mention or refer to just about every political ideal which has found support in any part of the globe during the post-war years.

If the rule of law is the rule of the good law then to explain its nature is to propound a complete social philosophy. But if so the term lacks any useful function. We have no need to be converted to the rule of law just in order to discover that to believe in it is to believe that good should triumph. The rule of law is a political ideal which a legal system may lack or may possess to a greater or lesser degree. That much is common ground. It is also to be insisted that the rule of law is just one of the virtues which a legal system may possess and by which it is to be judged. It is not to be confused with democracy, justice, equality (before the law or otherwise), human rights of any kind or respect for persons or for the dignity of man. A non-democratic legal system, based on the denial of human rights, on extensive poverty, on racial segregation, sexual inequalities, and religious persecution may, in principle, conform to the requirements of the rule of law better than any of the legal systems of the more enlightened Western democracies. This does not mean that it will be better than those Western democracies. It will be an immeasurably worse legal system, but it will excel in one respect: in its conformity to the rule of law.

Given the promiscuous use made in recent years of the expression 'the rule of law' it is hardly surprising that my claim will alarm many. We have reached the stage in which no purist can claim that truth is on his side and blame the others for distorting the notion of the rule of law. All that I can claim for my account is, first, that it presents a coherent view of one important virtue which legal systems should possess and, secondly, that it is not original, that I am following in the footsteps of Hayek and of many others who understood 'the rule of law' in similar ways.

[2] Clause 1 of the report of Committee I of the International Congress of Jurists at New Delhi, 1959.

1. THE BASIC IDEA

'The rule of law' means literally what it says: the rule of the law. Taken in its broadest sense this means that people should obey the law and be ruled by it.[3] But in political and legal theory it has come to be read in a narrower sense, that the government shall be ruled by the law and subject to it. The ideal of the rule of law in this sense is often expressed by the phrase 'government by law and not by men'. No sooner does one use these formulas than their obscurity becomes evident. Surely government must be both by law and by men. It is said that the rule of law means that all government action must have foundation in law, must be authorized by law. But is not that a tautology? Actions not authorized by law cannot be the actions of the government as a government. They would be without legal effect and often unlawful.

It is true that we can elaborate a political notion of government which is different from the legal one: government as the location of real power in the society. It is in this sense that one can say that Britain is governed by The City or by the trade unions. In this sense of 'government' it is not a tautology to say that government should be based on law. If the trade union ruling a country breaks an industrial relations law in order to impose its will on the Parliament or if the President or the F.B.I. authorize burglaries and conspire to pervert justice they can be said to violate the rule of law. But here 'the rule of law' is used in its original sense of obedience to law. Powerful people and people in government, just like anybody else, should obey the law. This is no doubt correct, and yet does it exhaust the meaning of the rule of law? There is more to the rule of law than the law and order interpretation allows. It means more even than law and order applied to the government. I shall proceed on the assumption that we are concerned with government in the legal sense and with the conception of the rule of law which applies to government and to law and is no mere application of the law and order conception.

The problem is that now we are back with our initial puzzle. If government is, by definition, government authorized by law

---

[3] Cf., on this sense of the phrase, Jennings, *The Law and the Constitution* (London, 1933), pp. 42–5.

the rule of law seems to amount to an empty tautology, not a political ideal.

The solution to this riddle is in the difference between the professional and the lay sense of 'law'. For the lawyer anything is the law if it meets the conditions of validity laid down in the system's rules of recognition or in other rules of the system.[4] This includes the constitution, parliamentary legislation, ministerial regulations, policemen's orders, the regulations of limited companies, conditions imposed in trading licences, etc. To the layman the law consists only of a subclass of these. To him the law is essentially a set of open, general, and relatively stable laws. Government by law and not by men is not a tautology if 'law' means general, open, and relatively stable law. In fact, the danger of this interpretation is that the rule of law might set too strict a requirement, one which no legal system can meet and which embodies very little virtue. It is humanly inconceivable that law can consist only of general rules and it is very undesirable that it should. Just as we need government both by laws and by men, so we need both general and particular laws to carry out the jobs for which we need the law.

The doctrine of the rule of law does not deny that every legal system should consist of both general, open, and stable rules (the popular conception of law) and particular laws (legal orders), an essential tool in the hands of the executive and the judiciary alike. As we shall see, what the doctrine requires is the subjection of particular laws to general, open, and stable ones. It is one of the important principles of the doctrine that *the making of particular laws should be guided by open and relatively stable general rules.*

This principle shows how the slogan of the rule of law and not of men can be read as a meaningful political ideal. The principle does not, however, exhaust the meaning of 'the rule of law' and does not by itself illuminate the reasons for its alleged importance. Let us, therefore, return to the literal sense of 'the rule of law'. It has two aspects: (1) that people should be ruled by the law and obey it, and (2) that the law should be such that people will be able to be guided by it. As was noted above, it is with the second aspect that we are concerned: the law must be capable of being obeyed. A person conforms with

[4] I am here following Hart, *The Concept of Law* (Oxford, 1961), pp. 97–107.

the law to the extent that he does not break the law. But he obeys the law only if part of his reason for conforming is his knowledge of the law. Therefore, if the law is to be obeyed *it must be capable of guiding the behaviour of its subjects*. It must be such that they can find out what it is and act on it.

This is the basic intuition from which the doctrine of the rule of law derives: the law must be capable of guiding the behaviour of its subjects. It is evident that this conception of the rule of law is a formal one. It says nothing about how the law is to be made: by tyrants, democratic majorities, or any other way. It says nothing about fundamental rights, about equality, or justice. It may even be thought that this version of the doctrine is formal to the extent that it is almost devoid of content. This is far from the truth. Most of the requirements which were associated with the rule of law before it came to signify all the virtues of the state can be derived from this one basic idea.

2. SOME PRINCIPLES

Many of the principles which can be derived from the basic idea of the rule of law depend for their validity or importance on the particular circumstances of different societies. There is little point in trying to enumerate them all, but some of the more important ones might be mentioned:

(1) *All laws should be prospective, open, and clear.* One cannot be guided by a retroactive law. It does not exist at the time of action. Sometimes it is then known for certain that a retroactive law will be enacted. When this happens retroactivity does not conflict with the rule of law (though it may be objected to on other grounds). The law must be open and adequately publicized. If it is to guide people they must be able to find out what it is. For the same reason its meaning must be clear. An ambiguous, vague, obscure, or imprecise law is likely to mislead or confuse at least some of those who desire to be guided by it.

(2) *Laws should be relatively stable.* They should not be changed too often. If they are frequently changed people will find it difficult to find out what the law is at any given moment and will be constantly in fear that the law has been changed since they last learnt what it was. But more important still is the fact that people need to know the law not only for short-term decisions

(where to park one's car, how much alcohol is allowed duty free, etc.) but also for long-term planning. Knowledge of at least the general outlines and sometimes even of details of tax law and company law are often important for business plans which will bear fruit only years later. Stability is essential if people are to be guided by law in their long-term decisions.[5]

Three important points are illustrated by this principle. First, conformity to the rule of law is often a matter of degree, not only when the conformity of the legal system as a whole is at stake, but also with respect to single laws. A law is either retroactive or not, but it can be more or less clear, more or less stable, etc. It should be remembered, however, that by asserting that conformity to the principles is a matter of degree, it is not meant that the degree of conformity can be quantitatively measured by counting the number of infringements, or some such method. Some infringements are worse than others. Some violate the principles in a formal way only, which does not offend against the spirit of the doctrine. Secondly, the principles of the rule of law affect primarily the content and form of the law (it should be prospective, clear, etc.) but not only them. They also affect the manner of government beyond what is or can usefully be prescribed by law. The requirement of stability cannot be usefully subject to complete legal regulation. It is largely a matter for wise governmental policy. Thirdly, though the rule of law concerns primarily private citizens as subject to duties and governmental agencies in the exercise of their powers (on which more below), it is also concerned with the exercise of private powers. Power-conferring rules are designed to guide behaviour and should conform to the doctrine of rule of law if they are to be capable of doing so effectively.

(3) *The making of particular laws (particular legal orders) should be guided by open, stable, clear, and general rules.* It is sometimes assumed that the requirement of generality is of the essence of the rule of law. This notion derives (as noted above) from the literal interpretation of 'the rule of law' when 'law' is read in its lay connotations as being restricted to general, stable, and open law. It is also reinforced by a belief that the rule of law

[5] Of course, uncertainty generated by instability of law also affects people's planning and action. If it did not, stability would not have any impact either. The point is that only if the law is stable are people guided by *their knowledge of the content of the law.*

is particularly relevant to the protection of equality and that equality is related to the generality of law. The last belief is, as has often been noted before, mistaken. Racial, religious, and all manner of discrimination are not only compatible but often institutionalized by general rules.

The formal conception of the rule of law which I am defending does not object to particular legal orders as long as they are stable, clear, etc. But of course particular legal orders are mostly used by government agencies to introduce flexibility into the law. A police constable regulating traffic, a licensing authority granting a licence under certain conditions, all these and their like are among the more ephemeral parts of the law. As such they run counter to the basic idea of the rule of law. They make it difficult for people to plan ahead on the basis of their knowledge of the law. This difficulty is overcome to a large extent if particular laws of an ephemeral status are enacted only within a framework set by general laws which are more durable and which impose limits on the unpredictability introduced by the particular orders.

Two kinds of general rules create the framework for the enactment of particular laws: those which confer the necessary powers for making valid orders and those which impose duties instructing the power-holders how to exercise their powers. Both have equal importance in creating a stable framework for the creation of particular legal orders.

Clearly, similar considerations apply to general legal regulations which do not meet the requirement of stability. They too should be circumscribed to conform to a stable framework. Hence the requirement that much of the subordinate administrative law-making should be made to conform to detailed ground rules laid down in framework laws. It is essential, however, not to confuse this argument with democratic arguments for the close supervision of popularly elected bodies over law-making by non-elected ones. These further arguments may be valid but have nothing to do with the rule of law, and though sometimes they reinforce rule of law type arguments, on other occasions they support different and even conflicting conclusions.

(4) *The independence of the judiciary must be guaranteed.* It is of the essence of municipal legal systems that they institute judicial

bodies charged, among other things, with the duty of applying the law to cases brought before them and whose judgments and conclusions as to the legal merits of those cases are final. Since just about any matter arising under any law can be subject to a conclusive court judgment, it is obvious that it is futile to guide one's action on the basis of the law if when the matter comes to adjudication the courts will not apply the law and will act for some other reasons. The point can be put even more strongly. Since the court's judgment establishes conclusively what is the law in the case before it, the litigants can be guided by law only if the judges apply the law correctly.[6] Otherwise people will only be able to be guided by their guesses as to what the courts are likely to do—but these guesses will not be based on the law but on other considerations.

The rules concerning the independence of the judiciary—the method of appointing judges, their security of tenure, the way of fixing their salaries, and other conditions of service—are designed to guarantee that they will be free from extraneous pressures and independent of all authority save that of the law. They are, therefore, essential for the preservation of the rule of law.

(5) *The principles of natural justice must be observed.* Open and fair hearing, absence of bias, and the like are obviously essential for the correct application of the law and thus, through the very same considerations mentioned above, to its ability to guide action.

(6) *The courts should have review powers over the implementation of the other principles.* This includes review of both subordinate and parliamentary legislation and of administrative action, but in itself it is a very limited review—merely to ensure conformity to the rule of law.

(7) *The courts should be easily accessible.* Given the central position of the courts in ensuring the rule of law (see principles 4 and 6) it is obvious that their accessibility is of paramount importance. Long delays, excessive costs, etc., may effectively turn the most enlightened law to a dead letter and frustrate one's ability effectively to guide oneself by the law.

---

[6] I am not denying that courts also make law. This principle of the rule of law applies to them primarily in their duty to apply the law. As law-makers they are subject to the same principles as all law-makers.

(8) *The discretion of the crime-preventing agencies should not be allowed to pervert the law.* Not only the courts but also the actions of the police and the prosecuting authorities can subvert the law. The prosecution should not be allowed, for example, to decide not to prosecute for commission of certain crimes, or for crimes committed by certain classes of offenders. The police should not be allowed to allocate its resources so as to avoid all effort to prevent and detect certain crimes or prosecute certain classes of criminals.

This list is very incomplete. Other principles could be mentioned and those which have been mentioned need further elaboration and further justification (why—as required by the sixth principle—should the courts and not some other body be in charge of reviewing conformity to the rule of law? etc.).[7] My purpose in listing them was merely to illustrate the power and fruitfulness of the formal conception of the rule of law. It should, however, be remembered that in the final analysis the doctrine rests on its basic idea that the law should be capable of providing effective guidance. The principles do not stand on their own. They must be constantly interpreted in the light of the basic idea.

The eight principles listed fall into two groups. Principles 1 to 3 require that the law should conform to standards designed to enable it effectively to guide action. Principles 4 to 8 are designed to ensure that the legal machinery of enforcing the law should not deprive it of its ability to guide through distorted enforcement and that it shall be capable of supervising conformity to the rule of law and provide effective remedies in cases of deviation from it. All the principles directly concern the system and method of government in matters directly relevant to the rule of law. Needless to say, many other aspects in the life of a community may, in more indirect ways, either strengthen or weaken the rule of law. A free press run by people anxious to defend the rule of law is of great assistance in preserving it, just as a gagged press or one run by people wishing to under-

---

[7] Similar lists of principles have been discussed by various authors. English writers have been mesmerized by Dicey's unfortunate doctrine for too long. For a list similar to mine see Lon Fuller's *The Morality of Law*, 2nd ed., ch. 2. His discussion of many of the principles is full of good sense. My main reason for abandoning some of his principles is a difference of views on conflicts between the laws of one system.

mine the rule of law is a threat to it. But we need not be concerned here with these more indirect influences.

3. THE VALUE OF THE RULE OF LAW

One of the merits of the doctrine of the rule of law I am defending is that there are so many values it does not serve. Conformity
to the rule of law is a virtue, but only one of the many virtues
a legal system should possess. This makes it all the more important to be clear on the values which the rule of law does serve.

The rule of law is often rightly contrasted with arbitrary
power. Arbitrary power is broader than the rule of law. Many
forms of arbitrary rule are compatible with the rule of law. A
ruler can promote general rules based on whim or self-interest,
etc., without offending against the rule of law. But certainly
many of the more common manifestations of arbitrary power
run foul of the rule of law. A government subjected to the rule
of law is prevented from changing the law retroactively or
abruptly or secretly whenever this suits its purposes. The one
area where the rule of law excludes all forms of arbitrary power
is in the law-applying function of the judiciary where the courts
are required to be subject only to the law and to conform to
fairly strict procedures.[8] No less important is the restraint
imposed by the rule of law on the making of particular laws
and thus on the powers of the executive. The arbitrary use of
power for personal gain, out of vengeance or favouritism, is
most commonly manifested in the making of particular legal
orders. These possibilities are drastically restricted by close
adherence to the rule of law.

'Arbitrary power' is a difficult notion. We have no cause to
analyse it here. It seems, however, that an act which is the exercise of power is arbitrary only if it was done either with in-
difference as to whether it will serve the purposes which alone
can justify use of that power or with belief that it will not serve
them. The nature of the purposes alluded to varies with the
nature of the power. This condition represents 'arbitrary
power' as a subjective concept. It all depends on the state of
mind of the men in power. As such the rule of law does not
bear directly on the extent of arbitrary power. But around

[8] The rule of law itself does not exclude all the possibilities of arbitrary law-making
by the courts.

its subjective core the notion of arbitrary power has grown a hard objective edge. Since it is universally believed that it is wrong to use public powers for private ends any such use is in itself an instance of arbitrary use of power. As we have seen the rule of law does help to curb such forms of arbitrary power.

But there are more reasons for valuing the rule of law. We value the ability to choose styles and forms of life, to fix long-term goals and effectively direct one's life towards them. One's ability to do so depends on the existence of stable, secure frameworks for one's life and actions. The law can help to secure such fixed points of reference in two ways: (1) by stabilizing social relationships which but for the law may disintegrate or develop in erratic and unpredictable ways; (2) by a policy of self-restraint designed to make the law itself a stable and safe basis for individual planning. This last aspect is the concern of the rule of law.

This second virtue of the rule of law is often, notably by Hayek, identified as the protection of individual freedom. This is right in the sense of freedom in which it is identified with an effective ability to choose between as many options as possible. Predictability in one's environment does increase one's power of action.[9] If this is freedom well and good. The important thing is to remember that this sense of freedom differs from what is commonly meant by political freedom. Political freedom consists of: (1) the prohibition of certain forms of behaviour which interfere with personal freedom and (2) the limits imposed on the powers of public authorities in order to minimize interference with personal freedom. The criminal offences against the person are an example of the first mode of protecting personal freedom, the disability of the government to restrict freedom of movement—an example of the second. It is in connection with political freedom in this sense that constitutionally guaranteed rights are of great importance. The rule of law may be yet another mode of protecting personal freedom. But it has no bearing on the existence of spheres of activity free from

[9] But then welfare law and governmental manipulation of the economy also increase freedom by increasing—if successful—people's welfare. If the rule of law is defended as the bulwark of freedom in this sense, it can hardly be used to oppose in principle governmental management of the economy.

governmental interference and is compatible with gross violations of human rights.

More important than both these considerations is the fact
that observance of the rule of law is necessary if the law is to
respect human dignity. Respecting human dignity entails treating humans as persons capable of planning and plotting their
future. Thus, respecting people's dignity includes respecting
their autonomy, their right to control their future. A person's
control over his life is never complete. It can be incomplete in
any one of several respects. The person may be ignorant of his
options, unable to decide what to do, incapable of realizing
his choices or frustrated in his attempts to do so, or he may
have no choice at all (or at least none which is worth having).
All these failures can occur through natural causes or through
the limitations of the person's own character and abilities.

Naturally, there are many ways in which one person's action
may affect the life of another. Only some such interferences will
amount to an offence to the dignity or a violation of the
autonomy of the person thus affected. Such offences can be
divided into three classes: insults, enslavement, and manipulation. (I am using the last two terms in a somewhat special sense.)
An insult offends a person's dignity if it consists of or implies
a denial that he is an autonomous person or that he deserves
to be treated as one. An action enslaves another if it practically
denies him all options through the manipulation of the environment. (Though it may be for a length of time—as in real slavery—I mean to include here also coercing another to act in
a certain way on a single occasion.) One manipulates a person
by intentionally changing his tastes, his beliefs or his ability to
act or decide. Manipulation—in other words—is manipulation of the person, of those factors relevant to his autonomy
which are internal to him. Enslavement is the elimination of
control by changing factors external to the person.

The law can violate people's dignity in many ways. Observing the rule of law by no means guarantees that such violations
do not occur. But it is clear that deliberate disregard for the
rule of law violates human dignity. It is the business of law to
guide human action by affecting people's options. The law
may, for example, institute slavery without violating the rule
of law. But deliberate violation of the rule of law violates human

dignity. The violation of the rule of law can take two forms. It may lead to uncertainty or it may lead to frustrated and disappointed expectations. It leads to the first when the law does not enable people to foresee future developments or to form definite expectations (as in cases of vagueness and most cases of wide discretion). It leads to frustrated expectations when the appearance of stability and certainty which encourages people to rely and plan on the basis of the existing law is shattered by retroactive law-making or by preventing proper law-enforcement, etc. The evils of uncertainty are in providing opportunities for arbitrary power and restricting people's ability to plan for their future. The evils of frustrated expectations are greater. Quite apart from the concrete harm they cause they also offend dignity in expressing disrespect for people's autonomy. The law in such cases encourages autonomous action only in order to frustrate its purpose. When such frustration is the result of human action or the result of the activities of social institutions then it expresses disrespect. Often it is analogous to entrapment: one is encouraged innocently to rely on the law and then that assurance is withdrawn and one's very reliance is turned into a cause of harm to one. A legal system which does in general observe the rule of law treats people as persons at least in the sense that it attempts to guide their behaviour through affecting the circumstances of their action. It thus presupposes that they are rational autonomous creatures and attempts to affect their actions and habits by affecting their deliberations.

Conformity to the rule of law is a matter of degree. Complete conformity is impossible (some vagueness is inescapable) and maximal possible conformity is on the whole undesirable (some controlled administrative discretion is better than none). It is generally agreed that general conformity to the rule of law is to be highly cherished. But one should not take the value of the rule of law on trust nor assert it blindly. Disentangling the various values served by the rule of law helps to assess intelligently what is at stake in various possible or actual violations. Some cases insult human dignity, give free rein to arbitrary power, frustrate one's expectations, and undermine one's ability to plan. Others involve only some of these evils. The evil of different violations of the rule of law is not always the same despite the fact that the doctrine rests on the solid core of its basic idea.

4. THE RULE OF LAW AND ITS ESSENCE

Lon Fuller[10] has claimed that the principles of the rule of law which he enumerated are essential for the existence of law. This claim if true is crucial to our understanding not only of the rule of law but also of the relation of law and morality. I have been treating the rule of law as an ideal, as a standard to which the law ought to conform but which it can and sometimes does violate most radically and systematically. Fuller, while allowing that deviations from the ideal of the rule of law can occur, denies that they can be radical or total. A legal system must of necessity conform to the rule of law to a certain degree, he claims. From this claim he concludes that there is an essential link between law and morality. Law is necessarily moral, at least in some respects.

It is, of course, true that most of the principles enumerated in section 2 above cannot be violated altogether by any legal system.[11] Legal systems are based on judicial institutions. There cannot be institutions of any kind unless there are general rules setting them up. A particular norm can authorize adjudication in a particular dispute, but no number of particular norms can set up an institution. Similarly retroactive laws can exist only because there are institutions enforcing them. This entails that there must be prospective laws instructing those institutions to apply the retroactive laws if the retroactive laws are to be valid. In the terminology of H. L. A. Hart's theory one can say that at least some of the rules of recognition and of adjudication of every system must be general and prospective. Naturally they must also be relatively clear if they are to make any sense at all, etc.

Clearly, the extent to which generality, clarity, prospectivity,

[10] In *The Morality of Law*, 2nd ed. (Yale, 1969), Fuller's argument is complex and his claims are numerous and hard to disentangle. Many of his claims are weak and unsupportable. Others are suggestive and useful. It is not my purpose to analyse or evaluate them. For a sympathetic discussion see R. E. Sartorius, *Individual Conduct and Social Norms* (Encino, California, 1975), ch. 9.

[11] I am not adopting here Fuller's conception of the law, but rather I am following my own adaptation of Hart's conception. Cf. Hart's *The Concept of Law* and my *Practical Reason and Norms* (1975), pp. 132–54. Therefore, the discussion which follows is not a direct assessment of Fuller's own claims.

etc., are essential to the law is minimal and is consistent with gross violations of the rule of law. But are not considerations of the kind mentioned sufficient to establish that there is necessarily at least some moral value in every legal system? I think not. The rule of law is essentially a negative value. The law inevitably creates a great danger of arbitrary power—the rule of law is designed to minimize the danger created by the law itself. Similarly, the law may be unstable, obscure, retrospective, etc., and thus infringe people's freedom and dignity. The rule of law is designed to prevent this danger as well. Thus the rule of law is a negative virtue in two senses: conformity to it does not cause good except through avoiding evil and the evil which is avoided is evil which could only have been caused by the law itself. It is thus somewhat analogous to honesty when this virtue is narrowly interpreted as the avoidance of deceit. (I do not deny that honesty is normally conceived more broadly to incorporate other virtuous acts and inclinations.) The good of honesty does not include the good of communication between people, for honesty is consistent with a refusal to communicate. Its good is exclusively in the avoidance of the harm of deceit—and not deceit by others but by the honest person himself. Therefore, only a person who can deceive can be honest. A person who cannot communicate cannot claim any moral merit for being honest. A person who through ignorance or inability cannot kill another by poison deserves no credit for it. Similarly, that the law cannot sanction arbitrary force or violations of freedom and dignity through total absence of generality, prospectivity, or clarity is no moral credit to the law. It only means that there are some kinds of evil which cannot be brought about by the law. But this is no virtue in the law just as it is no virtue in the law that it cannot rape or murder (all it can do is sanction such actions).

Fuller's attempt to establish a necessary connection between law and morality fails. In so far as conformity to the rule of law is a moral virtue it is an ideal which should but may fail to become a reality. There is another argument, however, which establishes an essential connection between the law and the rule of law, though it does not guarantee any virtue to the law. Conformity to the rule of law is essential for securing whatever purposes the law is designed to achieve. This statement should be qualified. We could divide the purposes a law is intended to serve into two kinds: those which are secured by conformity with the law in itself and those further consequences of conformity with the law or of knowledge of its existence which the law is intended to secure.[12] Thus a law prohibiting racial discrimination in government employment has as its direct purpose the establishment of racial equality in the hiring, promotion, and conditions of service of government employees (since discriminatory action is a breach of law). Its indirect purposes may well be to improve race relations in the country in general, prevent a threat of a strike by some trade unions, or halt the decline in popularity of the government.

Conformity to the rule of law does not always facilitate realization of the indirect purposes of the law, but it is essential to the realization of its direct purposes. These are achieved by conformity with the law which is secured (unless accidentally) by people taking note of the law and guiding themselves accordingly. Therefore, if the direct purposes of the law are not to be frustrated it must be capable of guiding human behaviour, and the more it conforms to the principles of the rule of law the better it can do so.

In section 2 we saw that conformity to the rule of law is one among many moral virtues which the law should possess. The present consideration shows that the rule of law is not merely a moral virtue—it is a necessary condition for the law to be serving directly any good purpose at all. Of course, conformity to the rule of law also enables the law to serve bad purposes. That does not show that it is not a virtue, just as the fact that a sharp knife can be used to harm does not show that being sharp is not a good-making characteristic for knives. At most it shows that from the point of view of the present consideration it is not a moral good. Being sharp is an inherent good-making characteristic of knives. A good knife is, among other things, a sharp knife. Similarly, conformity to the rule of law is an inherent value of laws, indeed it is their most important inherent value. It is of the essence of law to guide behaviour through rules and courts in charge of their application. Therefore, the rule of law is the specific excellence of the law. Since conformity to the rule of law is the virtue of law in itself, law as law regard-

[12] See further on this distinction Essay 9 above.

less of the purposes it serves, it is understandable and right that the rule of law is thought of as among the few virtues of law which are the special responsiblity of the courts and the legal profession.

Regarding the rule of law as the inherent or specific virtue of law is a result of an instrumental conception of law. The law is not just a fact of life. It is a form of social organization which should be used properly and for the proper ends. It is a tool in the hands of men differing from many others in being versatile and capable of being used for a large variety of proper purposes. As with some other tools, machines, and instruments a thing is not of the kind unless it has at least some ability to perform its function. A knife is not a knife unless it has some ability to cut. The law to be law must be capable of guiding behaviour, however inefficiently. Like other instruments, the law has a specific virtue which is morally neutral in being neutral as to the end to which the instrument is put. It is the virtue of efficiency; the virtue of the instrument as an instrument. For the law this virtue is the rule of law. Thus the rule of law is an inherent virtue of the law, but not a moral virtue as such.

The special status of the rule of law does not mean that conformity with it is of no moral importance. Quite apart from the fact that conformity to the rule of law is also a moral virtue, it is a moral requirement when necessary to enable the law to perform useful social functions; just as it may be of moral importance to produce a sharp knife when it is required for a moral purpose. In the case of the rule of law this means that it is virtually always of great moral value.

5. SOME PITFALLS

The undoubted value of conformity to the rule of law should not lead one to exaggerate its importance. We saw how Hayek noted correctly its relevance for the protection of freedom. We also saw that the rule of law itself does not provide sufficient protection of freedom. Consider, however, Hayek's position. He begins with a grand statement which inevitably leads to exaggerated expectations:

The conception of freedom under the law that is the chief concern of this book rests on the contention that when we obey laws, in the sense of general abstract rules laid down irrespective of their application to us we are not subject to another man's will and are therefore free. It is because the lawgiver does not know the particular cases to which his rules will apply, and it is because the judge who applies them has no choice in drawing the conclusions that follow from the existing body of rules and the particular facts of the case, that it can be said that laws and not men rule.... As a true law should not name any particulars, so it should especially not single out any specific persons or group of persons.[13]

Then, aware of the absurdity to which this passage leads, he modifies his line, still trying to present the rule of law as the supreme guarantor of freedom:

The requirement that the rules of true law be general does not mean that sometimes special rules may not apply to different classes of people if they refer to properties that only some people possess. There may be rules that can apply only to women or to the blind or to persons above a certain age. (In most instances it would not even be necessary to name the class of people to whom the rule applies: only a woman, for example, can be raped or got with child.) Such distinctions will not be arbitrary, will not subject one group to the will of others, if they are equally recognized as justified by those inside and those outside the group. This does not mean that there must be unanimity as to the desirability of the distinction, but merely that individual views will not depend on whether the individual is in the group or not.[14]

But here the rule of law is transformed to encompass a form of government by consent and it is this which is alleged to guarantee freedom. This is the slippery slope leading to the identification of the rule of law with the rule of the good law.

Hayek's main objection is to governmental interference with the economy:

We must now turn to the kinds of governmental measures which the rule of law excludes in principle because they cannot be achieved by merely enforcing general rules but, of necessity, involve arbitrary discrimination between persons. The most important among them are decisions as to who is to be allowed to provide different services or commodities, at what prices or in what quantities—in other words, measures designed to control the access to different trades and occupations, the terms of sale, and the amounts to be produced or sold.

There are several reasons why all direct control of prices by government is irreconcilable with a functioning free system, whether the

[13] F. A. Hayek, *The Constitution of Liberty* (Chicago, 1960), pp. 153–4.
[14] Ibid., p. 154.

government actually fixes prices or merely lays down rules by which the permissible prices are to be determined. In the first place, it is impossible to fix prices according to long-term rules which will effectively guide production. Appropriate prices depend on circumstances which are constantly changing and must be continually adjusted to them. On the other hand, prices which are not fixed outright but determined by some rule (such as that they must be in a certain relation to cost) will not be the same for all sellers and, for this reason, will prevent the market from functioning. A still more important consideration is that, with prices different from those that would form on a free market, demand and supply will not be equal, and if the price control is to be effective, some method must be found for deciding who is to be allowed to buy or sell. This would necessarily be discretionary and must consist of *ad hoc* decisions that discriminate between persons on essentially arbitrary grounds.[15]

Here again it is clear that arguments which at best show that certain policies are wrong for economic reasons are claimed to show that they infringe the rule of law and the making of supposedly misguided but perfectly principled particular orders is condemned as an arbitrary exercise of power.

Since the rule of law is just one of the virtues the law should possess, it is to be expected that it possesses no more than prima facie force. It has always to be balanced against competing claims of other values. Hence Hayek's arguments, to the extent that they show no more than that some other goals inevitably conflict with the rule of law, are not the sort of arguments which could, in principle, show that pursuit of such goals by means of law is inappropriate. Conflict between the rule of law and other values is just what is to be expected. Conformity to the rule of law is a matter of degree, and though, other things being equal, the greater the conformity the better—other things are rarely equal. A lesser degree of conformity is often to be preferred precisely because it helps realization of other goals.

In considering the relation between the rule of law and other values the law should serve, it is of particular importance to remember that the rule of law is essentially a negative value. It is merely designed to minimize the harm to freedom and dignity which the law may cause in its pursuit of its goals however laudable these may be. Finally, regarding the rule of law

---

[15] F. A. Hayek, *The Constitution of Liberty*, pp. 227–8.

as the inherent excellence of the law means that it fulfils essentially a subservient role. Conformity to it makes the law a good instrument for achieving certain goals, but conformity to the rule of law is not itself an ultimate goal. This subservient role of the doctrine shows both its power and its limitations. On the one hand, if the pursuit of certain goals is entirely incompatible with the rule of law, then these goals should not be pursued by legal means. But on the other hand one should be wary of disqualifying the legal pursuit of major social goals in the name of the rule of law. After all, the rule of law is meant to enable the law to promote social good, and should not be lightly used to show that it should not do so. Sacrificing too many social goals on the altar of the rule of law may make the law barren and empty.

Part IV

Moral Attitudes to the Law

12

THE OBLIGATION TO OBEY
THE LAW

I shall argue that there is no obligation to obey the law. It is generally agreed that there is no absolute or conclusive obligation to obey the law. I shall suggest that there is not even a prima facie obligation to obey it.[1] Such a view may be the outcome of a very pessimistic outlook on the value of law and the possibilities of its reform. My argument will not be based on such pessimistic assumptions. I shall argue that there is no obligation to obey the law even in a good society whose legal system is just. In other words, whatever one's view of the nature of the good society or the desirable shape of the law it does not follow from those or indeed from any other reasonable moral principle that there is an obligation to obey the law.

No general argument will be offered to show that there is no such obligation. Instead it is hoped that a more indirect approach may suggest that the duty does not exist. In the first section the nature of the claim that one has an obligation to obey the law will be discussed. The following two sections will examine the case for the existence of such an obligation arising first from moral and secondly from prudential considerations. Finally the last section clarifies the role of the law in society in a way which explains why one should not expect a good law to give rise to an obligation to obey it.

1. THE CHARACTER OF THE OBLIGATION

An obligation to obey the law entails a reason to do that which the law requires. But the converse does not hold. Many reasons to do that which the law requires have nothing to do with an obligation to obey the law. One has reasons not to kill, assault, rape, or imprison other people which have no connection with

---

[1] A very powerful and persuasive case showing that there is no obligation to obey the law is presented by M. B. E. Smith, 'Is there a Prima Facie Obligation to Obey the Law?', *Yale Law Journal* 82 (1973), p. 950. Cf. also R. Wasserstrom, 'The Obligation to Obey the Law' in R. S. Summers (ed.), *Essays in Legal Philosophy* (Oxford, 1968).

the law and depend entirely on the fact that such acts are against the will or interests or (moral) rights of others. Yet such reasons are reasons to do that which the law requires, for the law requires to refrain from murder, assault, rape, and imprisonment. The obligation to obey the law implies that the reason to do that which is required by law is the very fact that it is so required. At the very least this should be part of the reason to obey.

It is easy to find many examples where the fact that the law requires an act is a reason to perform it. A person may be expelled from school or lose his job if rumours that he broke the law become known to his headmaster or employer. His criminal act(s) may greatly aggrieve his much-loved parents or spouse, etc. Such considerations do not even tend to show that there is an obligation to obey the law. For although in these cases the law (i.e. the fact that the law requires an action) is a reason for conforming behaviour it is an incidental reason existing for a particular person, applying under certain special circumstances. The obligation to obey the law is a general obligation applying to all the law's subjects and to all the laws on all the occasions to which they apply. To look for an obligation to obey the law of a certain country is to look for grounds which make it desirable, other things being equal, that one should always do as the law requires. These grounds need not be the same for everyone or for every occasion, but they should be of sufficient generality so that a few general sets of considerations will apply to all on all occasions. The search for an obligation to obey the law of a certain country is an inquiry into whether there is a set of true premisses which entail that everyone (or every citizen? every resident?) ought always to do as those laws require and which include the fact that those actions are required by law as a non-redundant premiss.

Liberal political theory usually assumes that an obligation to obey the law implies nothing more than a prima facie reason to obey. The concept of an obligation, however, imports a practical necessity more stringent than that of a prima facie reason. I have argued elsewhere[2] that an action is obligatory

---

[2] On the analysis of 'obligation' see my 'Promises and Obligations' in *Law, Society and Morality*, Essays in honour of H. L. A. Hart, edited by P. M. S. Hacker and J. Raz (Oxford, 1977).

only if it is required by a protected reason[3] which does not derive merely from the fact that adherence to it facilitates realization of the agent's goals. No doubt one may be content with inquiring whether or not there is a prima facie reason to obey the law which applies to all the law's subjects on all occasions to which the law applies. It will be suggested below that even in this 'modest' sense there is no obligation to obey the law. But it is of interest to note that for most people an obligation to obey the law (and most people believe themselves to be under such an obligation) means something far more demanding than a prima facie reason. It means a peremptory reason best explained in keeping with my general analysis of obligation, as a categorical protected reason. The prevalence of this 'strong' notion of an obligation to obey, far from resting on naïve and unreflective political attitudes, reflects a coherent and sober understanding of essential features of the political situation which has long been conveniently overlooked by most political theorists.

The question of the proper attitude to the law is a central preoccupation of political philosophy. One aspect of it is the inquiry whether there is an obligation to comply with the claims of the law for obedience, whether one has a duty to obey the law as it, i.e. the law, demands to be obeyed. It is this obligation which is generally thought of by the general public as the obligation to obey the law. Quite apart from this terminological point there can be little doubt of the importance of an inquiry into whether it is justified to comply with the claims of the law for obedience.

The law's claims for obedience are very different from the current philosophical conception of the obligation to obey the law as a prima facie reason to obey. Most of the current philosophical writings assume that the obligation to obey the law is not violated when an offence is committed in circumstances where there are strong moral reasons for committing it even though its commission is liable to lead to a conviction in a court of law. One can imagine, for example, unlawfully obtaining or stealing a medicine necessary to cure a patient and which for various reasons cannot be lawfully obtained (suppose that the man is a tourist with very little money in a country whose

[3] Cf. Essay 1 above for the explanation of 'protected reasons'.

language he does not speak, etc.). Obviously such an act is a violation of an obligation to obey the law if that is understood as an obligation to obey the law as it requires to be obeyed. On that interpretation any act which is a breach of law is also a violation of the obligation to obey the law.

Two points are involved here. The first is that through its rules and its adjudicative machinery the law assumes the right to determine in what conditions legal requirements are defeated by other considerations. The courts apply various doctrines such as conscientious objection, self-defence, necessity, etc., to absolve people from blame for breach of law. To a certain extent prosecutorial discretion is designed, in certain countries, to serve the same purpose. So that while it is true that legal requirements are not, in law, absolute, the law itself claims to determine their proper import, to fix the conditions in which they are overridden. Therefore, an obligation to obey the law interpreted as a 'strong' obligation, i.e. to obey it as it requires to be obeyed, includes acknowledging more than a prima facie reason to obey the law. It includes admission that the reasons to obey have the weight and implications which the law determines for them. In other words it entails a reason to obey in all circumstances defeated only by considerations which are legally recognized as excusing from prosecution or conviction.

This may sound like claiming that the obligation to obey the law is absolute. But, and here is the second point, this is a mistake. The essay on 'The Claims of Law' provided arguments for holding that the law claims not absolute but exclusionary status. Courts need not deny the weight of moral reasons which sometimes argue for breaking the law but which are not provided for by the law and are not allowed to count as excuses or justifications. But the courts do maintain that neither they nor the individual are entitled to break the law on such occasions. They claim that one should disregard those countervailing considerations, however weighty.[4] The legislator or the executive may have to take some action. But so long as they have not done so the individual should disregard those counter-

---

[4] That the offender was motivated by them may, quite properly, count as either mitigating or aggravating consideration when it comes to sentencing. But sentencing is governed by its own principles, which do not affect the present issue.

vailing considerations. In other words the law claims that its rules and rulings are authoritative. To establish an obligation (in the strong sense) to obey the law, as commonly understood, is to establish that its claim is justified, that the law indeed has the legitimate authority it claims to have.

2. MORAL REASONS TO OBEY

There is no denying that some people have moral reasons to obey the law. Some people (e.g. the Archbishop of Canterbury) have such a position of pre-eminence in the community that their actions have profound influence on the attitudes and behaviour of many people. As a result any breach of the law on their part may have grave consequences and thus they have a general moral reason to obey the law. A reformed criminal may promise his girl-friend never to break the law again if she marries him. If she does he will be under an obligation to obey resting on moral reasons. Similar in some respects is quasi-estoppel. Occasionally a person presents himself as law-abiding in order to induce other people to obey the law. If he succeeds in moving other people to obey the law in an expectation of some benefits (peace, prosperity, etc.) which will accrue to them if both they and he abide by the law, he may well have a moral reason to obey the law so as not to deprive them of those benefits, especially if by inducing them to obey the law he made them forgo some other benefits or undertake certain extra burdens.

Several philosophers have attempted to found a general obligation to obey the law on extensions of these considerations. They tried to show that *every* person present or living in a country is bound, by considerations of one or the other of these kinds, to obey its law. Disobedience, even to a bad law, it is sometimes argued, sets an example and inclines other people to disobey. And those affected may not be discriminating or may lack sound judgment and may be inclined to break good laws as well as bad ones. Hence one has an obligation to obey. This is an important argument and I do not wish to appear to belittle its weight. It is all too easy to dismiss it on the ground that the action of one private individual has too little impact to be worth considering. A public atmosphere of respect for law rests on the cumulative effect of individual behaviour. Though most of us cannot influence public attitudes in the way the Archbishop of Canterbury can, we do affect other people's attitudes even if in smaller measure. While this is undoubtedly an important argument it can hardly be sufficient to establish a general obligation to obey the law. First, at best it provides an ordinary prima facie reason to obey, not a pre-eminent reason amounting to an obligation, to a recognition of the authority of the law. Secondly, though the argument applies in many cases it fails to apply to many others. There are offences which when committed by certain people or in certain circumstances do actually revolt people and strengthen the law-abiding inclinations in the population. In other cases the example set is a good one because on the whole it encourages disobedience only when it is justified. But of all such cases it may be said that to the extent that the offence tends also to act as a bad example for some the argument applies even if overridden by other considerations. There are, however, countless offences the commission of which is never known. Countless traffic offences and many small tax offences, for example, are never detected at all. Moreover, in many cases it is practically certain in advance that the offence, if committed, will remain undetected. Such offences naturally do not set any example whatsoever. Hence the argument from setting a bad example fails to apply to many instances of possible offences. Though an important consideration, it does not even establish a 'weak' general obligation to obey.

It is no objection to these considerations that most of the offences which do not serve as a bad example are either minor offences or victimless crimes or ones which (like tax offences) do not have a direct or identifiable victim. The obligation to obey the law is supposed to be general. Moreover its practical implications are more likely to be decisive in such cases. In major offences or those causing direct harm to identifiable individuals there are usually plenty of direct forceful reasons for (or against) conformity to the law which do not depend on the fact that the act is legally required.

The repeated attempts to base an obligation to obey the law on promises or other undertakings are even less persuasive. True enough, some people are made to take an oath of allegiance, sometimes including an undertaking to keep to the law.

Often such undertakings are given in conditions amounting to coercion or duress which deprive them of any moral validity (e.g. when conscripts are made, on pain of severe penalties, to take an oath of allegiance in a country not recognizing an adequate right of conscientious objection). But in other circumstances such an oath may impose a moral obligation to obey (e.g. when voluntarily undertaken prior to assuming an office of state which one is under no compulsion or great pressure to assume). Most people, however, do not commit themselves in this way. Can one interpret the ordinary submission to the law of the normal citizen as amounting to such an undertaking? Certainly not. Promises and other voluntary commitments are created by an expressed intention to be bound.[5] It is clear that the ordinary life of normal citizens includes nothing amounting to a promise or a voluntary undertaking.

Nor is the third type of consideration mentioned above more likely to provide a basis for a general obligation to obey the law. Estoppel and various forms of quasi-estoppel are indeed independent grounds for action. If by his behaviour a person knowingly induces another to rely on him then he should not, other things being equal, frustrate the expectations of that other person if doing so affects him adversely. Thus if, for example, I knowingly induce another to obey the law by words or actions which lead him to believe that I will obey the law myself, then I should, other things being equal, not let him down by breaking the law. But this argument applies only if by breaking the law I adversely affect the man who relied on me. This can be by harming him or his interests or even by causing him distress and disappointment. The degree of harm is one key factor in assesssing the weight of this consideration as a reason for a particular action. Herein lies one difficulty in basing a general obligation to obey on such a consideration: one's violation of the law does not always affect anybody, however minimally and however indirectly. But the main objection to this argument for an obligation to obey is that by and large we do not induce that kind of reliance in others and we certainly do not do it knowingly. This last point is a point of fact which I can but state: Even if it is true that one's behaviour induces others to obey the law, it is certainly not something that people are

[5] On the nature of promises see my 'Promises and Obligation', ibid.

normally aware of. Most people do not believe that others obey the law because they expect them to do so.[6]

The reason people do not believe that they induce others to obey is that they do not, at least not in any morally relevant sense. It is true that up to a point, and especially in certain areas of the law, people are encouraged to obey by the expectation that others will generally do likewise. But this is no more a reason for me to obey than the fact that many Londoners are encouraged to remain in London by the expectation that many people will continue to live there is a reason against any person leaving the city.

The arguments from promising and quasi-estoppel of the kinds considered above are not only intellectually misguided; they are also morally pernicious. They suggest that every individual is inevitably obliged to obey the law of his society regardless of how good or bad that law may be. The arguments from setting a bad example, on the other hand, presuppose—but do not in themselves establish—that the law has rules whose violation will be morally bad. Several kinds of arguments attempt to establish an obligation to obey all law because all legal systems are morally good (natural law arguments) or to obey the laws of a legal system if it is essentially just or morally good.

It was argued above[7] that many kinds of natural law theories are misconceived. But the arguments there presented left unaffected the thesis that every legal system has some moral merit. Even if the law is necessarily good in some respects and to some degree no obligation to obey it follows. If the facets of law which make it morally valuable are pervasive, systemic features, e.g. that it—the law—is a way of securing public order through subjecting social activity to a framework of openly ascertainable rules, then it affects an individual's reasons only to the extent that his action will tend to undermine the law. Such reasons are mostly derived from the argument from setting a bad example and it has already been argued that such reasons are not capable of generating an obligation to obey.

[6] It is true that one has reason to save others from harm even where that harm is not caused by one knowingly inducing them to behave in a certain way. But here one no longer relies on the semi-estoppel argument but on a general obligation to save others from harm. Such argument will often lead one to conform to the law but only occasionally to obey the law because it is the law.

[7] Cf. Essay 3 above and also *Practical Reason and Norms*, ch. 5, section 3.

Alternatively, the necessarily present and universally worthwhile aspects of the law may be manifested in some of its laws or institutions, e.g. if all legal systems contain laws protecting worthwhile life. If so then one has reason to obey those laws (which does not depend on their being legally valid, but derives from their moral content) but no reason to obey other laws, except in so far as not doing so is setting a bad example leading to offences against the good laws. And we are back with the inadequate argument from setting a bad example.

For similar reasons the duty to support and uphold good institutions, the existence of which need not be denied, is insufficient to establish an obligation to obey. It extends directly to those laws setting up and maintaining the just institutions (e.g. those guaranteeing the functioning of a democratic government in the society). It provides reasons to obey other laws only to the extent that by doing so one sets a good example or that by failing so to act one sets a bad example: that is, only to the extent that obedience to these other laws strengthens or prevents weakening the laws on which the democratic character of the government is founded.

Peter Singer's *Democracy and Disobedience* (Oxford, 1973) is among the most interesting discussions of the difference the democratic character of the government makes to the existence of reasons to obey the law. He sees two grounds for a prima facie obligation to obey the law of a perfect democracy. One arises out of participation (pp. 45 ff.). Singer's argument is one of estoppel: 'The legal doctrine of estoppel, then, serves as a useful illustration of what I am saying about voting. In voting, one's voluntary behaviour leads others to the reasonable belief that one consents to the majority decision-procedure. After the event one cannot say that one never consented.' (p. 52.) Here its factual assumption is simply false. People generally know that non-democrats do participate in democratic elections.

Singer's second argument (pp. 30 ff.) regards democratic procedure as a fair way of achieving a compromise between competing and legitimate claims. One therefore has reason to support it and accept its results as fair. There are, however, two reasons for which democratic procedures can be thought to be fair. One is valid but insufficient to create an obligation to obey; the other is misguided. The valid reason is that in some countries democratic decisions are more likely to produce fair results and to be acceptable to the public than any alternative. Such considerations establish that democratic government is a just government in those countries and should be supported. But as was pointed out above the duty to support just institutions is insufficient to establish an obligation to obey the law. (On p. 38 Singer indicates that he relies on the duty to support just institutions.)

The other interpretation of Singer's argument takes it to imply that the very fact that a solution was reached by a democratic procedure makes it a just solution (even while conceding that other features of it may make it unjust). This seems to me to be plainly false. The rejection of this view does not depend on a purely instrumental view of democracy. One may approve of it as expressing trust in the mature judgment of the population, or as necessary for self-expression and for the development of a free person, etc., and yet not acknowledge that each one of its decisions ought to be obeyed just because it was democratically reached (compare: the fact that a decision was taken by an official who followed all the rules of natural justice does not render it just, even though natural justice is valuable both instrumentally and in itself).

Such sketchy refutations of popular arguments as here provided are far from sufficient to show that there is no way of persuasively arguing for a moral obligation to obey. But probably no master argument can prove the non-existence of such a moral obligation. All that can be done is to illustrate the kind of difficulties such an argument has to overcome and to examine some popular arguments. Having done that the discussion in the rest of the book will be based on an assumption that there is no general obligation to obey.[8]

3. PRUDENTIAL REASONS TO OBEY

Most people have good prudential reasons to obey the law most of the time. There is the risk of incurring legal sanctions, crimi-

---

[8] Some further moral reasons to obey the law are discussed in the next essay on 'Respect for Law'. As will be there seen, they do not undermine the negative conclusion of the present section.

nal or other, which are unwelcome to most people most of the time, and there are numerous other 'social sanctions' which, though affecting different people in different ways and to different degrees, affect most people to a considerable extent. Furthermore, all those reasons are of the right kind. They are reasons to do that which the law requires because it requires it; hence they are unlike many moral reasons which are reasons to do that which the law requires for grounds not dependent on the fact that the law requires them.

It is plain that these primary prudential considerations are not sufficiently extensive. If they are the only prudential considerations then it is clear that all of us have opportunities to break the law where no prudential reasons against such action apply. There are, however, secondary prudential considerations which apply more widely. These considerations are parasitic on primary considerations in the following way: Suppose that it is known that primary considerations apply to some or all of the cases within a certain class of cases, e.g. that on some or all of the occasions in which one can break the law one has a prudential reason for not doing so. And suppose that the attempts to establish whether the consideration applies in each individual case, and if so whether it defeats all the contrary considerations which may also apply to the case, involve costs (time, effort, risk of reaching the wrong conclusion, etc.). In such a case it is sometimes best to adopt a policy or a rule that all the cases belonging to that class of cases are to be determined as if the reason which may be present in them is present and as if it defeats all contrary considerations.[9] In our case it means that one may have a prudential reason to act on a policy of always obeying the law rather than examine in every case whether it is or is not governed by a (primary) prudential reason. Whether or not one has sufficient reason to adopt such policies depends on numerous considerations, such as the kind and amount of cost to be incurred if one rejects the policy and relies on an examination of each case individually and the nature of the conflicting considerations likely to apply to cases in the class, etc.

---

[9] Such a policy is a mandatory rule in the sense analysed in *Practical Reason and Norms*, ch. 2.

Such prudential policies extend the scope of the prudential considerations to obey the law. They are probably more important than is generally realized. Understandably, one is more clearly aware of the character of one's reasons if one acts on the merits of the case than when one relies on a general policy. Then the reason for the action is often expressed in general and vague terms such as 'I just don't do such things'. Such an answer does not reveal the sort of considerations on which the policy rests. People are often vague about the reasons for which they maintain certain rules without this meaning that they have none. Many people just do not break the law in normal situations and such policies are often based on secondary prudential reasons of the kind mentioned above and yet this fact does not surface very often and they often are quite vague about their own reasons.

Even prudential policies, however, do not provide an adequate foundation for an obligation to obey the law, and this for several reasons. The obligation to obey the law is generally thought of as a moral obligation. Prudential grounds do not in themselves give rise to moral obligations. Even those who consider prudence a moral virtue will agree that on most occasions it is at best praiseworthy but not obligatory to exhibit it in one's behaviour. Furthermore, the extent to which one has secondary prudential reasons for adopting prudential policies of abiding by the law vary from person to person: some are more likely than others to miscalculate the risks in individual cases, some are more easily upset by having to contemplate such risks, by the very tensions generated by the deliberation. Those have stronger prudential reasons to adopt policies of conformity to law. Others have less reason to do so. More important still is the fact that almost nobody has reason to adopt an all-embracing policy of this sort. So far as prudence is concerned, almost everyone, though he has reason to follow a conformist policy in most areas, is free to exempt certain very low-risk areas from them: minor offences against the property of one's employer, minor violations of tax law, etc. Each has certain areas of law where the risks he runs by breaking the law are minimal and where prudential considerations would support adopting a policy of disregarding it altogether, and acting as if there is no prudential reason against breaking the law.

4. GOOD LAW WITHOUT AN OBLIGATION TO OBEY

The view that there is no obligation to obey the law in a country with a good and just legal system has the air of paradox. Its paradoxical appearance is responsible to a large degree for our reluctance to abandon the belief in the existence of such an obligation. The appearance of paradox is illusory. It stems from two closely connected sources: we think of a decent or a moral citizen as one who among other things obeys the laws of a just legal system and we think of the good legal system as the one whose laws ought to be obeyed (are obeyed by good citizens). The proper moral attitude of a good citizen to the law forms the topic of the next essay. Here it is useful to contemplate the possibility of judging a legal system good without acknowledging an obligation to obey its laws.

A couple of preliminary points first. It goes without saying that one has more often independent moral reasons for conforming to the laws of a good legal system than to those of a bad legal system. If a legal system is morally good then it contains morally good laws and those are often laws prescribing behaviour which is morally obligatory independently of the law (e.g. prohibiting murder, rape, libel, invasion of privacy, breach of promises under certain conditions, certain kinds of deception, etc.). One has moral reasons to act in conformity with the laws of a good system more often than with those of a bad system even if there is no special moral obligation to obey the laws of a just legal system.

It is also true that the fact that a legal system is in general good and just is a reason to trust its law-making and judicial institutions. If one knows that in general the laws are such that one has independent moral reasons to do as they require, then with respect to any individual law one has, other things being equal, reason to believe that there is independent moral reason to conform to it too. Thus the general moral quality of the system encourages conformity by being a reason to believe and trust the moral value of each individual law. Again no special obligation to obey the law is involved.

These two points, however, do not touch on the essence of the apparent paradox: how is it that the fact that a legal system is just is not a reason to obey it. To dispel the appearance of paradox one has to consider the essential role of the law in society. The essay on 'The Functions of Law' suggested a scheme of classification of the substantive functions of law. But how are those functions fulfilled? What is the law's technique of securing its own proper functioning?

Kelsen said that the legal technique is that of providing motivation for conformity to its own standards through the stipulation of sanctions for violations of the law. This is certainly a most important legal technique even though it is not unique to the law as Kelsen asserted. But the previous section of this essay suggested that in fact prudential considerations (and they include all those derived from fear of sanctions and others besides) are not sufficient to provide even a prima facie reason for obedience in all cases. Should we conclude that there should be no law where legal sanctions are unlikely to provide a reason for action? It is true that sometimes it is quite properly said that a law which is generally disregarded should be repealed. And if it is known in advance that a law, if made, will be generally disregarded, then it should not be made. But such arguments depend on existing or foreseeable disregard for the law resulting from the failure of any kind of consideration to secure conformity. They cannot be cited as evidence that it is generally believed that where *legal sanctions* are ineffective or unlikely to be effective then there should not be law. But if this is not a common belief then though legally provided sanctions are beyond doubt an important legal technique, they are not normally thought to be the only one.

There are in fact two basic legal techniques, two ways in which the law serves its functions (there may also be further minor techniques). One is the provision of reasons for compliance through the stipulation of sanctions. The other is the marking, in a publicly ascertainable way, of standards required by the organized society (i.e. claimed to be required by the society by the legally qualified institutions and organs of the society). In the first technique the law creates reasons for conformity, in the second it relies on independent reasons and invokes and directs them by openly declaring certain standards as the proper ones to be followed by all who are motivated by those invoked reasons. The independence of the second technique is often overlooked. It seems that the fact that legal standards are publicly ascertainable[10] is readily explained by the need to provide a publicly ascertainable standard for the sanction technique to be efficient and fair. Nor do I wish to deny the importance of regulating the use of public power by publicly ascertainable standards.[11] It has, however, to be pointed out that this is not the only role of publicly ascertainable standards. Consider the law regulating the activities of courts and other high-ranking state officers. Admittedly these officers are usually directly or indirectly connected with the application of legal sanctions. But the legal standards addressed to such officials are not there only to enable others to predict how the officials will act but primarily to guide the officials themselves (only because they do so can they also serve as a basis for predicting how the officials will act). But while it is intended that the officials will conform to the law, it is not expected that they should do so through desire to avoid the sanctions, but because they are predisposed by independent considerations to obey the law. The law's role here is merely to mark clearly the standards to which that independent motivation then attaches itself.

This distinction between the two legal techniques can be viewed as a reinterpretation of the traditional distinction between *mala per se* and *mala prohibita*. One role the law has is to prohibit and punish the performance of acts which should not be performed for independent reasons which neither depend on the existence of law nor are concerned with preserving other social practices (all of which are *mala per se*). Since some people fail to be motivated by those independent reasons as they should be, the law provides them through its sanctions with alternative reasons. A second role belonging to the law concerns participation in schemes of social co-operation (these duties are *mala prohibita*). I have here in mind cases where one has reason to act in a certain way because it contributes to an ongoing scheme of social co-operation. These are of a variety of kinds of which the following two are typical and pervasive: there are acts which are useful if a sufficiently large number of people behave in appropriate ways but are without any value if nobody does or if only few people do. Polluting the rivers is an example.

[10] For reasons to hold that all legal standards are publicly ascertainable and for an explanation of this condition cf. 'Positivism and the Sources of Law', above.
[11] See further 'The Rule of Law and its Virtue', above.

If a sufficiently large number of people refrain from polluting the rivers, they will be clean, and each person has a moral reason to contribute to keeping them clean.[12] But if most people pollute them and they are badly polluted there is normally no reason why I should refrain from polluting them myself.[13] Another kind of action one has reason to do because of the existence of schemes of social co-operation are cases where the particular form of the existing co-operative scheme concretizes a general obligation, gives it a particular shape. It can, for example, be agreed that each individual has a moral duty to contribute to the welfare of others. It can be argued that if there is a socially accepted and generally practised system of social welfare financed out of contributions by those who can afford it then each has a duty to contribute to the scheme as (partly or wholly) discharging his obligation to help others. He loses the option to do it any way he likes. He has moral reason to do it in the socially accepted way.[14]

The discussion of different kinds of schemes of co-operation is a fascinating and a very important subject giving rise to problems both in moral philosophy and in the theory of rational action. These, however, are not germane to the present issue. One need not even agree with the few remarks ventured above about the two kinds of co-operative schemes here exemplified. Only two points are pertinent to the present discussion. First, that the law is instrumental in setting up and maintaining schemes of social co-operation, and this not only by providing sanctions to motivate those who would not otherwise contribute their shares (first legal technique) but also through designating in an open and public way what the scheme is and what each

[12] In many cases an individual's action contributes to the results even if in only a very small measure. Sometimes, so long as there are enough other contributors an individual's action may not by itself causally contribute to the result. I am assuming that even in such cases one often has moral reasons, the basis or force of which need not detain us here, to participate in the co-operative enterprise.

[13] Except when there is a campaign starting to change public attitudes which has some chance of success, etc.

[14] A way of discharging one's duty may be the best way just because it is the common way. One's action may in those circumstances produce more direct benefits to those for whose sake the duty exists. One will, however, have other reasons as well for joining in the practice: This may strengthen the practice and thereby encourage other people to discharge their obligations. (It is easier to do so with the majority than on one's own.) Joining in the practice may also be desirable in itself. It is a way of manifesting a sense of belonging to the community.

has to do as his contribution to it (second legal technique), thus enabling those who are motivated by the appropriate reasons to take part in the co-operative enterprise. The second point is that the moral reasons affecting such cases derive entirely from the factual existence of the social practice of co-operation and not at all from the fact that the law is instrumental in its institution or maintenance. Consider the example of river pollution mentioned above. It matters not at all to one's moral reasoning whether the practice of keeping the rivers clean is sanctioned by law, is maintained by exhortations and propaganda undertaken by enthusiastic individuals, or whether it grew up entirely spontaneously. It is the existence of the practice that matters, not (except in special circumstances) its origins or surrounding circumstances. On the other hand, suppose that the law requires keeping the rivers clean but that nobody obeys and the rivers have turned into public sewers. The moral reasons for not throwing refuse into them that we have been considering do not exist in such circumstances notwithstanding the legal requirement not to do so.

The upshot of the discussion in this section is that the law is good if it provides prudential reasons for action where and when this is advisable and if it marks out certain standards as socially required where it is appropriate to do so. If the law does so properly then it reinforces protection of morally valuable possibilities and interests and encourages and supports worthwhile forms of social co-operation. But neither of these legal techniques even when admirably used gives rise to an obligation to obey the law. It makes sense to judge the law as a useful and important social institution and to judge a legal system good or even perfect while denying that there is an obligation to obey its laws.

13

RESPECT FOR LAW

I shall assume that there is no general obligation to obey the law, not even the laws of a good and just legal system. The question arises what should be the attitude of a conscientious citizen to the laws of a society whose legal system is by and large good and just? It may seem that, given that there is no obligation to obey, only one route is open to him. He should have no general moral attitude to the law. Every case of an action which is required or prohibited by law is to be assessed individually on its moral merits.[1] Sometimes the fact that the action is guided by law will make a moral difference, sometimes it will not. Since there is neither a general duty to obey nor a general duty to disobey the only proper general moral attitude there can be is not to have a general moral attitude.

The purpose of this essay is to suggest that one is not forced to this conclusion. The result of the absence of an obligation to obey the law is that one may have no general moral attitude to the law—even to the good law.[2] Having no general moral attitude is morally permissible. But there is another option equally permissible: to have respect for the law. It will be argued that there is an attitude to law, generally known as respect for it, such that those who have it have a general reason to obey the law, that their reason is their attitude, the fact that they so respect the law, and that it is morally permissible to respect the law in this way (unless it is a generally wicked legal system).

1. A PARADOXICAL CLAIM

The suggestion that those who respect the law are subject to an obligation from which others are exempt may look paradoxi-

---

[1] This need not involve spending time consciously deliberating what to do on every occasion.

[2] Perhaps I should qualify this. It may well be that there is a general reason to disobey the laws of certain wicked governments.

cal, and is in fact paradoxical given some of the common assumptions of current analytical moral philosophy. The present section explains the nature of the paradox. The next two sections dispel it and the final section examines the moral value of this attitude of respect for law.

The attitude we call respect for law is a complex one. For present purposes it is best divided into two components, each being a complex attitude in its own right. Let us call the two, which are often inseparably bound together in actual life, (primarily) cognitive respect and (primarily) practical respect. The primarily cognitive attitude consists in the appropriate cognitions concerning the moral value of law and affective and practical inclinations and dispositions appropriate to them. Both cognitions and affective and practical dispositions vary according to the case and the person whose attitude it is. They may consist, for example, in the belief that the law is democratic and fair, that it contributes to social progress or that it protects individual rights. They may include pride that the law of one's country is by and large enlightened and progressive, satisfaction that one lives under the protection of an adequate legal system, respect or even admiration for institutions or persons involved in creating or administering the law and for symbols of the law (the court house etc.). Among the secondary practical dispositions which the primarily cognitive respect may include could be a reluctance to support proposals for changing the structure of legal institutions unless on very convincing evidence that the change will be for the best, a willingness to recommend and encourage a similar attitude in others and to promote similar laws in other countries, etc.

These remarks are merely illustrative of the sort of beliefs and dispositions which make up the cognitive attitude of respect. The primarily practical attitude of respect consists largely of a disposition to obey the law (i.e. to do that which it requires because it so requires, because it is right as a matter of moral principle to obey it[3]) and a variety of affective and cognitive as well as further practical dispositions appropriate to it. Again these will vary from one person to another. They may include hostility to law-breakers, satisfaction when they are brought

---

[3] This condition is necessary to distinguish practical respect from a disposition to obey on prudential grounds.

to justice, approval of law-abiding behaviour and of people who obey the law, shame and guilt if one breaks the law, etc.

It was mentioned that an individual's respect for the law will usually include elements of both the primarily cognitive and the primarily practical attitudes and that they may be insepar-ably intertwined. It is also true that they are in principle separate both in thought and in life. A man may display the one without the other. An extreme example of a person having practical but not cognitive respect for law is one who believes that however bad the law may be one ought always to obey it. One should strive to reform it but is never entitled to break the law so long as it is in force. If such a man happens to believe that his country's law is very bad he will not have cognitive respect for it, but he is most likely to display extreme practical respect. Examples of separation in the reverse direction may be more common. An inhabitant of one country may have a mild cognitive respect for the law of a neighbouring country without having the practical attitude. He may believe that a citizen or a resident has an obligation to obey the laws of his own country but that tourists are under no such obligation. If by breaking the law they will not harm anyone they are morally free to disregard it when, perhaps, it imposes restrictions of which they are free in their own country.

It may seem that if there is no general obligation to obey the law then it is morally wrong to have a practical attitude of respect. No doubt people can and will continue to have it, but they should not. If there is a general obligation to obey the law then inculcating a practical attitude of respect is often justified as facilitating conformity to the obligation. Obedience comes naturally to one who practically respects the law and that obedience is generally justified by the obligation (it can be assumed that in reasonable legal systems it is rarely defeated). But if there is no general obligation to obey then this attitude is unjustified. It then becomes morally intolerable to cultivate a disposition of submission to legal demands. One should, instead, encourage an attitude of being generally on guard and always willing and ready to consider the merits of conformity or deviation on a case by case basis with no prior dispositions which may bias one's judgment.

Naturally, the absence of an obligation to obey the law does not affect the justifiability of having a cognitive attitude of respect. The law may be morally good and that fact justifies a cognitive attitude of moral respect. It seems, however, that there is no comparable moral fact which could justify a practical attitude of respect. This exposes the apparently paradoxical character of the claim defended below. According to it, the practical respect which some people have for the law is itself a reason to obey the law. The fact that this respect has no ordinary external foundation is acknowledged by the submission that there is no obligation to respect the law even of a good legal system. Respecting the law in such societies is merely permissible. Yet those who respect the law have a reason to obey, indeed are under an obligation to obey. Their attitude of respect is their reason—the source of their obligation. The claim is not merely that they recognize such an obligation, not merely that they think that they are bound by an obligation. It is that they really are under an obligation; they are really bound to obey.

Respect for law (the practical attitude) was identified as that kind of attitude involving recognition of moral reasons for obeying the law. Having concluded, in the previous essay, that there are no such general moral reasons it seems to follow that practical respect for law is an unjustifiable attitude. This conclusion is inescapable if practical respect is derivable from an independently based obligation to obey and is itself justified as being the attitude which facilitates compliance with that obligation. Practical respect is morally defensible only if one can reverse the order of justification and derive an obligation to obey from an independently defensible attitude of practical respect. This can be done if, for example, it is permissible to respect the law and the respect itself is a reason for obeying the law. But can it be that respect for law does not rest on an obligation to obey but is a substitute for it? Can one say that one's respect for the law obliges one to obey it? I shall defend this possibility through drawing an analogy with friendship.

2. FRIENDSHIP: AN ANALOGY

Imagine that one says 'I will help Mary because she is my friend'. That someone is one's friend depends, in part, on one's attitude to that person, but there is no surprise in invoking friendship as a reason for action. It is just what friends are expected to do on appropriate occasions. There are some obvious ways in which friendship can be or be cited as a reason. Two are most common. First, friendship implies a certain degree of goodwill. The agent may wish (has a spontaneous non-reason-based desire) to help his friend. His desire to do so is his reason. Saying 'because she is a friend' explains the context of his desire. Second, friendships create patterns of interaction and thus they generate expectations. The agent may believe that his friend expects him to help or even relies on him to do so (thus forgoing other avenues of securing the help he needs). It is the fact that it would be wrong to disappoint those expectations (or his spontaneous desire not to do so) which is his reason. Citing the friendship intimates that such expectations exist and how they arose (and perhaps it also indicates why it would be wrong to disappoint them).

The view of friendship on which the analogy is based assumes that these are not the only ways in which friendships can be or can generate reasons for action. In particular, it assumes that there are actions one must perform because failing to do so will be wrong given the friendship, but not because of the friend's reaction (emotionally or in action) upon learning of this failure. The friend may never discover the fact, to all outward appearances the friendship may remain intact, and yet the agent knows that he has failed on this occasion.

It is not possible here to provide an analysis or a defence of this view of friendship, but it is necessary to sketch it with a little more detail. No two friendships are alike. They vary with the intentions, personalities, and circumstances of the friends. And yet friendship is to a considerable degree a culturally determined form of human relationship. (There are of course not only one but several culturally recognized basic friendship patterns in our culture. The argument does not depend on there being only one.) When a relationship leading to friendship begins to develop between two or more people its future shape will be affected by the fact that each of them has a conception of what friendship is and what it implies (in his culture). This awareness gives, consciously or unconsciously, a direction to the developing relationship. To put it crudely, it will become a recognizable variation of the basic form, or fail. Few people can transcend the forms imposed by their culture. Their failure to do so is a main source of literary creation (cf. Anna Karenina).

The cultural pattern of friendship to which they conform includes notions as to how friends should behave to each other. They designate certain patterns of behaviour as fitting and others as unfitting between friends. It is part of our culture that a friend in need is a friend indeed or that friends should not be free to criticize friends in front of strangers, regardless of the justice of the criticism, etc. What precisely is fitting and what is not may differ from one culture to another. Common to all of them and part of the very concept of friendship is the fact that the fitting action is required of a friend regardless of whether or not he desires to perform it (I would much rather spend the evening by myself and have no desire to see Tom again, but I should really invite him because he is rather lonely and depressed these days). Similarly, the fitting action is sometimes required regardless of whether or not the friend will learn of it or be affected by it (I shouldn't confirm Dick's innuendoes even though Dick knows the truth and my confirmation will make no difference to anyone, and even though Tom will never hear of this).

If this is right then it is of the essence of friendship that friends regard their relationship as requiring actions independently of the desires of the agent or the interests of his friend. That a person is a friend is a reason simply because any other action is unsuitable between friends, inconsistent with the friendship. Naturally, if the agent is aware of the character of his action then he will be upset (at least if he desires the continuation of the friendship) by his unfitting actions. But his reason for not performing them is not his desire to avoid remorse or guilt but his belief that this is what is required by his friendship. I shall call reasons of this kind *expressive reasons*. Friendship is an expressive reason for those actions which are (in the agent's culture) fitting to the relationship and against the unfitting ones. It is, sometimes, an expressive reason for actions which one has no desire to perform and which even the expectations and reliance created by the friendship give no reason to perform. Expressive reasons are so called because the actions they require express the relationship or attitude involved. The fact that the agent regards himself as bound by such reasons is a criterion for his being a friend. Expressive reasons may require an action because it will benefit the friend (the invitation to Tom to spend the evening with me). They are then welfare reasons. But they may be independent of any benefit to anyone (not confirming the innuendoes about Tom), in which case they are symbolic reasons.

To claim that to be a friend involves belief in expressive reasons is to claim that the concept of expressive reasons has a use in explaining human relationships as we know them. It is not to claim that there are valid expressive reasons, i.e. that it is ever justified to have friends. Remember that the choice is not necessarily between being a friend and being a stranger; there are other relationships known to our culture and others still which may be created. I shall not try to justify friendship. Instead let it be assumed that friendship as a general form of human relation is morally defensible. On this assumption it is possible to summarize the main point of the discussion above and a few additional and relatively uncontroversial points about friendship.

(1) Friends have reasons which others have not. These, or some of them, arise independently of the relationship giving rise to or being accompanied by new interests or desires. They have reason to do that which is fitting and avoid that which does not befit their friendships. Their culture determines which actions fit that bill. Friendships generate expressive reasons (both of the welfare and of the symbolic varieties).

(2) It is morally permissible not to have friends at all and morally permissible not to be friends with any particular person. Barring exceptional circumstances it is not morally wrong for a person not to want to have nor to try to form friendships generally or respecting any particular person.[4]

(3) One's choice of friends is revealing of one's character and may be a manifestation of one's moral character as well. Though most friendships are not morally significant, some are. They reveal certain moral sensibilities or their absence, speak of moral strength or weakness, etc. Therefore, though one does

---

[4] The permission involved is an exclusionary permission. Therefore, the assertion in the text does not entail that there is no moral reason to have friends. Cf. *Practical Reason and Norms*, pp. 89 f.

no wrong in becoming or not becoming X's friend, it may be morally praiseworthy to do so, or be a moral blemish to refuse his advances.

(4) The obligations of friends are self-imposed. They depend on a relationship which one could have avoided and which one can terminate. Moreover, one can create and terminate the relation without doing anything wrong. (That is at least generally the case. It seems that in certain extreme circumstances it is not morally permissible to terminate a friendship.) Yet the obligations of friends differ from promises and other voluntary obligations in two crucial respects.

In the first place, they form a constitutive part of a relationship affecting, in characteristic cases, a whole dimension of one's life. Furthermore, the relationship has a cognitive and emotional aspect. Since the obligations are part and parcel of the relationship they cannot be assumed or renounced by one act (again—barring certain rare and untypical circumstances). The obligations derive from the friendship, not from an act of commitment. The friendship itself, involving an intricate web of reciprocal dispositions and attitudes, practical, emotional, and cognitive, cannot be created by an act of commitment. It has to grow, develop, and cement over time. The same is true of the termination of friendships. Normally no single act can put an end to the myriad elements making one person another's friend. These remarks should not be taken as implying that long periods are always necessary for the creation or severance of such ties. They merely suggest that periods, rather than single acts, are involved. It is a romantic and an adolescent fancy that friendships come and go in a flash or in an act of commitment. Such events can lead to the formation of friendships or their demise, since infatuation or commitment to become or cease to be friends may lead to friendship or its termination. But these events do not in themselves create a friendship nor put an end to one.[5]

Secondly, while promises and other voluntary obligations are undertaken by acts performed in order to undertake an obligation, friendships are not. Their practical consequences, the obligations they give rise to, are by-products of the relationship

---

[5] Thus, if the intial event has no continuation we do not have a short-lived friendship. At best we have a failed attempt to create one.

rather than its point and purpose. People may create a friendship in order to have someone to care for, but not, normally, in order to have an obligation to care for someone.

3. RESPECT FOR LAW: THE ANALOGY

Turning back to respect for law, one point must be made clear at the outset: it is not my intention to suggest that respect for law is a case of friendship. Obviously it is not. For one thing, friendship is a reciprocal relation whereas respect for law is not. Besides, friendship being a relationship between persons has very different emotional aspects from respect for an institution such as the law. But it is instructive to draw an analogy between friendship and respect for law. The analogy extends to the four points mentioned above. They will be taken in reverse order.

Respect for law is, like friendship, a complex and multi-faceted phenomenon. Naturally, such a complex attitude is not acquired or lost overnight. It grows or diminishes over time. At the same time whether or not one respects the law is up to the individual. A person may decide that the law deserves to be respected and that he will respect it or that it is better not to respect it any more. Such decisions do not create or terminate the attitude overnight, but they may signal the beginning of a process leading to its acquisition or loss, and they demonstrate one's control over its existence.

Whether or not one respects the law is, given information about the law and the society, revealing of one's character. It testifies to one's attitude to authority, to respectable institutions, the degree of one's socialization, etc. It may also speak, on occasion, of one's moral character. But not in every case is the existence or absence of the attitude morally significant.

Be that as it may, it is clear—given the conclusion of the previous essay—that there is no general obligation to respect the law. Nobody does any wrong in not respecting the law even in a good state. One may always avoid having any general moral attitude to the law. This may be more or less admirable than respecting the law but it is equally permissible. Here it seems there is an asymmetry between respect and its absence. While it is never wrong not to respect the law it is morally wrong to respect it in South Africa or other fundamentally iniquitous regions.[6]

Finally, respect is itself a reason for action. Those who respect the law have reasons which others have not. These are expressive reasons. They express their respect for the law in obeying it, in respecting institutions and symbols connected with it, and in avoiding questioning it on every occasion. Once again, as in the case of friendship, social conventions and cultural precepts partly determine the appropriate or fitting ways to express respect. It is here important to remember that just as there are qualified or partial friendships (golf friends, business friends, etc.) so there are possibilities of qualified respect (respect for law on all matters except women's rights, etc.).

It may be objected that there is one major disanalogy between friendship and practical respect, namely that the obligation of friends is but one aspect of a complex human relationship whereas practical respect is first and foremost a recognition of a reason to obey the law. Therefore while it is possible to conceive of certain actions as appropriate to express the friendship (i.e. the other aspects of the relationship) there is nothing which obedience for law can express. It therefore makes no sense—it can be alleged—to regard respect itself as an expressive reason. The objection is valid so far as the analysis of respect which was offered so far goes. It is further strengthened by the separation of practical respect from the cognitive one. But in truth practical respect is not an independent attitude. It is but one aspect of a complex attitude and style of life, relating not only to the law but to the community whose law it is. Respect for law is an aspect of identification with society (the reverse of alienation). Here we come to the root of our analogy. A person identifying himself with his society, feeling that it is his and that he belongs to it, is loyal to his society. His loyalty may express itself, among other ways, in respect for the law of the community. Friendship likewise presupposes mutual loyalty and there is therefore little surprise that both friendship and respect for law give rise to expressive reasons.

[6] The symmetry lies elsewhere. Just as one may not respect the law of an unjust system so one may not have an attitude of disrespect for a just one, though one may have no general practical moral attitude to it at all. Conventional reasons are always bound by non-conventional ones.

It would be wrong to suggest, however, that respect for law is inseparable from loyalty to the community and from identification with it. Identification and loyalty do express themselves in various ways. They may but need not manifest themselves through respect for the law. A person may express his loyalty in other ways only. It will not necessarily be incomplete for not including respect for law among its manifestations. Therefore, even if loyalty to one's community is obligatory, respect for law is not.

4. THE WORTH OF RESPECT

It is now possible to summarize the conclusions concerning the proper attitude to the law. There is no general moral obligation to obey it, not even in a good society. It is permissible to have no general moral attitude to the law, to reserve one's judgment and examine each situation as it arises. But in all but iniquitous societies it is equally permissible to have 'practical' respect for the law. For one who thus respects the law his respect itself is a reason for obeying the law. It is admittedly not very common to cite it as the reason. People would normally say 'because it is the law' or 'because it is *my* law', 'the law of *my* country'. Such explanations are in themselves incomplete. Often they allude to the person's respect for the law as the underlying factor.

It is never wrong not to respect the law in this practical sense. But it does not follow that where it is permissible both to respect and not to respect, it is also morally indifferent whether one does or not. Often indeed it is morally indifferent. In other circumstances it is not. A person who respects the law expresses in this way his attitude to society, his identification with and loyalty to it. Such a person may find it appropriate to express these attitudes to society, among other ways, through his attitude to the law. He may feel it is a fitting expression of his loyalty to acknowledge the authority of the law. He will then obey the law as it claims to be obeyed. But, as was mentioned above, respect can come in measures and in degrees and a person may regard a qualified respect as the appropriate expression of his attitude to his society. In any case, for the person who respects the law there is an obligation to obey. His respect is the source of this obligation.

It is not difficult to see why practical respect might be thought of as a proper expression of loyalty to the society. It is a manifestation of trust. A man who is confident that the law is just and good believes that he has reason to do as the law requires. If the law is really morally perfect it will not claim greater weight than is due to its laws, and it will allow as excusing conditions all those in which the reasons for the legally required act are defeated by other considerations. If a person places absolute trust in the law then he will acknowledge the authority of the law. It is natural therefore that loyalty to one's society can be expressed by behaving as one would if one trusted the law implicitly. Hence the attitude of respect is a manifestation of loyalty since it gives rise to such an obligation to obey, to such an acknowledgement of authority.

Which law is worthy of respect? What circumstances make it so? The questions about the conditions under which respect speaks well of the agent are important questions which cannot be explored here. Suffice it to say that it is not just a question of when one should be loyal to one's community. Even where loyalty to one's society is morally appropriate, or even obligatory, expressing it through respect for law may not be appropriate. Respect for law expresses loyalty through an attitude to certain institutionalized aspects of the community. Their moral character or behaviour may make them unfitting for the moral trust which respect for law expresses. After all, respect for law is a somewhat self-satisfied and complacent attitude to the law. It expresses confidence that the law is morally sound. Such confidence may or may not be misplaced. Loyalty to one's people may in certain countries require active opposition to the law as much as in others it may find proper expression in respect for the law. The question as to when the one or the other attitude is appropriate is no longer a question about the proper attitude to law; it is a question about the nature of the good society and the good law.

14

A RIGHT TO DISSENT?
I. CIVIL DISOBEDIENCE

The question to be considered in this essay and the next one is whether, and under what circumstances, there is a moral right to break the law for moral or political reasons. I shall assume that if there is such a moral right then there is a presumption for giving it legal recognition. The discussion will encompass some of the considerations affecting the form, if any, which legal recognition should have.

It may be thought that the view (which was defended in Essay 12) that there is no obligation to obey the law opens the way to an easy justification of disobedience on moral and political grounds and that this will be the main respect in which my conclusions will differ from those of most writers on civil disobedience and conscientious objection who assume a prima facie obligation to obey. But this is far from being the case. The argument for denying an obligation to obey turned in part on the fact that on numerous occasions the fact that an act is in breach of the law has no adverse consequences. This, however, is never (or hardly ever) true in civil disobedience (conscientious objection is often more like ordinary violations of law). Such acts are normally designed to catch the public eye and inevitably set people thinking of resorting to disobedience to achieve whatever changes in law or policy they find justified. Thus they have almost invariably some adverse consequences. No doubt, civil disobedience is sometimes justified and occasionally is even obligatory. But the reasoning pursued in the former essays supports the common assumption that in a reasonably just state any consideration in favour of disobedience has to overcome a presumption against it based on its accompanying undesirable results. Having said that, it must be added that the topic of this essay is not the justification of disobedience for political or moral reasons. It is the question whether there is, in certain circumstances, a moral right to such disobedience. The difference between these questions will be explained below, but first the main classes of disobedience for moral and political reasons must be distinguished.

1. FORMS OF DISSENT

Many cases of law-breaking are not backed by a claim that they are justified. The agent may have acted wrongly knowingly or in ignorance. Consideration of such cases and the question of the proper legal attitude to them does not belong to this essay. It is concerned only with cases of law-breaking with respect to which the agent denies that he acted wrongly. Many such cases, probably the vast majority, can be dubbed 'cases of occasional disobedience'. These are breaches of law which the agent thinks, given the character of the law involved and of the particular circumstances in which he acted, were morally permissible (and for which he had what he considered some good reasons). Such occasional disobedience, though claimed to be morally justified, is not undertaken for moral or political reasons. Moral considerations merely render it permissible. Its motivation comes from other considerations. The present essay deals with morally motivated disobedience only.

It is convenient to follow the traditional classification of morally and politically motivated disobedience into three categories: revolutionary disobedience, civil disobedience, and conscientious objection.

Revolutionary Disobedience is a politically motivated breach of law designed to change or to contribute directly to a change of government or of the constitutional arrangements (the system of government).

Civil Disobedience is a politically motivated breach of law designed either to contribute directly to a change of a law or of a public policy or to express one's protest against, and dissocation from, a law or a public policy.

Conscientious Objection is a breach of law for the reason that the agent is morally prohibited to obey it, either because of its general character (e.g. as with absolute pacifists and conscription) or because it extends to certain cases which should not be covered by it (e.g. conscription and selective objectors and murder and euthanasia).

There is little point in a very extensive discussion and defence of these definitions. No claim is here made that they represent the ordinary meaning of the defined terms. They are presented as a useful classification of certain cases of disobedience. The classification does not exhaust all cases of morally and politically motivated disobedience. It does not, for example, include breach of law in protest against morally unacceptable actions or policies of private agents (trade unions, banks, private universities, etc.). Nor is the classification exclusive. The categories are partly overlapping. A person may break the law on a single occasion for a combination of reasons making his action simultaneously a revolutionary one and a case of civil disobedience (e.g. he wishes to protest against a particular law and thereby directly contribute to a change of government). Selective conscientious objection to the war in Vietnam in the U.S.A. during the Sixties provided many illustrations of people combining civil disobedience and conscientious objection in one act.

These categories are most easily applied to the analysis of action by individuals. But they can be applied to the analysis of action by groups, the character of a demonstration or a sit-in involving breach of law being determined by the reasons of its organizers, or the bulk of its participants. It is important, however, to remember that the character of the reasons and therefore of the actions of individual participants may differ.

Revolutionary acts and civil disobedience are cases of political action, they are essentially public actions designed to have a political effect. Conscientious objection is not. It is essentially a private action by a person who wishes to avoid committing moral wrong by obeying a (totally or partially) morally bad law. Note that not every case of breach of law which is morally obligatory is a case of conscientious objection. Sometimes it is wrong not to participate in civil disobedience involving breach of a reasonable law. Only where a claim that the law itself is wrong (or at least certain aspects of it) motivates violation of it does one have an instance of conscientious objection.

Civil disobedience can be aimed to be effective or expressive (or both). It is designed to be effective if it is justified as part of a plan of action which is likely to lead to a change in law or public policy. But civil disobedience includes also breaches of law the perpetrators of which know to be ineffective, provided they are justified as expressions of protest against or a public disavowal of a law or a public policy. Given that revolutionary and civil disobedience are political actions, they normally involve public, open, action. This is normally necessary for them to achieve their purpose (be it expressive or effective). But only the fact that an act of disobedience occurred and (at least in most cases of civil disobedience) the nature of its motivation have to be made publicly known. There is no general reason why individuals engaged in those activities should make their identity known or voluntarily submit to punishment. Though such reasons may well exist on occasion, such action proves the purity of one's motives; a trial or a term in gaol may serve as a focal point for the mobilization of more opposition to the law or policy protested against, etc.

Some writers have included submission to punishment in their definition of civil disobedience. This is just one respect in which the definition endorsed here is wider than most of the definitions canvassed in recent years. This definition relates to the reason for the disobedience and nothing more. The justification for such a wide definition is that it is meant to characterize civil disobedience as a certain type of political action. Like all political action it is aimed at a law or a public policy and it is distinguished from other political acts by using violations of law as a means (and from revolutionary action by not being designed to lead to a change of government or of the system of government). The main motivation for the more restrictive definition is to identify the conditions under which political breach of law is justified (only if open, non-violent, etc.). But this definition is not meant to single out a class of *legitimate* political action. I am assuming a definition which is value-neutral so as to separate the classification of types of political acts from the discussion of their justification. Furthermore, and more to our point, I wish to argue in the next section that discussions of civil disobedience favouring a narrow understanding of the expression make sense only on the assumption that there is a right to civil disobedience. I shall then proceed to argue that there is no such general right.

2. COMMON PHILOSOPHICAL ATTITUDES TO
CIVIL DISOBEDIENCE

It is common ground to most discussions of the subject, and one which I share, that civil disobedience is sometimes justified or even obligatory. Many authors do tend to favour a stronger view which they often fail clearly to separate from this one, namely that one has, under certain conditions, a right to civil disobedience. It is, therefore, necessary to clarify the difference between these claims.

Consider an analogous case. People have, let us assume, a moral right to freedom of expression. That right extends to cases in which one should not exercise it. One should not repeat stories about people which one does not believe to be true. But one has a right to do so. The right to free expression is not recognized in the law of the Soviet Union despite the fact that it is permissible there to express views agreeable to the Soviet Communist Party. The reason one says that the right is there denied is not because the views of the Communist Party are wrong and should not be expressed. Even one who accepts their truth will have to admit that there is no freedom of expression in the Soviet Union, though he may find no fault in this. Freedom of expression is denied there not because one cannot express true beliefs but because one cannot express false ones, beliefs which one should not have nor express. This and nothing less is implied by the common observation that the freedom is to express any view one wishes (subject to a certain small number of restrictions such as that against libel).

At first blush it may be thought surprising that one should have a right to do that which one ought not. Is it not better to confine rights to that which it is right or at least permissible to do? But to say this is to misunderstand the nature of rights. One needs no right to be entitled to do the right thing. That it is right gives one all the title one needs. But one needs a right to be entitled to do that which one should not. It is an essential element of rights to action that they entitle one to do that which one should not. To say this is not, of course, to say that the purpose or justification of rights of action is to increase wrongdoing. Their purpose is to develop and protect the autonomy of the agent. They entitle him to choose for himself rightly or wrongly. But they cannot do that unless they entitle him to choose wrongly.[1]

Herein lies the difference between asserting that civil disobedience is sometimes right and claiming that one has, under certain conditions, a right to civil disobedience. The latter claim entails, as the first does not, that one is, under those conditions, entitled civilly to disobey even though one should not do so.

I have said that more writers than those who openly endorse such a right gravitate towards supporting its existence. This tendency is manifested in their concern with setting formal limits on the permissible forms of civil disobedience. Consider one often discussed limitation: civil disobedience, it is often said, must be non-violent. It is clear that, other things being equal, non-violent disobedience is much to be preferred to violent disobedience. First, the direct harm caused by the violence is avoided. Secondly, the possible encouragement to resort to violence in cases where this would be wrong, which even an otherwise justified use of violence provides, is avoided. Thirdly, the use of violence is a highly emotional and explosive issue in many countries and in turning to violence one is likely to antagonize potential allies and confirm in their opposition many of one's opponents. All these considerations, and others, suggest great reluctance to turn to the use of violence, most particularly violence against the person. But do they justify the total proscription of violence as a means to achieving a political aim? They do not. The evil the disobedience is designed to rectify may be so great, may indeed itself involve violence against innocent persons (such as the imprisonment of dissidents in labour camps in the Soviet Union), that it may be right to use violence to bring it to an end. It may be relevant here to draw attention to the fact that certain non-violent acts, indeed some lawful acts, may well have much more severe consequences than many an act of violence: consider the possible effects of a strike by ambulance drivers.

Some people do of course reject the use of violence absolutely regardless of any other considerations. Pacifists take such a

---

[1] These comments on rights to act are in keeping with the general analysis of rights developed in several articles by H. L. A. Hart, even though they do not commit me to all the details of his views. Cf., for example, 'Bentham on Legal Rights' in A. W. B. Simpson (ed.), *Oxford Essays in Jurisprudence*, 2nd series (Oxford, 1973).

view. But on any other basis violence for political gains cannot be rejected absolutely.[2] Many writers have argued for similar conclusions. My aim is not to vindicate the use of violence, which I would hope to see used only very rarely and with great caution. My aim is to point to the (often silent) presuppositions of the argument to condemn all violent civil disobedience by people who are not pacifists and do not reject all violence as wrong absolutely. This rejection of violence is due no doubt to a certain extent to a somewhat confused apprehension of the various considerations mitigating against violence mentioned above, but to a certain extent they are inspired by a feeling that if civil disobedience is justified then there is a right to it.

To say that there is a right to civil disobedience is to allow the legitimacy of resorting to this form of political action to one's political opponents. It is to allow that the legitimacy of civil disobedience does not depend on the rightness of one's cause. The comments above make clear that by all accounts the rightness of civil disobedience does not depend only on the rightness of the cause it is meant to support. There is always the question of the appropriateness of the means. Will they not contribute to an even greater evil, are there not less harmful or less risky ways of supporting the same cause, etc.? Those who hold that there is a right to civil disobedience are committed to the view that in general[3] the rightness of the cause contributes not at all to the justification of civil disobedience. Such a view leads quite naturally to a consideration of formal limits on the forms such disobedience may take.

The logic of such reasoning becomes transparent once one considers the similar line of reasoning concerning lawful political action. Liberal states do not make the legitimacy of political action dependent on the cause it is meant to serve. People may support political aims of all complexions.[4] But the right to political action is circumscribed in such states by limitations as to the form of the permissible actions. Given that we are used to thinking in this way of lawful political action, it is only

---

[2] Some will say that violent action cannot be considered civil disobedience because by its meaning civil disobedience does not apply to such action. But even if right this is irrelevant. Such a linguistic point cannot prove the wrongness of my action.

[3] Many if not all political theories rule out certain political goals as altogether illegitimate and do not extend to them any toleration.

[4] Subject to the proviso above.

natural to extend the same approach to unlawful political activity. Such an attitude regards pursuit of political goals of all kinds—good as well as bad—through civil disobedience as justified provided one observes the forms of permissible action.

Considered against this background it is understandable that so much intellectual effort has been invested in an attempt to articulate and justify a doctrine of the permissible forms of civil disobedience. It must be used as a measure of last resort after all other means have failed to obtain one's desired goal; it must be non-violent; it must be openly undertaken; and its perpetrators must submit to prosecution and punishment; such acts must be confined to those designed to publicize certain wrongs and to convince the public and the authorities of the justice of one's claims; it should not be used to intimidate or coerce. Such and similar conditions have been much discussed and often favoured. All of them are open to objections similar to those deployed above against the non-violence requirements. Why, for example, should civil disobedience be always thought of as a measure of last resort? True, other things being equal, it has by-products (setting a bad example even if the act is justified in the instant case) which lawful political action does not have. But other things are rarely equal and sometimes civil disobedience should be preferred to lawful action even when that action will be effective. Which is worse: a miners' march in London which perpetrates various offences such as obstruction to the highway, or a lawful lengthy miners' strike?

Such objections are correct. But to be completely successful they must tackle directly the reasoning which leads to such apparently arbitrary restrictions on legitimate civil disobedience. It is necessary to examine the question of the right to civil disobedience.

3. A RIGHT TO POLITICAL PARTICIPATION

There are some bad arguments for a right to civil disobedience:

(1) It could be argued that since one's own acts of civil disobedience may well encourage others to break the law in pursuit of their wrong political objectives one is not entitled to engage in such activities unless they are similarly entitled. This is a *non sequitur*. If one's otherwise justified disobedience may lead others to disobey in circumstances where it is wrong to

do so, then one's own disobedience is permissible only if it is justified to run the risk of this happening, that is only if the advantages of one's disobedience are sufficient to outweigh this as well as all the other resulting disadvantages. It does not follow that others have a right to disobey for wrong objectives, only that one should be cautious in considering disobedience for it may lead others to do so.

(2) It could be argued that there is a right to civil disobedience, for the contrary is conceivable only if there is a moral authority to judge which causes are right and which are wrong. Since there are no such moral authorities, since everyone has an equal right to judge for himself what is right and what is wrong, it follows that everyone has a right to civil disobedience in support of a cause which he finds to be right, even if it is in fact wrong. But this argument is valid only if it follows from the admitted fact that there are no general moral authorities, that each person is an ultimate and unchallengeable authority concerning the morality of his own actions. But in fact all that follows is that nobody is. Therefore, moral disagreements cannot be resolved by appeal to authority—not even that of the individual concerning his own actions—but, if at all, only by resort to substantive rational argument. Therefore, it does not follow that there is a right to disobedience, though it is true that there are no moral authorities who can judge whether the disobedience is justified or not.

(3) It could be argued that since it is unfair to deny to others what one allows oneself, it follows that if one allows oneself to resort to civil disobedience in support of one's political goals one should allow others the right to use civil disobedience to support theirs. But this is at best an argument *ad hominem*. People who defend their own disobedience by reference to their right to pursue their political goals by such means cannot in fairness deny a similar right to their political opponents. But a person who supports his action by argument to show that it is in defence of a just cause can without unfairness deny a right to civil disobedience. He allows others to perform similar actions in pursuit of similarly just aims. He denies both himself and others the right to disobey in support of morally wrong aims.

(4) Some may argue from relativism. Since there is no rationally conclusive proof of moral right and wrong, one could

not defend civil disobedience by relying on the rightness of one's cause. It cannot be proved and hence if one is justified in acting on one's beliefs one must, to be consistent, allow others the right to act in support of their beliefs. This argument is flawed. If interpreted in the spirit of radical scepticism it leads to the conclusion that no moral conclusions can ever be rationally held or defended and therefore it is rationally impossible to hold or defend the view that there is a right to civil disobedience. Interpreted as an argument for relativism rather than scepticism, it means that though one can rationally hold moral views one cannot conclusively prove their validity so that people presented with the evidence will be irrational not to endorse the conclusion. But then if one rationally believes a certain political ideal to be invalid, the fact that others are not irrational to reject this view does not entail that one cannot hold them immoral for acting on it. On the contrary, by one's very (rational) commitment to the view that the ideal is wrong, one is committed to the view that so is action based on it. No right to civil disobedience can be established in this way.[5]

We need to make a new beginning, to find a way of relating the general principles governing the right to lawful political activity to the question of civil disobedience. But it is not possible to return here to first principles. Instead I shall take it for granted that every person has a right to political participation in his society. Let me call this the liberal principle. I do not call it the democratic principle for in itself it does not commit one to a democratic government, only to a right to a certain degree of political participation. Nothing in the argument that follows depends on one's assessment of the precise limits of the right and I shall not attempt to specify them. It is clear, nevertheless, that the right to political participation is limited. It is limited because of the need to respect the same right in others and because the right to political participation is neither the only nor an absolute value and it has to be limited in order to safeguard other values. It is further clear that, subject to certain limited possible objections, the limitations on the scope of the right are independent of the political objective sought. The right means nothing if it does not mean the right of every

[5] This argument shows that nothing in this essay presupposes either the truth or falsity of relativism.

member of a society to try to get his society to endorse, at least to some degree, political objectives which he supports, be they what they may. Given that by and large the limitations on the right are independent of the political objectives the right is used to support, they must inevitably turn on the means used to support such objectives. It must be a right confined to certain forms of action and not to others.

The most direct implication of the limited right to political participation is that it is binding on law-makers. It should be recognized and defended by the law. In other words the law should set limits to one's legal right to political activity and these should coincide with those which are right on moral and political grounds. To say this is not to imply that the extent of the moral right should affect but not itself be affected by legal rules. Many alternative determinations of the precise boundaries of the right may be largely equivalent in value and many more possible determinations are better or worse than the optimum by small margins. Furthermore, it is greatly desirable to have the limits declared in an open and public way by a generally accepted authority. Therefore if the legally declared boundaries of the right of political action fall within the area of reasonable potential determinations the fact that they are legally declared makes them morally binding. An argument in favour of an otherwise slightly superior potential solution will not succeed in undermining the morally binding force of an otherwise slightly inferior but legally endorsed boundary. In this way the law affects one's moral right to political action. But principally it should be moulded by it.

All states can accordingly be divided into those in which the liberal principle is adequately recognized and protected in law and those in which it is not. Let states of the first kind be called 'liberal states' and the others 'illiberal states'. The main presupposition of this essay is that all states ought to be liberal states. The two main conclusions entailed by this view are that (1) there is no moral right to civil disobedience in liberal states; (2) normally there is such a right in illiberal states.

4. CIVIL DISOBEDIENCE IN A LIBERAL STATE

Given that the illiberal state violates its members' right of political participation, individuals whose rights are violated are entitled,, other things being equal, to disregard the offending laws and exercise their moral right as if it were recognized by law. Of course, other things are rarely equal. In the illiberal state to exercise one's right may involve breaking the law and such action will sometimes have undesirable consequences which would have been avoided had the action been lawful. Therefore, the illiberality of the illiberal state may have the effect of narrowing down the *moral* right to political action of its members. However, subject to this reservation, members of the illiberal state do have a right to civil disobedience which is roughly that part of their moral right to political participation which is not recognized in law.

The case is reversed in a liberal state. Here there can be no right to civil disobedience which derives from a general right to political participation. One's right to political activity is, by hypothesis, adequately protected by law. It can never justify breaking it. Put it another way: Every claim that one's right to political participation entitles one to take a certain action in support of one's political aims (be they what they may), even though it is against the law, is *ipso facto* a criticism of the law for outlawing this action. For if one has a right to perform it its performance should not be civil disobedience but a lawful political act. Since by hypothesis no such criticism can be directed against the liberal state there can be no right to civil disobedience in it.

This conclusion does not mean that civil disobedience in a liberal state is never justified. A liberal state was defined in a rather technical and narrow sense. It is simply one which respects the right to political participation. It may contain any number of bad and iniquitous laws. Sometimes it will be right to engage in civil disobedience to protest against them or against bad public policies. The practical implications of the argument above concerning disobedience in a liberal state are as follows:

Generally two kinds of arguments are relevant for judging another person's action, two kinds of argument that a man can use to convince another rationally that he is entitled to perform a certain act. He can show that the act is right (or that there is reason to think that it is) or he can show that he has (or that there is reason to think that he has) a right to perform it. To show that the act is right is to get the other person to approve its performance. To show that one has a right to it is to show that even if it is wrong he is entitled to perform it. In a liberal state the second argument is not available in defence of civil disobedience. It can be rationally supported by people who approve its aims, but it has no claim to the toleration of those who do not. There could, for example, be no claim that the general public or public authorities shall not take action to prevent the disobedience or to punish its commission (provided such action is proportionate to the offence, etc.) which is based on a right to toleration.[6] The only moral claim for support or non-interference must be based on the rightness of the political goal of the disobedient.[7]

I said that the practical implications of the absence of a right to civil disobedience in a liberal state affect one person's judgment of another's action and the agent's way of defending his action to others. Does it not affect the agent's own practical deliberations? Having a right to perform an action is no reason to do it. One has to be convinced that the action is right. Otherwise one's action will be an abuse of one's rights. But it is sometimes thought that having a right to act is, in general, a precondition for its being right to do so. No doubt this is sometimes the case. For example, since one has no right to interfere in a stranger's private affairs it is never (or almost never) right

[6] If the state authorities come to share (to a sufficient degree) the views of the civil disobedients they should not, other things being equal, prosecute them, for people should not be punished for doing the right thing. If a judge or a prosecutor comes to side with the protesters against the authorities he may find it necessary to resign or civilly disobey or both.

[7] Two possible objections should be mentioned and dismissed. It may be said that the law cannot set the right limits to political action for it cannot set limits to specifically political action. If a road is closed it must be closed to all. If it is open it will be open to all. It cannot be closed to some and open to others, closed to the general public and open to demonstrators. The answer to this objection is just to deny its premiss. It is often possible and practical to permit action for political reasons where similar action for other reasons is proscribed. Admittedly sometimes this is impractical, but there is no reason to think that, given the many alternative forms political action can take, the law cannot set reasonable boundaries to political action.

Some may think that the argument in the essay disregards the desirability of encouraging pluralism in the society. Pluralism would lead to dissent and to civil disobedience and if it is desirable its inevitable consequences should be tolerated. The fallacy in this argument is to suppose that pluralism must lead to dissent and disobedience. It will do so if the law does not allow for pluralistic forms of life to flourish. If the law encourages and respects pluralism it need not lead to dissent from law. It can find adequate expression within it.

to do so, even though having a right to interfere in one's wife's private affairs does not mean that it is generally right to do so. But whether or not having a right to act is a precondition of the rightness of the act depends on the underlying reasoning supporting the claim of a right and its limitation. The reason for the limits on the right to political participation is to set a boundary to one's toleration of unjustified political action. It therefore does not affect the agent's own reasoning so long as he is confident that his action is justified.

Yet more indirectly the absence of a right to civil disobedience in liberal states does affect even the agent's own reasoning. First, he may be less than certain that his action is justified and, therefore, caution may advise desisting from an action to which one may not be entitled. Secondly, civil disobedience is a very divisive action. It is all the more so because of the absence of a right to it (in liberal states). In taking a civilly disobedient action one steps outside the legitimate bounds of toleration and this in itself adds to its disadvantages and should make one very reluctant to engage in it.

The argument above explains the sense in which civil disobedience is an exceptional political action. It is exceptional, in liberal states, in being one beyond the bounds of toleration, beyond the general right to political action. It is not necessarily, as is sometimes said, justified only as an action of last resort. In support of a just cause it may be less harmful than certain kinds of lawful action (e.g. a national strike, or a long strike in a key industry or service). It may be wrong not to resort to civil disobedience and to turn to such lawful action first, or give up any action in support of a just cause. The claim that civil disobedience is justified only when all else has failed or is certain to fail, like the claims that it should be open and non-violent, etc., reflects a failure to conceive its true nature. It is an attempt to routinize it and make it a regular form of political action to which all have a right. Its exceptional character lies precisely in the reverse of this claim, in the fact that it is (in liberal states) one type of political action to which one has no right.

15

A RIGHT TO DISSENT?
II. CONSCIENTIOUS OBJECTION

The main conclusion of the above discussion of civil disobedience is that there should not be a moral right to such disobedience. If in the circumstances of a certain state there is a right to civil disobedience it is a reflection of the inadequacy of its law in not setting the right limit to lawful political activity. Nothing in the arguments leading to this conclusion suggest that it can be extended to the problem of conscientious objection. Civil disobedience is a political act, an attempt by the agent to change public policies. Conscientious objection is a private act, designed to protect the agent from interference by public authority. The two classes of action overlap, but their justification is bound to take different routes; an individual entering the public arena in the name of his right to participate in making collective decisions in the one case as against an individual asserting his immunity from public interference in matters which he regards as private to himself. The case for a right to conscientious objection seems much stronger. Reflection on the nature of liberalism, it seems, may suggest that the very narrow definition of the liberal state given above should be widened to include the institution of a general legal right of conscientious objection, that is, a state is liberal only if it includes laws to the effect that no man shall be liable for breach of duty if his breach is committed because he thinks that it is morally wrong for him to obey the law on the ground that it is morally bad or wrong totally or in part. Though the case for such a view is very strong, so are the considerations weighing against it, and I find myself unable to advocate a general view based on general political principles. The following discussion will be rather inconclusive. It explores in a general way various considerations for and against such a right and various alternative solutions. These when coupled with detailed information concerning the political and social circumstances of a certain country may lead to definite conclusions as to the legal institutions appropriate for that country. No attempt at such application will be made here.

1. CONSCIENCE AND RESPECT FOR PERSONS

Conscientious objection is most often discussed nowadays in connection with military service. There may be practical reasons why it is difficult to extend the right to conscientious objection to other fields of the law, but whatever principles or moral reasons there are for recognizing it with regard to conscription apply also to other areas of law.[1] Even if it is true that the duty of military service is the only one which requires individuals to kill or to participate in killing and even if this duty requires greater sacrifice of personal goals and desires than any other legal duty, these facts do not make conscientious objection uniquely suitable to conscription. Conscientious objection seems not to be based on a desire to protect individuals from far-reaching consequences to their life due to the law. It is moral objection, not objection in the name of one's own interest in preserving one's basic life-style and one's fundamental plans for the future. Nor does the fact that killing is a matter of grave moral concern matter. This in itself does not raise any doubt in the justification of requiring a man to kill (or indeed to put his own life at risk). The point is not that military service is morally justified. It may not be, but that debate is irrelevant to the present purpose. The point is that if one holds that military service can in principle be justified (by considerations such as the need to prevent death or indignity to other people) then once one is convinced that it is required in certain circumstances the gravity of the requirement does not in itself give rise to any right to conscientious objection. The only way to base such a right on moral principles is to concede that because somebody *wrongly* believes that military service is morally prohibited for him he should be allowed to opt out.

Here lies the main difficulty in justifying conscientious objection. It involves showing that a person is entitled not to do what it would otherwise be his moral duty to do simply because he wrongly believes that it is wrong for him to do so. There are,

---

[1] There are historical reasons for the way Western thought concerning conscientious objection has developed. But this essay deliberately ignores the history of the subject. It aims to present several considerations towards a systematic treatment of the subject.

of course, other kinds of arguments which could be used to justify conscientious objection in some cases. It could, for instance, be argued that to force pacifists to serve in the army is counter-productive for they will make bad soldiers and will spread dissension in the ranks (or alternatively live at public expense in gaol). In totalitarian and similar states the right to conscientious objection is sometimes demanded as a compromise. The real solution to the moral iniquities of those states can only come with the overthrow of the government and the repeal of many laws. This being impossible, let those who feel the oppression most strongly have the partial relief which a right to conscientious objection can bring. This and similar arguments are often valid and valuable. But the purpose of this essay is to examine the principal moral arguments for a general right to conscientious objection, a right to be recognized even in the good state. Therefore, the argument must proceed on the assumption that the law is morally valid and that one should (morally) comply with it. The conscientious objector, it will be assumed, proposes to act wrongly. Should he have a right to do the wrong thing because he sincerely holds mistaken or wrong moral views?[2] If there is reason to allow people such a right it is likely to apply to matters other than military service as well. Some time ago a very religious parent objected to his daughter attending school wearing a skirt. Eventually he preferred to emigrate rather than to submit. This shows the depths of his conviction. But he was not a pacifist and would not have objected to military service as such. Surely if there is a right to do the wrong thing because of one's convictions it should apply to this parent as well. The fact that he prizes highly what we do not does not weaken his case. It is precisely this fact that lies at the heart of the principle of conscientious objection.

So much by way of clarifying the nature of the problem. Set in this way it is easy to see the outline of a utilitarian solution. Even if performing an action would, disregarding the agent's own attitude to it, be morally obligatory, it may not be so once his attitude to it is taken into account. If the person prefers not

[2] For the reasons explained in the previous essay no coherent relativist position concerning moral matters affects this presentation of the issue. Coherent relativism allows the agent to hold moral views. Therefore, it must allow him to reject incompatible beliefs as misguided and wrong. Hence the problem of why one should allow another to act immorally just because he holds misguided views.

to perform it, his preference affects the moral reckoning and may tip the balance. This is most likely to be the case where the preference not to perform the act is intense and where the utility of reluctant performance is small.[3] In some such way a utilitarian may defend the right to object to military service without wishing to justify its extension to other areas. In contemporary Western societies conscription is likely to be the only legal requirement which arouses a depth of opposition among pacifists such that the suffering caused to them by insisting on their service outweighs their contribution to security (especially given the availability of acceptable and useful forms of alternative service).

This is hardly the place to consider the truth of utilitarianism. Let me mention four features of utilitarian arguments for conscientious objection, two of which I find attractive and two unattractive. The two attractive features are: First, though every individual's desire to act in accordance with his wrong moral convictions is recognized, it is not allowed absolute force. It has to be considered against other interests and values (for the utilitarian these are all preferences of people—perhaps even other preferences of the would-be objector himself). Second, there is, for the utilitarian, a similar case to allow a person freedom to pursue other preferences and goals. The first drawback of the utilitarian view is in fact the root of its second advantage. The utilitarian exempts the objector not because of his moral belief but because of his desire to act according to it. Any desire, for a mink coat, for a polygamous marriage, etc., gives rise to the same considerations of principle. Only the relatively easy and harmless way in which the objector's claim can be satisfied and the difficulty or impossibility of satisfying other desires without harm to others distinguish them. Most people reflecting on conscientious objection tend to the view that the right of the objector, if he has any, rests on respect for his moral beliefs. To be sure, the objector desires to conform to his beliefs, but it is the fact that those desires reflect a moral belief which distinguishes them from other desires of his and endows them with

[3] A utilitarian may wish to defend conscientious objection on the ground that it encourages a propensity to stand up to intolerant government. But it seems to me that it is rather difficult to make out a reasonable case as to how respect for conscientious objection by a liberal government will encourage people to stand by their principles in general or in the face of an illiberal government in particular.

a special claim to our respect. Finally, this, like any other utilitarian argument, presupposes that every desire which any person may conceive is a reason for action for any other person (provided he can do something about it). This is a highly questionable assumption which it is extremely difficult to justify.

Utilitarianism is only one form of humanism, i.e. of the view which prizes the well-being of persons very highly. Contemporary philosophers prefer to talk of 'respect for persons'. Respect for persons can and, I think, should be interpreted in ways incompatible with utilitarianism.[4] Once more it has to be admitted that this is not the place to propound and defend any view of the requirements entailed by respect for persons. It is necessary again to begin by making a bold and undefended assumption. It is that humanism calls for respecting the autonomy of persons, that is, their right and ability to develop their talents and tastes and be able to lead the kind of life they are committed to. The areas of a person's life and plans which have to be respected by others are those which are central to his own image of the kind of person he is and which form the foundation of his self-respect.

These considerations are here outlined briefly and crudely. But even so they point to the familiar conclusion that inasmuch as respect for persons leads to valuing personal autonomy, it also leads to valuing pluralism. This takes two fundamental forms: first, the creation and protection of conditions for developing people's talents and tastes in accordance with their nature, in a way which opens for them possibilities of satisfying lives subject to the constraints imposed by the necessities of social co-operation and of securing similar opportunities to all; second, with respect to people with formed tastes and inclinations, creating an environment which enables them to pursue them in any way they like, subject to those same constraints.

It is from this second aspect of pluralism that the argument for conscientious objection derives its force. It concerns people with formed moral views and it claims their right to be faithful to them even if they are misguided. To establish the claim it

[4] It is difficult to know to what extent the view of the foundation of a right to conscientious objection stated below leads to practical conclusions different from a utilitarian argument for a right to object. There is a considerable overlap between them, but they may diverge to a greater or lesser degree depending on the conditions of the society under consideration.

is not enough to point, as the utilitarian does, to the fact that people generally prefer to conform to their moral views. It is necessary to explain why and how it is that a person's ability to avoid wrongdoing is central to his self-respect. It is necessary to contrast one's inability to satisfy many personal goals and desires which is regarded as bad luck and unfortunate and is felt as disappointing and frustrating, with one's inability to conduct normal life (i.e. out of gaol) while avoiding moral wrongdoing which is perceived as humiliating and degrading.

As was indicated above it is not part of my case that moral convictions, however wrong, have a claim to respect superior to all personal goals. On the contrary, most adults' vision of themselves is built around some aspects of their life or personality and around some goals such that the preservation of these is crucial to their sense of identity and self-respect. Such personal goals have an equal claim to respect by the state. A law preventing dedicated novelists from pursuing their vocation with the freedom essential to it is as bad, and bad for the same reasons, as a law conscripting pacifists to the army. The same is true of laws making the tenure of offices of state or pursuit of certain professional occupations dependent on declarations of allegiance which people may find incompatible with their moral principles. Here people are faced with a choice of being false to their moral convictions or sacrificing what may well be essential personal goals. Both alternatives are equally evil.

Humanism leads to the ideal of individual autonomy and this to pluralism. These in turn provide much guidance to the general purpose and features of the law and among other consequences they provide a firm foundation for the claim that the law should not coerce a person to do that which he holds to be (however misguidedly) morally wrong. But—and here again the argument outlined agrees in principle with the utilitarian approach—the right not to have one's conscience coerced which is thus established is merely a prima facie right. It can be overridden to protect other values and ideals. This is inevitable, given that it is a right to do that which is in fact morally wrong which is given to people who will use it for that very purpose. To give it absolute importance is to prefer the morally wrong to the morally right whenever the agent has misconceived moral ideas however wicked. A sufficient number of sufficiently wicked people will be able to create, even if they are a mere minority, a most iniquitous state just by the use of the right to conscientious objection. Surely one does not wish to allow Hitler to perpetrate his atrocities simply because he thinks it his moral duty to do so.

2. CONSCIENCE AND THE PURPOSE OF LAW

The prima facie character of these considerations canvassed above seems sufficient to justify (at least partly) one limitation on one's right not to have one's conscience coerced by law. It was noted in the preceding essay that not every case of breach of law which is held by the agent to be morally obligatory for him is a case of conscientious objection. Only when the ground is that the law itself is wrong (at least in part) is it such a case, but not if the obligation to violate the law is thought to be due to a rare combination of circumstances or to any other conditions which cannot be expected to be met by amending the law. This may be no more than an arbitrary distinction or one which at best is justified in terms of the administrative difficulty of extending a right to object to such circumstances. But it is perhaps possible to justify the exclusion on the ground that such cases are most often avoidable by the agent. The circumstances which lead to the conflict between the law and one's perceived moral duty are normally subject to one's control and if one desires to remain faithful to one's moral principles one could, even if at a cost to oneself, prevent them from arising. Hence, especially given the prima facie nature of the claim that the law should not coerce one's conscience, society is entitled to require the individual to shoulder the burden of his convictions rather than require society itself, which regards them as wrong convictions, to do so.

One important category of such occasional conflict between law and conscience in which the agent has no control over the circumstancces giving rise to the conflict is that where one's moral principles require political action whether revolutionary or by way of civil disobedience, in defiance of the law. Here, given the potentially grave consequences of such actions, they should be governed by the principles explained in the previous essay which, in a liberal state, do not allow the claim of an erroneous conscience to be tolerated. Too much is usually at stake in such cases.[5]

A humanistic society will in general allow the imposition of duties on people only if these are justified on one or more of the following grounds: It must be in the interest of the person subjected to the duty, or in the interest of other identifiable individuals, or in the interest of the public. A duty is in the public interest if its observance benefits, or is likely to benefit, unidentifiable individuals. A duty benefits identifiable individuals if and only if an explicit and non-norm-dependent[6] description of the act constituting breach of duty entails the occurrence of harm to an individual (it need not identify the individual in any way other than as the victim of that violation). Murder, rape, theft, assault, libel, breach of contract are examples of this kind. Refraining from speeding, spying, circulating counterfeit currency, polluting the rivers are examples of duties protecting the public. A particular offence may well harm individuals, but whether or not it has done so cannot be deduced from a description of the occurrences of the violation by itself. If there were other drivers around then one's speeding may have alarmed them or put them at risk; if not, not.

The ground for having a particular legal duty is of great importance in assessing the force of the claim to recognize a right to conscientious objection. The claim is strongest with respect to paternalistic laws, i.e. those whose justification is predominantly in terms of the interests of the persons bound by them (each person's duty being in his own best interests). It is hard to imagine a situation in which coercing the conscience of a normal adult by law in his own interest could be justified. If the ideals of autonomy and pluralism are not enough to enable a person to pursue his moral convictions at his own expense then they count for very little indeed.[7]

---

[5] This should not be read as a call for severe sentences in such cases. They should simply be governed by normal penal considerations. Such considerations do suggest that crimes of principle often require a more severe sentence effectively to deter potential offenders, but this is not always so.

[6] This condition is meant to rule out description of the act as 'an offence against the Criminal Law Act no. ...', etc.

[7] In recent years some members of the Sikh community conducted a brave campaign to be allowed to wear turbans rather than crash-helmets when riding motor-cycles. It could be said that this is an avoidable duty and that it is not purely paternalistic, being partly in the public interest (to avoid the cost of looking after injured motor-

The objector's claim to respect carries least conviction with regard to laws protecting the interests of identifiable individuals. We are hardly likely to tolerate murder, rape, libel, or even violation of property or contractual rights because of a misguided moral belief on the part of the offender. The reason is simple enough.

The legal consequences of such breaches of duty may be a liability to pay damages, they may involve an enforcement of the duty through injunction or specific performance, and they may involve penal measures. As was noted before, it is normally right to expect the conscientious objector to bear the cost to others of his adherence to his principles and therefore there will be little reason in a humanistic state for exemption in normal cases from liability for damages. But often even penal and enforcement measures may be justifiably directed against him. In a humanistic society it is assumed that the law will respect pluralism and will restrain individual freedom of action only rarely, only when vital interests of other people are involved. When this is the case those others should not be made to pay for the conscience of objectors. Hence their liability in damages. Furthermore, in a humanistic society direct enforcement and penal measures will be prescribed only where (1) damages are not adequate compensation, (2) the matter affects sufficiently vital interests of the victim to justify the further intrusion into the liberty of the offenders which such measures involve. When these conditions are satisfied the right to object is normally overridden.

This argument anticipates some of the points raised in the next section. It is an argument based on the prima facie nature of the case for a right to object. It does not deny the force of the claim but insists that in most cases penal and enforcement measures should anyway be invoked only to protect vital interests and in such cases the autonomy of the offender will norm-

---

cycle riders). Still it seems a pathetic example of bureaucratic insensitivity. Their case highlights a growing problem in contemporary Western societies. Increasingly the state is thought to have an obligation to care for the victims of various misfortunes and consequently also a duty to prevent such misfortunes. The necessary measures are defended both on grounds of interest and of paternalistic protection. Unfortunately such measures often involve restrictions of individual freedom. Such restrictions, though sometimes justified, are often excessive because, among other reasons, they create problems of conscientious objection.

ally be overridden. Where less vital interests are at stake
liability should anyway be for compensation only and these are
not in most cases excluded by the claim to autonomy. They
are a reasonable price for it. They can be thought of as the equivalent of the alternative service normally accepted as a justified
price for exemption from conscription. The reasoning is similar:
the alternative duty (alternative service, damages) is beneficial
(to the public, to the harmed individual); it is not harder to
bear than the original duty avoided by the objector but borne
by others; it serves more or less indirectly the same or related
goals, and it avoids coercing the objector's conscience. Naturally, these conditions sometimes cannot be met and then
alternative service may not be justifiable.

When the person whose interests the law is designed to protect voluntarily agrees to the breach of duty, the case, though
formally of the second category (protecting the interest of identifiable others), becomes in essence the same as that of paternalistic duties. This is the reason why a person who claims, however
erroneously, that it was his moral duty to aid a friend to commit
suicide or to commit voluntary euthanasia has an overwhelming claim that his offence shall not make him liable to the
normal legal consequences. His claim must be recognized as
exceptionally strong even by those who support the existence
of such laws.

Different considerations arise in connection with duties to
protect the public interest. Here the claim not to have one's
conscience coerced encounters less powerful opposition from
other considerations. The reason is not that the interests of unidentifiable individuals count for less than those of identifiable
ones. Obviously these are the same individuals and their interests count equally regardless of the legal technique of protecting
them. The reason is that laws protecting the public interest
normally allow for certain flexibility because of the insignifi-
cance of each individual's contribution. Consider taxation,
anti-pollution laws, etc. Most of the time exempting a single
individual from the duty will make little or no discernible difference to the protected good. This is generally the case in all
public-interest laws concerned with the provision of common
goods, whose availability to an individual does not depend on
his personal contribution and where the value of individual

contributions to the generally available benefits is small. Similar considerations affect other public-interest laws such as inchoate offences and others. These very often are concerned with easing the job of the law-enforcing agencies (enabling the police to prosecute for conspiracy or for unlawful possession of firearms people who probably will or did commit serious offences but where this cannot be proved). Here, where the objection affects the inchoate offence but not the complete one there is an obvious case for protecting the objector from criminal liability. (If he objects to the main offence and the connection between the inchoate offence and the main offence is close, then the argument does not apply.) Public-interest laws often concern reducing risk of harm and these often have (as with rules for safe driving) the characteristics of laws providing for common goods.

These comments are very general. I have not picked on examples which are particularly likely to be objected to on conscientious grounds. My intention was simply to point to the flexibility such laws allow and which makes them particularly suitable for an exception based on a right of conscientious objection. There is little surprise therefore that laws protecting public interest have traditionally been the main focus of attention of those who claim a right to conscientious objection. Remember, however, that here as elsewhere one is concerned with balancing the right to autonomy as against other interests. Thus if too many people will, in a particular society and at a particular period, claim the right to object they may defeat the interest served by the law and this may be indefensible.

3. FREEDOM OF CONSCIENCE AND A RIGHT TO OBJECT

In the first section we saw that a prima facie right not to have one's conscience coerced by law is implied by an appropriate interpretation of humanism. The section included various general considerations concerning the kind of laws which it is reasonable to suppose should be subsumed under this right, that is laws which even when right in all other respects should not be enforced against conscientious objectors. No very precise conclusions are possible concerning such balancing questions. All one can say is that generally laws of one category should be subjected to the right while generally laws of another category should not. There is another problem, however, which has to be discussed if only in the same general and tentative way: What legal form should the recognition of a right not to act against one's conscience take?

One simple and radical solution is to introduce a special and unified legal doctrine granting a right of conscientious objection which can be invoked to obtain exemption from liability for breach of any of a number of laws. Let us suppose that with respect to some laws the burden is on the objector to apply for a certificate of exemption from an appropriate judicial authority, whereas with respect to other laws there is a choice of applying for an exemption in advance or of raising a defence of conscientious objection when sued for breach of law. Henceforth when talking of a right of conscientious objection I shall have in mind a legal doctrine of this kind. Such a doctrine is a way of recognizing one's right not to have one's conscience coerced by law or the right to freedom of conscience, as I shall now call this aspect of the ideal of respect for personal autonomy. But is it the only way? Is it a good way?

Three major drawbacks seem to be inevitable concomitants of a right to conscientious objection.

First, such a right is wide open to abuse. Entitlement for it depends on a person's moral convictions. Such matters are hard to establish by independent evidence. The word of the person invoking the right is almost invariably the only direct evidence. The opportunities for abuse are countless.

Second, the existence of the right encourages self-doubt, self-deception, and in general undesirable forms of introspection. The exact nature of one's motives is a matter concerning which even the agent himself may not be too confident. This is especially so in the numerous cases in which one acts out of mixed motives. And almost all one's important decisions are like that. By making the application of the law to one's case dependent on one's motives for action in matters which are normally of some consequence to one's life the right to object encourages self-doubt, self-deception, and morbid introspection.

Third, unless the right is applied on the basis of a simple declaration by the objector (a method making abuse all the more easy) the institution of a right to object involves sanctioning some degree of public intrusion into the private affairs of individuals. The police or other investigating agencies will have appropriate powers to pry and the individual himself will have to account for his moral life before public officials (and possibly in public). It is no adequate answer to this objection that one's exposure is self-inflicted, since nobody is compelled to apply for exemption. The very existence of the right constitutes an encouragement for individuals to apply for it and in any case freedom of conscience is compromised if it is guaranteed only through compromising other aspects of one's autonomy, and self-respect, i.e. one's privacy and one's dignity.

For these reasons it is preferable to protect freedom of conscience in other ways which are free of such objections. A right to conscientious objection should be introduced only very sparingly and only in the absence of better ways of protecting freedom of conscience.

The main device for protecting freedom of conscience is and must in any case be the avoidance of laws to which people are likely to have conscientious objection. A state which does not impose an obligation of public worship according to state religion will not have to deal with objection to such a duty. Freedom of conscience and the pluralistic character of a state are guaranteed by its self-restraint from dictating action in areas known to be subject to sensitive moral convictions and by the provision of facilities and services as required by people of different moral and religious convictions (adequate possibilities of choice in education, freedom of marriage to members of different religions, etc.). All this is of course very familiar wisdom. The point I am urging is that a right to object should in so far as is possible be avoided in favour of general exemptions from law for categories of people identified independently of their moral views. Rather than allow Muslim employees to stay away from work on Fridays, all employees should have the freedom to choose their rest day (or their second rest day). All doctors should have the right to refuse to abort (without having to state any reasons) and so on. Naturally, it will not always be possible to get round the need to have a right to object in this way. It is better, other things being equal, not to have conscription and thus avoid the problem of conscientious objection. But sometimes other things are not equal and conscription is justified. It then becomes imperative to recognize the right of objection on moral grounds.[8]

In summary, there is a strong case for avoiding coercion of even an erroneous conscience. The case is, however, merely a prima facie case. It may be right to compromise and override it in favour of other goals. It is, however, particularly strong respecting paternalistic laws and public-interest laws (at least unless the number of objectors is large enough to jeopardize the goal of the law). In devising ways of recognizing the right, the institution of a right of conscientious objection has inevitable undesirable results. It is better to shape the controversial law in a way which avoids its application to controversial cases or, if this is not possible, by exempting potential objectors in ways not dependent on their declared moral beliefs. Within limited boundaries there is, however, room for a right to conscientious objection as one way of protecting autonomy and pluralism.

---

[8] Modern states tend on the whole to avoid imposing specific duties of service on citizens. These have been to a large extent replaced with the levying of taxes, enabling the state to pay for the services it requires which are then provided on a voluntary basis. This trend helps avoid the problem since individuals are not directly responsible for potentially controversial services. It is true that one may object to taxation because of the use made of the money, but this can be sincerely done only by a person who finds that the wrong of contributing money to bad causes outweighs the wrong of withholding taxation and denying his contribution to many worthwhile services.

INDEX

A

advising, 13–14, 21–2
Alchouron, C. E., 54
Altham, J. E. J., 3
American Realists, 53, 85
analytical legal philosophy, methodological considerations, 37–52, 79–85, 103–5, 132–3
Antley, K., 3
arbitrary power, 219–20
Atiyah, P. S., 180
Austin, J., 53, 79, 85, 99
authoritative decisions, 108–9, 111
authority
  to act, 19–20
  de facto, 5, 7, 9, 26–8
  having—and being an authority, 19
  law's claim to authority, 29–33, 116–17
  legitimate, 3–27
  over people, 19
  political, 8–9
  and power, 19–21
  and reasons, 12–16
  relativized, 9–11
  theoretical, 8

B

Baker, G., 53
basic norm, the, 69, 122–45
Bentham, J., 53, 85, 99, 101, 154, 166
Blackburn, S., 77
Bowring, J., 166
Bronaugh, R., 3
Bulygin, E., 54

C

civil disobedience, 262–76
closure rules, 61, 72, 75–7
Cohen, L. J., 3
command, *see* orders
conflicts
  in the law, 59–61, 201
  of reasons, 74–5
conscientious objection, 263–4, 276–89
conventional reasons, 254–5, 259

courts, their role, 48–50
Cross, R., 181, 184

D

Davidson, D., 3
declaratory judgments, 111
Dicey, A. V., 100
dignity, 221–2, 278–82
disputes, unregulated, 45–6, 96, 172–5, 181–3
distinguishing, 183–9
Dworkin, R. M., 37, 45–6, 57–60, 67, 73–4, 77, 173, 205–6

E

estoppel, 237, 239–40
exclusionary reasons, 17, 22–3, 26–7, 32–3
expressive reasons, 255

F

Feinberg, J., 3
Finnis, J. M., 37, 98
Foot, P. R., 3, 18
freedom, 220
friendship, 253–8
Fuller, L., viii, 40, 164, 218, 223–4
functions, of law, 163–79, 246–9

G

gaps, legal, 58, 60–1, 63–4, 70–7
Gray, J. C., 85, 89

H

Hacker, P. M. S., 3, 54, 184, 234
Hart, H. L. A., 41, 44, 53, 69, 79, 85, 89–94, 96, 98, 101, 128, 134, 145, 151, 153–5, 173, 177–9, 213, 223, 267
Hayek, F. A., 210, 220, 226–8
Hodgson, D. H., 181
Holland, T. E., 89
Holmes, O. W., 89
Honoré, A. M., 180
Hutchinson, D., 210

I

identity of legal systems, 78–102, 113–14, 120, 127–9, 148–9
indeterminacy in the law, 49, 72–4, 113, 193, 208
individuation of laws, 63n., 80

J

Jennings, I., 212
judicial discretion, 96, 113, 173
  system of absolute, 111–12, 115
judicial law-making, 194–201, 207–9
judicial reasoning
  analogy in, 201–9
  in closure rule cases, 192–3
  distinguishing, 183–9
  in English law, 180–209
  extending rules, 207
  overruling, 189–92
  ratio decidendi, 183–4
  in unregulated disputes, 193–4
  in the use of its discretion, 194–209

K

Kant, 130, 132
Kaplan, A., 86–7
Kelsen, H., vii, 44, 53–4, 69, 79, 85–7, 99, 122–45, 150–2, 155–7, 164, 175, 246
Kiefer, H. E., 92, 128

L

Laslett, P., 7
Laswell, H., 86–7
Law
  comprehensivity, 116–18
  exclusionary force, 30–3, 236–7
  existence and efficacy, 85–90, 103–4, 111
  functions, 163–79, 246–9
  guiding behaviour, 30–3, 50–2, 112, 246–9
  identity, 78–102, 113–14, 120, 127–9, 148–9
  institutional character, 43–5, 88, 105–16
  justification of laws, 245–9, 271–2, 282–9
  limits, 45, 88, 111–15, 120
  and morality, 31–2, 38–9, 46–8, 50–2,
    104, 137–44, 219–26
  normativity of, 134–7, 145, 150, 158–9
  openness of, 101–2, 119–20
  respect for, 250–61
  social basis of, 38–52
  sources of, 45–54, 62–3, 65–6
  and state, 97–102, 105
  supremacy of, 118–19
law-applying organs, 87–9, 105–11
law-enforcing organs, 107–8
law-making
  v. law-applying, 49, 90–7, 109, 183–94, 206–9
  judicial, 194–201, 207–9
legal point of view, 112, 140–3
legal statements, 54–77, 158–9
  complete description of a legal system, 80–1
  detached, 140–3, 153–7
  internal and external, 154–5
  pure, 62, 80
  reductive explanations of, 53, 154
  total set of, 80
liberal state, 268, 271–4
Libling, D., 47
Llewellyn, C., 89, 164
Lucas, J., 11–12
Lukes, S., 7
Lyons, D., 47

M

McCrudden, C., 180
Miers, D., 184
Munitz, M. K., 92, 128

N

natural law, 39, 44, 129–32, 144, 150, 158–9, 240
Nowell-Smith, P. H., 3

O

Oberdiek, H., 44
obligation
  to obey the law, 233–49
  voluntary, 257–8
orders, 14–15, 21–4
overruling, 189–92

P

permissions
  and authority to act, 20
  cancelling, 18, 67
  conclusive, 64–5, 67
  and conflict of reasons, 75
  exclusionary, 256
  explicit, 64–7
  repealing laws, 57
  strong and weak, 117
Plato, 130
positivism, legal, 37–55, 59, 62, 150, 153, 157–9
Pound, R., 164
power, 16–19
  and authority, 19–21
primary institutions, 105–11
prohibitions, 57–60
protected reasons, 18, 21–3

R

ratio decidendi, 55, 183–4
reasons
  and authority, 12–16, 19
  conclusive, 64–5, 67–8
  conventional, 254–5, 259
  exclusionary, 17, 22–3, 26–7, 32–3
  expressive, 255
  friendship as a reason, 255–7
  and power, 16–19
  protected, 18, 21–3
  respect for law as, 259
  second order, 17
  statements of, 64
  symbolic, 256
Reid, Lord, 190, 198
relativism, moral, 271, 278
requesting, 14–15, 21–2, 24
res judicata, 110–11
respect
  for law, 250–61
  for persons, *see* dignity
rights, 266–7, 274–5

rule of law, the, 210–29
rule of recognition, the, 69, 90–8
rules, 146–8
  acceptance of, 154
  closure, 61, 72, 75–7, 192–3
  ultimate legal, 68–9, 96–7

S

Salmond, J. W., 89
Sartorius, R., 210, 223
Simpson, A. W. B., ix, 98, 163, 185, 267
Singer, P., 241–2
Skinner, Q., 7
Smith, M. B. E., 233
Soper, P., 47
sources of law, 45–54, 62–3, 65–6
Stone, J., 185
Summers, R. S., 233
symbolic reasons, 256

T

Tiles, M. E., 77
Tuck, R., 6–7, 19
Twining, W., 184

U

ultimate legal rules, 68–9, 96–7
utilitarianism, on conscientious objection, 278–80

V

vagueness, 73–4
validity, 15, 95, 146–59
  systemic, 150–3
violence, 267–8
void and voidable, 146

W

Wasserstrom, R., 233
Wilberforce, Lord, 198
Wolff, R. P., 11, 26–7